the Rodale
Guide to
Composting

the Rodale
Guide to
Composting

by Jerry Minnich, Marjorie Hunt, and
the editors of *Organic Gardening®* magazine

 **Rodale Press,** Emmaus, Pa.

Illustrations by Jerry O'Brien
Photos by the Rodale Press Photography Department
Book design by Barbara Field

Library of Congress Cataloging in Publication Data

Minnich, Jerry.
The Rodale guide to composting.
Bibliography: p.
Includes index.
1. Compost.   I. Hunt, Marjorie Lesher, 1921-
joint author.   II. Organic gardening and farming.
III. Title.
S661.M56   631.8′75   78-27650
ISBN 0-87857-212-0

Printed in the United States of America on recycled paper, containing a high percentage of de-inked fiber.

2 4 6 8 10 9 7 5 3 1

Contents

part one

The How and Why of Composting: Essentials of Understanding

1

Composting throughout History

Composting is, in broadest terms, the biological reduction of organic wastes to humus. Whenever a plant or animal dies, its remains are attacked by soil microorganisms and larger soil fauna, and are eventually reduced to an earthlike substance that forms a beneficial growing environment for plant roots.

This process, repeated universally and continuously in endless profusion and in every part of the world where plants grow, is part of the wheel of life, the ever-recurring natural process that supports all terrestrial life. The entire composting process, awesome in its contribution to all plant and animal life, is probably impossible to contemplate in its full dimensions. Let's just say that compost and composting are, like water and air, essentials of life.

The initial origin of compost is similarly difficult to contemplate. Who can imagine the birth and death of the earth's first primitive plant, its minute remains transformed into life-giving substance by a small number of unseen and unheard bacteria? In these thoughts, we are dealing with the very origins of life, a seemingly mystical event of which compost was an integral part. Compost, then, spans the entire course of life on earth. It is and always has been essential to the sustenance and forwarding of life as we know it.

Man and Compost

A different, more common, definition of compost requires man's participation in the process. Ordinarily, when we speak of compost and composting, we are referring to the process by which we transform organic wastes into a soil-building substance for farm, orchard, or garden.

1

Even when considering this common definition, however, the origins of man's composting activities quickly become buried in the sands of prehistory. The best we can surmise is that sometime after man began to cultivate food to augment his hunting and food gathering activities, he discovered the benefits of compost, probably in the form of animal manure. Noting, perhaps, that food crops grew more vigorously in areas where manure had been deposited, he made the connection between the two phenomena and began a more selective application of the composting process.

Probably the oldest existing reference to the use of manure in agriculture is to be found on a set of clay tablets of the Akkadian Empire, which flourished in the Mesopotamian Valley a thousand years before Moses was born. Akkadia was overthrown by Babylon, which in turn fell to Cyrus, but though empires crumbled, the knowledge and practice of organic fertilizing increased.

Compost was known to the Romans; the Greeks had a word for it, and so did the Tribes of Israel. From the first glories of the Garden of Eden to the somber shadows of the Garden of Gethsemane, the Bible is interspersed with references to the cultivation of the soil. The terms "dung" and "dunghill," used by the theologians who translated the scriptural Hebrew and Greek into English, have numerous variants in the original. Dung was used as fuel, and (more importantly for us) as fertilizer. Manure was sometimes spread directly onto the fields. It was also composted along with street sweepings and organic refuse on the dunghill (more correctly compost pile) outside the city wall. Sometimes straw, trampled to reduce its bulk, was soaked in liquid manure (literally "in dung-water").

In the parable of the fig tree—Luke 13:8—the gardener pleads for delay until he can "dig about it and put on manure." This is a reference to a method of fertilizing trees by digging holes about the roots and filling the spaces with manure, a custom still practiced in southern Italy. The *Talmud* tells us "They lay dung to moisten and enrich the soil; dig about the roots of trees; pluck up the suckers; take off the leaves; sprinkle ashes; and smoke under the trees to kill vermin." From other sources we learn that soil was enriched by adding ashes, straw, stubble and chaff, as well as with the grass and brambles which sprung up in the sabbatical (seventh) year. During this year, compost was not allowed to be removed from the pile. An exception was granted under certain circumstances to graze cattle upon land in need of their manure for fertilizer. Normally, sheep manure was collected from walled-in sheep-folds and used as a fertilizer.

Another *Talmud* passage tells us of the use of blood as fertilizer. The blood of the sacrifice, poured out before the altar, drained through an underground channel to a dump outside the city wall. Here it was sold to gardeners on payment of a trespass offering. Without this fee, its use for common purpose was prohibited as it retained the sanctity of dedication at the altar.

According to *Talmud*, raw manure was not to be handled by the truly religious because it was unclean. A *Talmud* commentator set down the rule for the faithful: "Do not use your manure until some time after the outcasts have used theirs," thus advocating the use of rotted or composted manure instead of fresh animal matter.

Much of the agricultural wisdom of the ancients survived the blight of the Dark Ages, to reappear—along with other fundamental scientific knowledge—in the writings of learned Arabs. Ibn al Awam, variously assigned to the 10th and 12th centuries, goes into extensive detail on the processing and use of compost and other manures in his *Kitab al Falahah* or *Book of Agriculture.* He recommends blood for its fertilizing properties and casually endorses the superiority of human blood for this purpose. The manure value of crushed bones, waste wool, wood ash and lime is recognized in other old manuscripts as well.

The medieval Church was another repository of knowledge and lore where, thanks to the efforts of a few devoted monks, the feeble flame of truth was kept alive. Within monastery enclosures sound agricultural practices were preserved and applied, and in some instances taught to the neighboring farmers by the Abbot, acting as a sort of medieval county agent. It is but natural that the charters of two old English Abbeys, St. Albans (1258) and the Priory of Newenham (1388) should enjoin the use of compost for soil fertility.

References to compost in Renaissance literature are numerous; space restricts us to only a few quotations. William Caxton, pioneer 15th century printer, relates ". . . by which dongyng and compostyng the feldes gladeth." Three other renowned Elizabethans reveal in their writings that compost was a familiar word. Shakespeare's *Hamlet* advises ". . . do not spread the compost on the weeds, to make them ranker," and in *Timon of Athens,* Timon rages "the earth's a thief, that feeds and breeds by a composture stolen from general excrement." Sir Francis Bacon tells in his "Natural History" that plants degenerate by

". . . removing into worse earth, or forbearing to compost the earth." The unfortunate Raleigh, awaiting execution, writes of the soil "He shall have the dung of the cattle, to muckle or composture his land." (Our word "compost" comes from Old French, but in the 16th and 17th centuries various spellings are encountered—compass, compess, compast, composture, etc.)

Tusser (1557) was a real organic enthusiast and advised "One aker well compast, is worth akers three" and "Lay on more compass, and fallow again." Detail is given us by Pultenham (1589) "The good gardiner seasons his soyle by sundrie sorts of compost; as mucke or marle, clay or sande . . . bloud, or lees of oyle or wine." Evelyn (1693) defines it "Compost is rich made mold, compounded with choice mold, rotten dung, and other enriching ingredients." A mere 130 years ago Bingley wrote "The neighboring farmers made them (herring) up into compost, and manured their ground with them."

Early Use in the United States

On the North American continent, compost was used by native Indian tribes and by Europeans upon their initial settlement. Public accounts of the use of stable manure in composting date back to the 18th century. Early colonial farmers abandoned the fish-to-each-hill-of-corn system of fertilizing when they discovered that by properly composting two loads of muck and one load of barnyard manure, they obtained a product equivalent to three loads of manure in fertilizing value. By the middle of the 19th century, this knowledge was thoroughly ingrained in Yankee agricultural philosophy, and Samuel W. Johnson, Professor of Analytical and Agricultural Chemistry at Yale College, asserted that "this fact should be painted in bold letters on every barn door in Connecticut."

Many New England farmers found it economical to use the white fish or Menhaden abundant in Long Island Sound as well as manure in their compost heaps. Stephen Hoyt and Sons of New Canaan, Connecticut, made compost on a large scale, using 220,000 fish in one season. A layer of muck one foot in thickness would be spread on the ground, then a layer of fish on top of that, a layer of muck, a layer of fish, and so on, topped off with a layer of muck, until the heap reached a height of 5 or 6 feet. Their formula required 10 or 12 loads of muck to 1 of fish. This was periodically turned until fermentation and disintegration of the fish (excepting the bones) had been completed. The resulting compost was free of odors and preserved perfectly all the manurial values of the fish.

Our first president was a skilled farmer and a strong advocate of proper composting methods. After the Revolutionary War, one of Washington's main concerns was the restoration of the land on his plantation. For this purpose he looked for a farm manager who was "above all, like Midas, one who can convert everything he touches into manure, as the first transmutation toward gold; in a word, one who can bring worn-out and gullied lands into good tilth in the shortest time."

According to Paul L. Haworth, author of the 1915 biography, *George Washington, Farmer*, Washington "saved manure as if it were already so much gold, and hoped with its use and with judicious rotation of crops to accomplish . . ." that. Washington carried out his own composting experiments, from which he concluded that the best compost was made from sheep dung and from "black mould from the Gulleys on the hillside which seemed to be purer than the other."

Our third president, Thomas Jefferson, was no less a skilled farmer, and equally inventive. In fact, Washington and Jefferson, when not otherwise occupied with affairs of state, often corresponded about mutual farming problems and observations.

Jefferson routinely depended on the use of manure to maintain the fertility of his fields. In *Thomas Jefferson's Farm Book*, Edwin Morris Betts, the editor, discusses Jefferson's use of various kinds of manure:

> Jefferson used dung in three different stages of decomposition—fresh or long dung, half putrified or short dung, and well-rotted dung. He does not state which condition of the dung he found most beneficial for his crops.

> Jefferson probably used very little manure of any kind on his lands in the early days of farming at Monticello and at his other plantations. The newly cleared land was plentiful and rich and brought forth abundant crops. He expressed this idea in a letter to George Washington on June 28, 1793. He wrote, ". . . Manure does not enter into this, *a good farm* because we can buy an acre of new land cheaper than we can manure an old acre. . . ." But later, after the soil had been robbed of its fertility by successive crops of corn and tobacco, fertilizing his soil became a necessity.

> Jefferson often followed a green dressing of buckwheat with dung in his crop rotations. In a plan of crop rotation which he sent

to Thomas Mann Randolph on July 28, 1793, he wrote, ". . . 3d. wheat, & after it a green dressing of buckwheat, and, in the succeeding winter put on what dung you have."

Jefferson was also an innovative farmer. Noting the difficulty and expense entailed in carrying manure to distant fields, he came upon the idea of stationing cattle for extended periods of time in the middle of the field which needed fertilization. Wrote Jefferson, ". . . a moveable airy cow house, to be set up in the middle of the field which is to be dunged, & soil our cattle in that thro' the summer as well as winter, keeping them constantly up & well littered. . . ."

James Madison, our fourth president, was also aware of the need to renew the fertility of crop lands. On May 12, 1818, in an address to the Agricultural Society of Albemarle, Virginia, he stated:

> Closely as agriculture and civilization are allied, they do not keep pace with each other. There is probably a much higher state of agriculture in China and Japan than in many other countries far more advanced in the improvements of civilized life. Nothing is more certain than that continual cropping without manure deprives the soil of its fertility. It is equally certain that fertility may be preserved or restored by giving to the earth animal or vegetable manure equivalent to the matter taken from it. That restoration to the earth of all that naturally grows on it prevents its impoverishment is sufficiently seen in our forests, where the annual exuviae of the trees and plants replace the fertility of which they deprived the earth. Where frequent fires destroy the leaves and whatever else is annually dropped on the earth, it is well known that land becomes poorer, this destruction of the natural crop having the same impoverished effect as removal of a cultivated crop. A still stronger proof that a natural restoration to the earth of all its annual produce will perpetuate its productiveness is seen where our fields are left uncultivated and unpastured. In this case the soil, receiving from the decay of the spontaneous weeds and grasses more fertility than they extract from it, is, for the time being, improved. Its improvement may be explained by the fertilizing matter which the weeds and grasses derive from the water and atmosphere, which forms a net gain to the earth. That individual farms do lose their fertility in proportion as crops are taken from them and return of manure

Thomas Jefferson stationed his cattle in the fields that needed fertilizing, moving them from field to field as necessary throughout the year.

neglected is a fact not likely to be questioned. The most logical mode of preserving the richness and of enriching a farm is certainly that of applying a sufficiency of manure and vegetable matter in a decomposed state; in order to procure which too much care cannot be observed in saving every material furnished by the farm. This resource was among the earliest discoveries of man living by agriculture; and a proper use of it has been made a test of good husbandry in all countries, ancient and modern, where its principle and profits have been studied.

George Washington Carver, the famed botanist-chemist-agriculturist, advised the farmer to compost materials and return them to the land. In an agriculture experiment station bulletin entitled, "How to Build Up and Maintain the Virgin Fertility of Our Soil," Dr. Carver says, "Make your own fertilizer on the farm. Buy as little as possible. A year-round compost pile is absolutely essential and can be had with little labor and practically no cash outlay."

Dr. Carver also stressed the importance of covering the heap to prevent the leaching away of nutrients by rain. He explained:

> It is easy to see that our farm animals are great fertilizer factories, turning out the cheapest and best known product for the permanent building up of the soil. In addition to this farmyard manure, there are also many thousands of tons of the finest fertilizer going to waste all over the South, in the form of decaying leaves of the forest and the rich sediment of the swamp, known as "muck." Every idle moment should be put in gathering up these fertilizers.

A Professor Johnson, in 1856, had written some articles for *The Homestead* which proved to be so thought-provoking and excited so much attention among readers of this journal that he was invited to address the annual meeting of the Connecticut State Agricultural Society in January, 1857, on the subject of "Frauds in Commercial Manures."

It was then established that "gross deceits had actually been practiced by parties soliciting the patronage of farmers in Connecticut, and the facilities for perpetrating further frauds were the subject of the lengthened exposition." A few years later, in 1859, Professor Johnson wrote a book entitled *Essays on Manure*, in which the subject of composting received prominent and favorable comment. Composting was said to develop the inert fertilizing qualities of muck itself, and a fermentation which began in the manure extended to and involved the muck, reducing the whole to the condition of well-rotted dung. It was pointed out that in this process of composting, the muck effectively prevented the waste of ammonia or nitrogen.

Relatively small quantities of plant material were composted in this period because there was plenty of barnyard manure. However, in some sections of the South, cotton seed was composted with muck. The heap was started with alternate 6-inch layers of muck, and 3-inch layers of cotton seed, finished off with a layer of muck. This was turned and re-piled once a month until complete decomposition of the cotton seed had been effected. Considerable watering was a prime requisite.

As America grew older, many of the sons and daughters of the early New England settlers trekked westward searching for more abundant,

George Washington Carver believed that, "A year-round compost pile is absolutely essential and can be had with little cash outlay."

lower-priced land. Some of them found soil so rich in organic matter from buffalo droppings, plants, grasses and dead animals, all nicely composted, that little thought was given to composting. Only a few farsighted settlers in this newly discovered land of plenty continued composting practices proven effective by farming poorer soil.

Start of the Organic Method

Composting has been a basis of the organic method of gardening and farming since the days of Sir Albert Howard, father of the organic method. Howard, a British government agronomist, spent the years from 1905 to 1934 in India, where he slowly evolved the organic concept. In making compost, Howard found by experiment that the best compost consisted of three times as much plant matter as manure. He devised the Indore method of compost-making, in which materials are layered sandwich fashion, then are turned (or are mixed by earthworms) during decomposition.

In 1942, J. I. Rodale, pioneer of the organic method in America, began monthly publication of *Organic Farming and Gardening*, assimilating the ideas of Howard and adding knowledge gained by further experimentation. From 1942, the organic method extolled the use of compost and stressed its importance as a garden necessity. Subsequent developments in composting included adding ground rock powders to the heap, sheet composting, shredding materials for quicker decomposition, digester composting, and numerous other innovations discussed later in this book.

The history of compost, then, is both ancient and modern. Compost was recognized, as early as ancient Rome and probably before, as a transitional force in the life cycle. For at least two thousand years, man depended on compost to sustain his croplands and to feed himself and others. It was not until the 19th century, in fact, that man began to substitute chemical fertilizers for compost in the new "scientific" method of farming.

The Frenchman Boussingault laid the foundations of agricultural chemistry in 1834. Then, in 1840, the great German scientist Justus von Liebig published his classic monograph on agricultural chemistry. Up until that time, the humus theory had prevailed. It was believed that plants actually ate humus in order to grow. Liebig disproved this theory, demonstrating that plants obtained nourishment from certain chemicals in solution. Since humus was insoluble in water, Liebig dismissed it as a significant factor in plant growth.

For the next hundred years, agricultural practice became increasingly chemical in nature. It is ironic that in 1940, exactly one hundred

J. I. Rodale introduced American gardeners to the value of composting as a means of building soil quality.

years after Liebig's classic work, Sir Albert Howard published his own magnum opus, *An Agricultural Testament,* which set in motion the movement to organic farming and gardening that now is widely accepted throughout the world. Even farmers who depend heavily and routinely on chemical fertilizers now know of the value of compost and organic matter.

Today, the organic method of farming and gardening is more popular than it has ever been, at least since the turn of the last century. Gardeners were the first to return to organic methods, and they are now being followed by increasing numbers of farmers, who are discovering that they can no longer afford to farm with expensive chemicals, and that returning to organic methods can restore life to the soil and actually increase yields, at less cost. More and more cities are turning their sludge and garbage into rich compost. Government agricultural experiment stations are, after years of reluctance, advocating the use of compost and distributing pamphlets on its preparation and application. Composting methods are becoming increasingly refined and effective. Just as the farmer can spread hundreds of tons of organic matter on his fields through sheet composting, now the city gardener can make quick compost for his flower and vegetable beds by using one of the new metal composting units designed for backyards. It seems clear that composting, which has sustained man since the very beginning of his history, is now entering into a bright new era in which the intelligent use of scientific methods will enhance the quality of life instead of destroying it. In this, compost and composting will find an increasingly welcome place.

2

The Benefits of Compost and Composting

Plants, animals, insects, and people are all inextricably linked in a complex web of interrelationships with air, water, soil, minerals, and other natural resources playing vital roles. Compost, too, plays an important role. There is a cycle, a continuity to life.

We are only at the very beginning of an understanding of all the parts of this cycle of life. But we are learning that upsetting the life patterns of only one kind of plant or animal, even in a seemingly minor way, can have effects on many other living things. All of the environmental problems we face are rooted in a failure to appreciate the need to understand the life cycle and to keep it intact. We can use our understanding of the interrelationships of living things in active ways, too, to increase the productivity of our fields, forests, orchards, and gardens. Composting is one way to use our understanding of life's cycle in the furthering of our welfare.

Compost is more than a fertilizer, more than a soil conditioner. It is a symbol of continuing life. Nature herself has been making compost since the first appearance of primitive life on this planet, eons before man first walked the earth. Leaves falling to the forest floor are soon composted, returning their nutrients to the tree that bore them. The dead grass of the meadow, seared by winter's frost, is made compost in the dampness of the earth beneath. The birds, the insects, and the animals of field and forest contribute their wastes and eventually their bodies, helping to grow food so that more of their kind may prosper. The greenness of the earth itself is strong testimony to nature's continuing composting program.

The compost heap in your garden is an intentional replication of the natural process of birth and death which occurs almost everywhere in

Nature has been making compost since the first forms of primitive life appeared on earth.

nature. It did not take man long to learn to imitate nature by building compost piles, as we saw in Chapter 1. It is ironic that composting, the oldest and most universally practiced form of soil treatment in the world, should today be claiming so many converts. Perhaps this is nature's Restoration—a reaffirmation that man does, indeed, live best when he lives in harmony with nature.

Because the compost heap is symbolic of nature's best efforts to build soil, and because compost is the most efficient and practical soil builder, it has become the heart of the organic method of farming and gardening. Composting is the single most important task of the organic gardener or farmer because the health of the soil depends on the composting treatment it receives, and success in gardening and farming depends on the health of the soil.

Compost builds good soil texture and structure, qualities that enable soil to retain nutrients, moisture, and air for the support of healthy crops. Compost helps control erosion that otherwise would wash topsoil into waterways. Compost is the best recycler of man's biological wastes, turning millions of tons of our refuse into a food-growing asset. Compost provides and releases plant nutrients, protects against drought, controls pH, supports essential bacteria, feeds helpful earthworms, stops nutrient loss through leaching, acts as a buffer against toxins in the soil, controls weeds, stretches the growing season, and conserves a nation's nonrenewable energy resources. Every gardener knows that compost is valuable—but, until we understand more fully all the benefits of compost, we can never understand why it must be the single most important part of gardening and farming. In this chapter, we will examine those benefits more closely.

The Great Recycler

Recycling garden and food wastes is important to a good environment because it is a natural process. Waste can be disposed of by chemical means (burning) or by largely physical means (landfill), but only when it is disposed of by biological means (composting) are plant nutrients conserved to the advantage of the entire ecosystem. Resources are conserved by returning wastes in the form in which they can be most efficiently used.

They are also conserved when the need to use chemical fertilizers is drastically reduced. Chemical fertilizers, unlike the natural fertilizer of compost, are manufactured from unrenewable natural resources. Principal among these resources, especially for the manufacture of ammonia-type fertilizers, is natural gas. Approximately 2 percent of the natural gas consumed in the United States goes into the manufacture of nitrogen fertilizer. Natural gas supplies, of course, are finite. Shortages have already occurred, and they will occur with increasing frequency in the years ahead. We are spending a rich inheritance of gas with little thought of tomorrow's needs and with no hope of getting more; all the while we are burying organic wastes in landfills or dumping them into the oceans.

Composting is a giant step toward recycling wastes, conserving precious energy reserves, and regaining control of our food supplies. Backyard composting is the first step and the easiest. Farm-scale composting is more difficult to effect, but potentially far more beneficial to society as a whole. Municipal composting—the transformation of a city's wastes into compost for farm and garden—is the most far-reaching and potentially beneficial of all.

THE DISPOSABLE SOCIETY

This realization of the proper place of compost in a complex society strikes many of us in different ways, and at different times. It struck Wayne H. Davis, a professor at the University of Kentucky, in June, 1971. He cancelled his garbage collection service after having carried two bags of garbage to the curb almost every week of his adult life up to that time. The idea of having to pay more for garbage collection than for his daily newspaper was part of his motivation, but the most important factor was "a desire to find an alternative to what I consider a self-destructive life-style that grew out of the country's 'use it once and throw it away' philosophy which replaced the hated rationings of World War II days and led economists into the practice of measuring progress by the rate at which we turn our natural resources into junk. Man's system of moving nutrients from the farm to the ocean by way of sewers and of moving industrial materials from the mines to landfills, is not a viable life-style."

Composting is an ideal form of recycling, returning organic wastes to the use of the land from which they originally came. It is one of the most basic means of conservation, assuring that future generations will have the same benefit of the earth as we do now. Composting can be seen, in one of its aspects, as an essential part of a responsible and efficient home management system.

Organic Gardening staff editor Steve Smyser stated the recycling ethic eloquently when he wrote: "Composting is perhaps the simplest example we have of man working in harmony with nature to keep his habitat in order and assure his own survival. The principle involved is really nothing more than the first law of good housekeeping, or good earthkeeping—when you're finished with something, put it back where it belongs!"

An anthropological study carried out by classes of Professor William L. Rathje at the University of Arizona reached some startling conclusions about household wastes. Originally a project designed to determine how much could be learned about the habits of people by examining their wastes, just as we examine debris of archaeological sites to make discoveries about past cultures, the project taught the students some pointed lessons.

It was discovered, by studying a sample of 380 representative household units, that Tucson's population of 450,000 was throwing away more than 9,500 tons of edible food each year. The average middle-income household in the study disposed of 10 percent of the food brought into the home. Students involved in the Tucson study became aware of the tremendous ecological impact of this waste and of its loss to the earth from which it originally came. In addition to loss of nutrients, energy is wasted once as the crops are grown, processed, and transported, and then again as they are transported as "waste" to the incinerator or landfill.

Like Mr. Davis, the man who cancelled his garbage service, many others have achieved a sense of independence and freedom and realized the satisfactions of sane management from dealing responsibly with their own wastes, through composting and other forms of recycling.

Building Soil Structure

Compost builds good soil structure.

In good garden soils, the individual particles of sand, clay, and silt will naturally group together into larger units called *granules* or *aggregates*. This process is necessary to a good garden soil, since it promotes aeration and water drainage. And the success of your soil in forming these aggregates is called its *structure*, or *crumb structure*. Sandy soils will have poor structure, since sand is too coarse to form aggregates, while a heavy clay soil compacts when wet, inhibiting good plant growth. Compost can correct a soil that is either too sandy or too clayey, thus helping to build good structure and a good environment for the growing of plants. Soils which have been chemically treated with little or no addition of organic matter will gradually lose structure, necessitating increased fertilization, cultivation, and irrigation.

Good structure allows a soil to breathe and facilitates circulation. A heavy clay soil tends to become waterlogged quickly, preventing water and air penetration. Adding compost helps to loosen this packed soil by opening up pore spaces that, like little tunnels, carry air and water down into the soil. A crumb structure is built, and a thin film of moisture is held on each crumb of soil where plant roots can utilize it as needed.

Sandy soils, which tend to let water drain away too rapidly, are also rebuilt by the addition of compost. The fine particles are united into larger ones that can hold greater quantities of water in films on their surfaces.

The higher the humus content, the more moisture a soil can absorb and retain. Soil with ample organic matter lets raindrops seep gently into it, instead of splattering and churning up soil particles. In the case

CLAY

CLAY WITH COMPOST

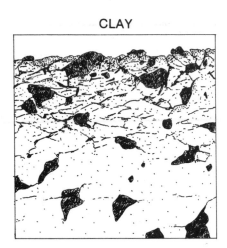
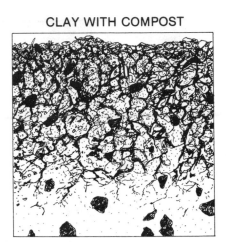

Compost helps to loosen heavy clay soil (above) by opening pore spaces that allow air and water to penetrate into the soil. The fine particles in sandy soil (below) are united into larger ones that can hold greater amounts of water in films on their surfaces.

SANDY

SANDY WITH COMPOST

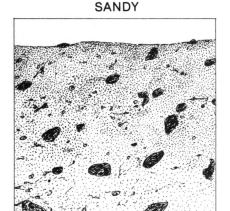
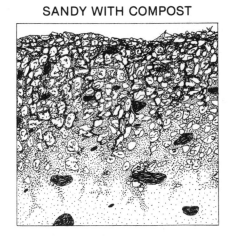

of packed, crusted soil, a muddy drop of water is formed which will run over the soil surface as the first stage of erosion. A heavy rainstorm may result in considerable runoff which carries away soil. And finally, disastrous floods can occur. Instead of huge dams for flood control, the best preventive is improving soil structure.

DROUGHT PROTECTION

The permeability of soils amply supplied with organic matter is thus a potent weapon against drought damage. Water is soaked up like a sponge and stored on the soil crumbs (100 pounds of humus holds 195 pounds of water). When the tiny hairs on plant roots can absorb all the water the plant needs from the films on these crumbs, they do not suffer from long rainless periods.

Crumb structure is built not merely by mechanical means, but with the help of soil bacteria and fungi. Here, the vital ecology of soil and compost comes sharply into focus.

The mystery of aggregate formation (crumbs) was solved in great part by two scientists from the National Institute of Agricultural Science, Tokyo, several decades ago. In tests made on the decomposition of organic matter and aggregate formation, it was learned that various soil fungi grow on the organic matter. Soil bacteria then come along to turn the fungal products into "cementing materials." These cementing mate-

Soil with ample organic matter is loose and crumbly. Good crumb structure, as in the soil shown here, improves the soil's aeration and moisture retention, thus providing the best possible environment for growing plants.

rials "glue" together tiny particles of soil into coarse grains or crumbs.

Soil microbiologist Dr. R. J. Swaby did extensive research on the mechanism of aggregation. At the beginning, Dr. Swaby reasoned that improved structure must be due to one or all of several things—the roots themselves, microorganisms associated with the roots, or to gums and resins produced by these organisms. So his experiments began.

First, he grew grasses in a sterilized soil and measured the structural changes. There were scarcely any. The grass roots were incapable of doing the job without the microorganisms which live and feed on them. These microorganisms were apparently the real soil binders, the grass roots acting merely as food.

Question number two—was it the microorganisms themselves or their gummy by-products which bound the soil into desirable water-stable aggregates? Microorganisms known to be gum and resin producers were isolated from soil and grown in laboratory cultures. Their gummy products were added to unstructured soil. There was little improvement in granulation. Apparently the gummy substances were not important.

One by one, the important groups of soil organisms were added to poorly structured, sterilized soil at this stage and allowed to grow and increase. The effect on structure was carefully measured. There was a remarkable improvement when some were added. The soil became granulated and permeable to water.

Easily the most effective organisms were the fungi or molds. Plants grown in poorly structured soil increased dramatically in size when these were added to the pots. Soil aeration was improved and water permeability increased. Microscopic bacteria had no such beneficial effects. The threadlike mycelium of the fungi apparently wound itself around soil particles and held them together.

Walking on Harpenden common, at Rothamsted, one late winter's morning, Dr. Swaby noticed that some earthworm casts on permanent grassland were more resistant to the disintegration action of thawing snow than were similar casts on nearby wheatland. So, the role of earthworms was investigated. Worm casts from various types of soils were collected and tested in the laboratory.

Results showed that earthworms improved the permanence of aggregation of all soils they devoured. Their casts on grassland soil were particularly stable. Evidently, binding substances were derived as grass roots present in the soil passed through the worm.

The extra organic matter in the grassland soil, with its greater number of roots, encouraged a vigorous microbial population in the worms' intestines. These glued the soil into very stable aggregates. Earthworms accounted for another small portion of the field aggregation, but there was still some to be explained. Also, there was still the mystery of the very permanent aggregates found in the field. These were more stable even than worm casts.

Now thinking in terms of humus, Dr. Swaby began to treat soil crumbs with certain humic extracts. One extract known as humic acid gave remarkable results. It not only improved aggregation but increased the permanence of the crumbs already formed.

Humic acid is a complicated product formed during the breakdown of organic matter in the soil. It has so far resisted attempts to unravel its involved chemical formula. In the presence of some minerals such as calcium and iron, a salt such as calcium humate was formed. This substance often proved more potent than humic acid as a means of increasing the permanence of aggregation, and explained the extreme stability of the crumb structure of some heavy red and black soils.

With X-ray analysis, chains of humic acid molecules could be detected inside actual clay particles, where they were held electrostatically. The presence of positively charged metals in solution increased the strength of the electrostatic bond and made the aggregate more permanent.

The picture was clearer now. Fungi which fed on plant roots bound soil particles into aggregates. Earthworms also helped to make soil aggregates. These aggregates were made stable by mobile humic acid compounds formed during the active breakdown of organic matter. Organic matter improved the quantity and quality of aggregation.

But even the strong, humus-bound crumbs are broken down by bacteria. When bacteria help break down organic matter to produce the humus extracts which aid aggregation, other bacteria destroy both these and aggregates bound together by fungal mycelia.

And what does this mean agriculturally?

It means that provision must be made in crop rotations to feed organic matter constantly back into the soil to replace that which is broken down by bacteria. If this is not done, the soil structure will suffer.

Stopping Erosion

A soil lacking good crumb structure is susceptible to erosion. Shortsighted agricultural practices have already led to the erosion and

Erosion is often the end result of a gradual loss of soil fertility. Compost helps to build the good crumb structure that encourages optimum fertility and resists erosion.

subsequent loss of frightening amounts of America's topsoil. Common estimates of annual United States soil loss run as high as 3 *billion* tons annually, as much as 700 million tons washing into the Gulf of Mexico alone. Some time ago, Dr. E. P. Dark stated the problem most eloquently. Writing in the *Medical Journal of Australia* ("The Haughley Experiment," October 25, 1978), and speaking of his own country while referring to the United States as well, he said:

> Mile high, those gloomy curtains of dust are the proper backdrop for the tragedy that is on the boards. The lustful march of the white race across the virgin continent strewn with ruined

forests, polluted streams, gullied fields, stained by the breaking of treaties and titanic greed, can no longer be disguised behind the camouflage which we call civilization.

. . . nearly all erosion is only the end result of a progressive loss of fertility; really fertile soil is very resistant to erosion, particularly wind erosion, being firmly bound together by its organic content into what is known as the crumb structure. That is soil as nature intended it to be, and can be seen at its best in any untouched rain forest. Such soil can be intensively farmed without destroying it as the Chinese have demonstrated during the past 4,000 years. In their farming all the wastes, from crops, animals, and humans, are returned to the soil as compost, which is as near as we can get to nature's method of growing grass on the prairies and trees in the forest.

The loss of crumb structure, then, is related closely to soil erosion, and the answer to good crumb structure is the incorporation of organic materials into the soil, along with other sound land management practices. It is a lesson that every farmer must learn, as must the increasing number of city dwellers who are buying rural land in an effort to preserve it. Unless sound land management practices are understood and applied conscientiously, erosion can deplete fertility with amazing rapidity. Organic matter—especially compost—can play an integral role in the fight against erosion.

Improving Aeration

Aeration is also extremely important to soil health. Air plays a vital role in the maintenance of soil productivity. Without air, soils tend to become alkaline, organic matter content decreases, active humus becomes deactivated, total and active humus content decreases, nitrogen content is reduced, and the carbon/nitrogen (C/N) ratio is lowered.

The presence of sufficient air in the soil is necessary for the transformation of minerals to forms usable by plants. Scientists have discovered that forced aeration increases the amount of potassium, one of the macronutrients, or elements most responsible for plant health, taken in by plants.

Many of the processes in the soil are oxidative—such as when sulfur is transformed to sulfur dioxide, carbon to carbon dioxide, ammonia to nitrate. Oxygen is essential in these processes and air is an

Hardpan results when the soil's crumb structure is too poor to allow the formation of air pockets. An extreme lack of organic matter can cause hardpan, and compost can correct it.

urgent need of the many beneficial soil organisms that aid in these transformations. In addition, aeration helps the formation of mycorrhiza, a fungus organism that acts in partnership with the roots of a plant to feed it valuable nutrients.

Compost helps to build soil structure that will allow for optimum aeration at all times. Without sufficient compost or other organic matter, soils will be unable to form the crumb structure that encourages air pockets. The result, in extreme cases, is a hardpan, inhospitable to all but the rankest of weeds. A true hardpan is formed by the compacting of soil grains into a hard, stonelike mass which is impervious to both air and water. Normally deep-rooted crops like alfalfa simply will not grow deeply in a shallow soil that overlies a hardpan or infertile subsoil. Conversely, shallow-rooted crops, given a deep, fertile soil, will go down deeply for minerals and water, producing higher yields of better quality. Breaking up hardpans with organic soil management practices, including plenty of compost, is the answer.

Nutrients When You Need Them

Compost is an excellent vehicle for carrying nutrients to your soil and plants. In a well planned and executed composting program, in fact, food crops and ornamentals will need no other form of fertilization besides good compost.

Further, the naturally occurring nutrients in compost are released slowly at a rate at which the plants can use them most profitably for optimum growth. Compost, then, is not only a source of nutrients, but a *storehouse* for them.

Compost doles out nutrients slowly when plants are small and at greater rates as soil temperatures warm up and the crops' major growth period begins. This is because soil microorganisms which release the nutrients from compost work harder as temperatures increase. Chemical fertilizer companies have tried to reproduce this effect by marketing their products in timed-release form. Rather than saturating a field with quickly available nitrogen, a major factor in nitrogen pollution of ground and surface waters, such fertilizers slowly release their nitrogen over a period of time. Unfortunately, they are horribly expensive—unlike compost.

For example, when composted, manure releases 50 percent of its nutrients in the first season and a decreasing percentage in subsequent years. This means that with constant additions of compost, the reserves of plant nutrients in the soil are being built up and up to the point where, for several seasons, little fertilizer of any kind may be needed. No chemical can claim that.

"I used to put raw manure in the holes I dug for tomato plants," wrote a Pennsylvania gardener to the editors of *Organic Gardening*. "Or, when I could afford it, a cupful of high-nitrogen commercial plant food. The plants grew to be green and massive, but there were very few tomatoes on them. Someone told me I was giving the plants too much nitrogen all at once."

This gardener started to use compost instead, and several years later reported that even when he had been unable to make and use compost for as long as two seasons, his tomatoes were still the best around.

"I think it's the buildup of nutrients in the soil and all the microorganisms and worms that are there now," he said. "The soil seems to feed the plants just what they need and when they need it."

The greater the variety of materials used in making compost, the greater will be the variety of nutrients contained in it. This includes not only the major elements, nitrogen, phosphorus, and potassium (N-P-K), but also the minor elements (often called trace elements).

Although trace elements are needed by plants in very small amounts in comparison to major elements, they are nevertheless just as essential to plant growth and reproduction. Trace elements commonly found to be deficient in many soils include iron, cobalt, manganese, boron, zinc, copper, molybdenum and iodine. Similarly, too much of these trace elements will also affect plant growth. As little as 25 parts per million of nickel will reduce the growth of an orange seedling, for example. Manure and compost usually contain a balanced amount of minor elements and farmers who still use large amounts of these materials are less likely to encounter deficiencies of minor elements.

K. J. McNaught in a technical report appearing in the *New Zealand Journal of Agriculture* says that a general survey of trace-element deficiencies in market garden crops definitely shows that organic materials produce better vegetables for market. They have more of the vital minerals in them.

McNaught points out that the survey showed that crops not fertilized and those fertilized with chemicals did not show the content of trace elements that the organically fertilized vegetables did. McNaught says that this is definitely an effect of the use of organic materials in gardening. Pastures and field crops, he states, are more often deficient in trace elements than garden crops for the same reason. Farmers don't add as much organic material to their farm lands as they do to their gardens.

COLLOIDS AND MINERALS

The medium by which organic matter transfers nutrients to plant roots is called base exchange. Colloidal (very tiny) humus particles are negatively charged and attract positive elements such as potassium, sodium, calcium, magnesium, iron, and copper. Colloidal clay particles have this same ability, but not to as great an extent as humus. When a tiny rootlet moves into contact with some humus, it exchanges hydrogen ions for equivalent quantities of the mineral ions. These are then taken up into the plant.

The mineral-holding capacity of colloidal particles is very important to the maintenance of soil fertility. Lack of soil colloids means that minerals are easily leached out by rain. As Dr. Ehrenfried Pfeiffer, originator of the bio-dynamic method, pointed out in *Bio-Dynamic Farming and Gardening:* "One can wash out a soil by frequent percolation until the filtrate no longer contains any minerals in solution. In many cases, the analysis of the soil before and after the washings does not correspond with the amount of minerals washed out. The holding capacity is quite different in soils with a high organic matter content

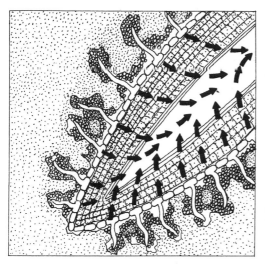

Diagram of base exchange.

➡ MINERAL IONS

🕸 HYDROGEN IONS

from that of soils with low organic matter. In fact, a soil with high organic matter loses very little through washing out. In the same procedure, a soil plus soluble mineral fertilizer loses not only the added minerals, but quite a bit of its own hidden reserves, too.

"One can pour seven times their weight in water through soils with high organic matter in 12 washings, and not lose any appreciable amount of minerals."

Dr. Pfeiffer explained that this is why crops on low-humus soils exhibit fast growth after a rain—they are absorbing the minerals in solution—but "when drought sets in these crops come to a standstill, and start to head out much too early. Organic soils result in a slower growth during the same period, but the plants continue to grow on into the dry season, head out later, and thus accumulate more weight." They are drawing on the minerals held on the colloids which are plentiful in a humus-rich soil.

Neutralizing Toxins

Another service of compost occurs in the neutralization of soil toxins. Authorities state, for example, that an overabundance of aluminum in the soil solution is highly toxic to plants, since it prevents them from taking up phosphorus. Actively decomposing organic matter results in more effective use of applied phosphorus in soils by the production of organic acids, some of which form stable complexes with iron and aluminum. The aluminum is thus "locked up" in a stable complex, unable to harm plants.

Selman Waksman in his book, *Humus*, says, "The toxicity of plant poisons becomes less severe in a soil high in humus than in a soil deficient in humus; high salt concentrations are less injurious; and aluminum solubility and its specific injurious action are markedly decreased."

Humus thus acts as a buffer in the soil. Garden and crop plants are less dependent upon a specific soil pH when there is an abundant supply of humus. For instance, in soils where the humus content is low, potatoes require acid conditions. If such soils are more alkaline, potatoes are highly susceptible to potato scab. In soils better supplied with humus, they suffer no potato scab even when the soil is slightly alkaline.

"Organic matter has a high capacity to fix heavy metals and many papers have been written on the subject," observed M. B. Kirkham, who conducted a study on organic matter and heavy metals at the University of Massachusetts. Kirkham concluded, "Indigenous soil organic matter and that added in sewage sludge, farmyard manures, composts, crop residues, and peat, bind heavy elements in soil. Most heavy metals which are associated with soil organic matter are in insoluble and stable combinations and are relatively unavailable for plant uptake. The ability of soil organic matter to hold heavy elements necessary for growth for a long time and release them as needed to crops is one of the most important benefits derived from its presence in soils."

pH Control

Carefully made compost can alter the pH (acidity or alkalinity) of soil.

Excessive alkalinity means that soil pH is abnormally high. This condition is common throughout the Southwest. It reduces microorganism life in the soil and makes raising acid-loving vegetables difficult or impossible.

One southwestern gardener who knows about alkaline soil, Regina Jones, used a compost made of sand, straw, and steer manure and succeeded in growing good rhubarb, strawberries, raspberries, and grapes—all crops which thrive in acid conditions.

"This year," she writes, "the grapes boast dark green foliage. They have climbed 6 feet and are loaded with fruit—another row of soldiers who battled alkali and won!"

In parts of New England, northern Michigan, northwestern Minnesota, northern Wisconsin, New York, New Jersey, and Alaska, sandy soil covers heavy colloidal clay and is in turn covered by a thin layer of acid humus. This condition, also inhospitable to many crops, can also be corrected by the use of compost.

A couple gardening in West Hatfield, Massachusetts, learned how to bring fertility to their acid soil. They applied lime and added humus to the soil. "The soil," they said, "is now rich and clean smelling, a dark brown in color and loose enough to dig a carrot with your fingers. And it yields as we never dreamed possible. Five of our cabbage heads can fill a bushel basket, and our potatoes are things to marvel at. All this from a hopeless leached-out soil that couldn't even support radishes."

EARTHWORMS HELP

Earthworms, in passing soil and organic matter through their bodies, gradually make acid soil less acid, and alkaline soil less alkaline, eventually drawing any out-of-balance soil into the neutral range. Compost feeds earthworms and allows them to multiply, thus enhancing their ability to correct soil pH. Earthworms and compost work together in many ways to improve soil for growing plants. This relationship is discussed more fully in Chapter 9.

Stretching the Growing Season

Compost can enable gardeners and farmers to plant earlier in the spring and harvest later in the fall, effectively stretching the growing season at both ends. Compost accomplishes this feat by making soil darker, thus allowing it to absorb more heat from the sun.

Paul Mahan, who lives in Florida, spreads 2 inches of compost over his garden every September and digs it into the soil. "The proof that plants respond to treatment is," he says, "that I picked kohlrabi in 35 days, snap beans in 45, tomatoes in 60, and all vegetables ahead of the time as stated in seed catalogs."

Even as far north as northern Ohio, the use of humus enables earlier and later than normal harvesting. One Ohio homesteader grows a wide variety of fruits and vegetables usually associated with warmer climates. His rhubarb and asparagus are ready to eat ahead of schedule. His celery gets a long enough growing season so that it resembles Florida celery more than the kind usually seen in northern gardens.

In October, when a hard frost has already occurred, the fall-bearing raspberries are still going strong. "Some years," he says, "we have raspberries straight from the garden with our Thanksgiving Day dinner."

Compost can also be used as a mulch, in which case it will act even more effectively as a moderator of soil temperature. At the end of the season, the compost mulch can be plowed or tilled under to provide a storehouse of nutrients for crops in following seasons. A compost mulch will also encourage the multiplication and good work of earthworms, especially red worms and brandling worms, neither of which can survive in soils without copious amounts of organic matter on the surface.

Growth Stimulators

Compost also produces compounds that act as growth stimulators. Experiments on wheat, barley, potatoes, grapes, tomatoes, beets, and other crops show that even in very low concentrations, humic acids act to stimulate plant growth. At concentrations as low as 0.01 to 0.1 percent, increased growth has been observed. Root systems in particular respond rapidly to the stimulating action of humic acids.

Tests to determine just how humic acids work revealed that they are in an ionically dispersed state. In this form they are readily assimilated by the plants as a nutrient over and above any normal mineral nutrition that plants get. Humic acids also improve oxygen assimilation. This is particularly noticeable in the early stages of plant growth.

It was also noted during tests with humic acids that plants are able to assimilate other physiologically active substances, including bitumens, vitamins, and vitamin-analogs. All of these substances, including the humic acids, are either supplied in fresh organic matter or derived from it during the decaying process.

Colors of Flowers

Even the colors of plants can be affected by compost. The pigments that make up the green chlorophyll of leaves, as well as all the colors of flowers, fruits and crops, are manufactured from substances in soil and air. Carbon dioxide, nitrogen, and magnesium are some of the elements that must be present in sufficient quantities to bring out the best colors. Compost-grown plants, because they get all they need of these elements, are more richly colored than plants that are grown without compost.

Chemicals vs. Compost

It should be obvious, if you have read this far about the benefits of compost, that chemical fertilizers are no substitute for compost. Chemicals supply major nutrients—period—in quick-release forms. Plants obtain fast growth, but long-term benefits are few. And living soil and living plants need far more than a few isolated chemical elements. Plants take their nourishment through infinitely complex biological processes which we still do not understand fully. To use chemical fertilizers to the neglect of compost is to disregard the soil's need for life.

Further, the chemical system of gardening and agriculture depends extensively on the use of dwindling energy reserves. In 1969 an average of 110 pounds of nitrogen fertilizer per acre was used on corn in this country, equivalent to using 42 gallons of gasoline for every acre. With nonrenewable energy supplies decreasing, their costs will continue to rise, making the use of chemical fertilizers ever more expensive.

Thirty-five percent of chemical nitrogen and from 15 to 20 percent of the phosphorus and potassium applied to land is lost because farmers and gardeners apply these chemicals in amounts greater than can be immediately assimilated by plants or soil. Since the chemical material, unlike the major constituents of compost, is immediately soluble, it is easily leached out during a rain.

Several years ago a biology class in a small midwestern college undertook as a term project the analysis of periodically taken and geographically distributed samples from a local river which had become polluted. It was not long before a variety of industrial chemicals and other wastes could be traced to their sources near factories and sewage outlets. Later on in the project, students became concerned about the large algae blooms in the river. These appeared regularly following rain and were particularly thick at one bend of the river under a steep bank. One day a group of students followed a small rivulet which emerged from the bank. They traced it uphill for nearly half a mile, and, at its source, they found the home and property of a part-time homesteader. The homesteader grew most of his own vegetables and also raised catfish in a small pond from which the rivulet flowed as an outlet. The pond had been dug a year or so before and since that time, the homesteader explained, he had had trouble with dirt washing into the pond from its surrounding banks. His aim was to grow grass on the banks to hold the soil, but he had had such difficulty getting grass started that he had begun throwing large quantities of high-nitrogen fertilizer on the seeded banks. From that seemingly innocent use of chemical fertilizer had come a sizable addition to the pollution of a river.

According to Dr. Barry Commoner, pollution by nitrates from inorganic fertilizers equals pollution from sewage. This pollution through leaching and accumulation in ground and surface waters promotes the growth of algae in streams, rivers, and lakes, eventually leading to the biological "death" of bodies of water.

Nitrates and other substances in synthetic fertilizers have also been linked to nitrate poisoning, cancer, deterioration of soils' healthy structures, creation of hardpans, and destruction of earthworms, azotobacters, and other helpful microorganisms. These chemicals can alter the vitamin and protein content of certain crops and make some crops more vulnerable to disease. Some experts have even said that vegetables grown with chemical fertilizers lose the power to reproduce in kind after a period of years. For example, Sir Albert Howard (one of the original promoters of composting) felt that new varieties would have to be introduced frequently from areas of the world where chemicals were not traditionally used if vegetable species were to maintain their strength when planted for several generations and nourished with chemicals.

The foundation of chemical agriculture and the chemical fertilizer industry rests on the assumption that what a plant removes from the soil can be analyzed and replaced in chemical form. Though this would seem to be a logical assumption, it fails to take into account the complex biological processes and mechanisms through which the chemical transactions are performed, processes and mechanisms aided by finely tuned and highly specialized living organisms whose operations cannot be duplicated or even completely understood by man. In general, the use of synthetic fertilizers trades short-term rapid growth for long-term gain in structure and soundness. Chemical fertilizer advertisements, you will notice, emphasize rapid crop growth and vegetable size, not vegetable texture and flavor or permanent advantage to soil structure.

3

Life inside a Compost Heap

The two most important aspects of a compost pile are the chemical makeup of its components and the population of organisms in it. Compost piles are intricate and complex communities of animal, vegetable, and mineral matter, all of which are interrelated, and all of which play a part in the breakdown of organic matter into humus. Composting is the result of the activities of a succession of organisms, each group paving the way for the next group by breaking down or converting a complex biodegradable material into a simpler or more usable material that can be utilized by its successor in the chain of breakdown. Generally speaking, the more "simple" is the molecular structure of the material, the more resistant it becomes to bacterial attack and hence, the more biologically stable it becomes. Whether the decomposition process takes place on the forest floor or in a gardener's compost heap, the biochemical systems at work are the same, and humus is always the result.

Humus

Humus, the relatively stable end product of composting, is rich in nutrients and organic matter, and highly beneficial to both the soil and crops grown in the soil.

As we saw in Chapter 2, the advantages of humus are twofold. First, when it is mixed with the soil, the resulting combination becomes a heterogeneous, loosely structured soil mixture allowing air and water to penetrate to soil organisms and growing plants. Because of its loose texture, humus-rich soil soaks up water in its pores so that less runoff occurs. Second, humus contains a number of chemical elements that enrich the soil with which it is mixed, providing nutrients for growing plants.

The major elements found in humus are nitrogen, phosphorus, potash, sulfur, iron and calcium, varying in amounts according to the original composition of the raw organic matter thrown on the heap. Trace elements are also present, again in varying amounts depending on the type of compost. The N-P-K percentages of finished compost are relatively low, but their benefit lies in the release of nitrogen and phosphorus in the soil at a slow enough rate that plants can use them, and they aren't lost through leaching.

Soil mixed with humus becomes a rich, dark color that absorbs far more heat than nonorganic soils, making it a more favorable environment in which to grow crops and ornamental plants.

How Compost Is Produced

The road from raw organic material to finished compost is a complex one, because both chemical and microbial processes are responsible for the gradual change from one to the other.

Decomposition of compost is accomplished by enzymatic digestion of plant and animal material by soil microorganisms. Simultaneously, chemical processes of oxidation, reduction, and hydrolysis are going on in the pile, and their products at various stages are used by microorganisms for further breakdown.

Bacteria use these products for two purposes: (1) to provide energy to carry on their life processes, and (2) to obtain the nutrients they need to grow and reproduce. The energy is obtained by oxidizing the products, especially the carbon fraction. The heat in a compost pile is the result of this biological "burning," or oxidation. Some materials can be broken down and oxidized more rapidly than others. This explains why a pile heats up fairly rapidly at the start. It is because the readily decomposed material is being attacked and bacterial activity is at its peak. If all goes well, this material is soon used up, and so bacterial activity slows down—and the pile begins to cool. Of course, if the mass of the material is big enough, it acts as an insulator to prevent heat loss, and the high temperature may thus persist for some time after the active period is over, especially if the pile is not turned. Persistent high temperatures are the result of uneven breakdown.

The raw materials that you add to your compost heap will have to be of biological origin in order to decompose down to finished compost. Wood, paper, kitchen trimmings including vegetable matter, crop leavings, weeds, manure, etc., can all be included in the heap. As compost is broken down from these raw materials to simpler forms of proteins and carbohydrates, it becomes more available to a wider array of bacterial species that will carry it to a further stage of decomposition.

Carbohydrates (starches and sugars) break down in a fairly rapid process to simple sugars, organic acids and carbon dioxide that are released in the soil. When proteins decompose, they readily break down into peptides, amino acids, and then to available ammonium compounds and atmospheric nitrogen. Finally, species of "nitrifying" bacteria change the ammonium compounds to nitrates, in which form they are available to plants.

At this stage of decomposition, the heap is near to becoming finished compost, with the exception of a few substances that still resist breakdown. Through complex, biochemical processes, these substances and the rest of the decomposed material form humus.

The microorganisms of the compost heap, like any other living things, need both carbon from the carbohydrates, and forms of nitrogen from the proteins in the compost substrate. In order to thrive and reproduce, all microbes must have access to a supply of the elements of which their cells are made. They also need an energy source and a source of the chemicals they use to make their enzymes. The principal nutrients for bacteria, actinomycetes, and fungi are carbon (C), nitrogen (N), phosphorus (P), and potassium (K). Trace elements are needed in minute quantities.

These chemicals in the compost pile are not in their pure form, and certainly not all in the same form at the same time. For example, at any given moment, nitrogen may be found in the heap in the form of nitrates and nitrites, in ammonium compounds, in the complex molecules of undigested or partly digested cellulose, and in the complex protein of microorganism protoplasm. There are many stages of breakdown and many combinations of elements. What's more, microorganisms can make use of nitrogen and other elements only when they occur in specific forms and ratios to one another.

Nutrients must be present in the correct ratio in your compost heap. The ideal C/N ratio for most compost microorganisms is about 25:1, though it varies from one compost pile to another. When too little carbon is present, making the C/N ratio too low, nitrogen may be lost to the microorganisms because they are not given enough carbon to use with it. It may float into the atmosphere as ammonia and be lost to the plants

One way to insure plenty of air in a compost heap is to thrust a board or pole into the middle of the heap, then withdraw it gradually as composting proceeds.

Another method is to build several rods or sticks right into the pile to be withdrawn as the heap heats up.

that would benefit by it when it would become part of humus. Materials too high in carbon for the amount of nitrogen present (too high C/N) make composting inefficient, so more time is needed to complete the process. When added to the soil, high-carbon compost uses nitrogen from the soil to continue decomposition, making it unavailable to growing plants.

Affecting the interwoven chemical and microbial breakdown of the compost heap are environmental factors that need to be mentioned here.

Composting can be defined in the terms of *availability of oxygen*. Aerobic decomposition means that the active microbes in the heap require oxygen, while in anaerobic decomposition, the active microbes do not require oxygen to live and grow. When compost heaps are located in the open air, as most are, oxygen is available and the biological processes progress under aerobic conditions. Temperature, moisture content, the size of bacterial populations, and availability of nutrients limit and determine how much oxygen your heap uses.

The *amount of moisture* in your heap should be as high as possible, while still allowing air to filter into the pore spaces for the benefit of aerobic bacteria. Individual materials hold various percentages of moisture in compost and determine the amount of water that can be added. For example, woody and fibrous material, such as bark, sawdust, wood chips, hay and straw have the capacity to hold up to 75 to 85 percent of moisture. "Green manure," such as lawn clippings and vegetable trimmings are able to hold 50 to 60 percent moisture. According to Clarence G. Golueke in *Composting*:

> The minimum content at which bacterial activity takes place is from 12 to 15 percent. Obviously, the closer the moisture content of a composting mass approaches these low levels, the slower will be the compost process. As a rule of thumb, the moisture content becomes a limiting factor when it drops below 45 or 50 percent.

Temperature is an important factor in the biology of a compost heap. Low outside temperatures during the winter months slow the decomposition process, while warmer temperatures speed it up. During the warmer months of the year, intense microbial activity inside the heap causes composting to proceed at extremely high temperatures. The microbes which decompose the raw materials fall into basically two categories: mesophilic, those that live and grow in temperatures of 50° to 113°F. (10° to 45°C.), and thermophilic, those that thrive under tempera-

You can gauge the progress of your compost by regularly checking the temperature inside the heap. The center of this pile has reached thermophilic temperatures, while higher up, heat is still in the mesophilic range.

tures of 113° to 158°F. (45° to 70°C.). Most garden compost begins at mesophilic temperatures, then increases to the thermophilic range for the remainder of the decomposition period. These high temperatures are beneficial to the gardener because they kill weed seeds and diseases that could be detrimental to a planted garden.

The bacterial decomposers in compost prefer a *pH range* of between 6.0 and 7.5, and the fungal decomposers between 5.5 and 8.0. Compost must be within these ranges if it is to decompose. Levels of pH are a function of the number of hydrogen ions present. (High pH levels, of course, indicate alkalinity; low levels, acidity.) In finished compost, a neutral (7.0) or slightly acid (slightly below 7.0) pH is best, though slight alkalinity (slightly above 7.0) can be tolerated.

Lime is often used to raise the pH if the heap becomes too acid. However, ammonia forms readily with the addition of lime, and nitrogen can be lost.

Compost Organisms

Since decomposition is the crux of the composting process, let's take a look at the various organisms that play such an essential role in the working compost heap. Most are microscopic, some are large enough to be observed with the unaided eye, but all are beneficial, each having a role in breaking down raw organic matter into finished compost. They are known as decomposers.

By far the most important microscopic decomposers are bacteria, who do the lion's share of decomposition in the compost heap. But there are other microscopic creatures such as actinomycetes, fungi, and protozoa, that also play an important role. Together, these microscopic decomposers change the chemistry of the organic wastes, and carry the name of chemical decomposers.

The larger fauna in the heap include mites, millipedes, flatworms, centipedes, sowbugs, snails, slugs, spiders, springtails, beetles, ants, flies, nematodes and, most importantly, earthworms. Collectively, these are called the physical decomposers since they bite, grind, suck, tear and chew the materials into smaller pieces, making them more suitable for the chemical work of the microscopic decomposers.

BACTERIA

The bacteria likely to be found in a compost heap are those that specialize in breaking down organic compounds; thrive in temperatures ranging up to 170°F. (77°C.) in the thermophilic range, and those that are aerobic, needing air to survive. Bacterial populations differ from pile to pile, depending upon the raw materials of the compost, degree of heat, amount of air present, moisture level, geographical location of the pile, and other considerations.

Bacteria are single-celled and can be shaped like a sphere, rod, or a spiral twist. They are so small that it would take 25,000 bacteria laid end to end to take up one inch on a ruler, and an amount of garden soil the size of a pea may contain up to a billion bacteria. Most bacteria are colorless and cannot make carbohydrates from sunshine, water, and carbon dioxide the way more complex green plants can. Some bacteria produce colonies; others are free-living. All reproduce by means of binary fission.

In binary fission, the nucleus splits in two and a new cell wall grows crosswise over the middle of the cell. Each half contains one of the two nuclei, so that a new individual is produced from a single bacterial cell.

Under the best conditions, a colony of bacteria can multiply into the billions in a very short time. The life span of one generation of bacteria is about 20 to 30 minutes, so that one cell may yield a progeny of billions of individuals in half a day.

Bacteria are the most nutritionally diverse of all organisms, which is to say, as a group, they can eat nearly anything. Most compost bacteria are heterotrophic, meaning that they can use living or dead organic materials, similar to fungi and animals. Some are so adaptable that they can use more than a hundred different organic compounds as their source of carbon because of their ability to produce a variety of enzymes. Usually, they can produce the appropriate enzyme to digest whatever material they find themselves on. In addition, respiratory enzymes in the cell membrane make aerobic respiration possible as an energy source for compost bacteria.

Since bacteria are smaller, less mobile and less complexly organized than most organisms, they are less able to escape an environment that becomes unfavorable. A decrease in the temperature of the pile or a sharp change in its acidity can render bacteria inactive or kill them. When the environment of a heap begins to change, bacteria that formerly dominated may be decimated by another species.

At the beginning of the composting process, mesophilic (medium temperature) bacteria and fungi predominate. They gradually give way to thermophilic (high temperature) bacteria as the pile becomes hotter; the more thermophilic bacteria that are present, breaking down compounds and releasing heat as a by-product, the hotter the pile becomes. As stability approaches, actinomycetes and fungi that have so far been confined to the cooler edges of the pile begin to dominate the compost and hasten it toward further stability.

ACTINOMYCETES

The characteristically earthy smell of newly plowed soil in the spring is caused by actinomycetes, a higher form of bacteria similar to fungi and molds. Actinomycetes are especially important in the formation of humus. While most bacteria are found in the top foot or so of topsoil, actinomycetes may work many feet below the surface. Deep under the roots they convert dead plant matter to a peatlike substance.

While they are decomposing animal and vegetable matter, actinomycetes liberate carbon, nitrogen and ammonia, making nutrients available for higher plants. They are found on every natural substrate, and the majority are aerobic and mesophilic. Five percent or more of the soil's bacterial population is comprised of actinomycetes.

The reason that bacteria tend to die rapidly as actinomycete populations grow in the compost pile is that actinomycetes have the ability to produce antibiotics, chemical substances that inhibit bacterial growth.

PROTOZOA

Protozoa are the simplest form of animal organism. Even though they are single-celled and microscopic in size, they are larger and more complex in their activities than most bacteria. A gram of soil can contain as many as a million protozoa, but compost has far fewer, especially during the thermophilic stage. Protozoa obtain their food from organic matter in the same way as bacteria do. In fact, they are so much like bacteria in every way, and so much less important to composting, that they need to receive only brief mention in the compost biological census.

FUNGI

Fungi are many-celled, filamentous or single-celled primitive plants. Unlike more complex green plants, they lack chlorophyll, and therefore lack the ability to make their own carbohydrates. Most of them are classified as saprophytes because they live on dead or dying material, and obtain energy by breaking down organic matter in dead plants and animals.

Like the actinomycetes, fungi take over during the final stages of the pile when the compost has been changed to a more easily digested form. The best temperature for active fungi in the compost heap is around 70° to 75°F. (21° to 24°C.) though some thermophilic forms prefer much greater heat and survive to 120°F. (49°C.).

The bacteria, actinomycetes, protozoa and fungi that we have looked at so far have to do mainly with chemical decomposition in the compost heap. The larger organisms, though, that chew and grind their way through the compost heap are higher up in the food chain, and are known as physical decomposers.

All of the organisms, from the microscopic bacteria to the largest of the physical decomposers, are part of a complex food chain in your compost pile. They can be categorized as first, second and third level consumers, depending upon whom they eat and whom they are eaten by. First level consumers attract and become the food of second level consumers, who in turn are consumed by third level consumers. The organisms comprising each level of the food chain serve to keep the populations of the next lower level in check, so that a balance can be maintained throughout the compost. For example, according to Daniel L. Dindal, in *Ecology of Compost*,

> . . . mites and springtails eat fungi. Tiny feather-winged beetles feed on fungal spores. Nematodes ingest bacteria. Protozoa and rotifers present in water films feed on bacteria and plant particles. Predaceous mites and pseudoscorpions prey upon nematodes, fly larvae, other mites and collembolans. Free-living flatworms ingest gastropods, earthworms, nematodes and rotifers. Third level consumers such as centipedes, rove beetles, ground beetles, and ants prey on second level consumers.

The following is a rundown of some of the larger physical decomposers that you may find in nearly any compost heap. Most of these creatures function best at medium or mesophilic temperatures, so they will not be in the pile at all times.

MITES

Mites are related to ticks, spiders, and horseshoe crabs because they have in common six leglike, jointed appendages. They can be free-living or parasitic, sometimes both at once. Some mites are small enough to be invisible to the naked eye while some tropical species are up to a half-inch in length.

Mites reproduce very rapidly, moving through larval, nymph, adult and dormant stages. They attack plant matter, but some are also second level consumers, ingesting nematodes, fly larvae, other mites and springtails.

MILLIPEDES

The wormlike body of the millipede has many leg-bearing segments, each except the front few bearing two pairs of walking legs.

The life cycles are not well understood, except that eggs are laid in the soil in springtime, hatching into small worms. Young millipedes molt several times before gaining their full complement of legs. When they reach maturity, adult millipedes can grow to a length of 1 to 2 inches. They help break down plant material by feeding directly on it.

CENTIPEDES

Centipedes are flattened, segmented worms with 15 or more pairs of legs—1 pair per segment. They hatch from eggs laid during the warm months and gradually grow to their adult size. Centipedes are third level consumers, feeding only on living animals, especially insects and spiders.

SOWBUGS

The sowbug is a fat-bodied, flat creature with distinct segments. In structure, it resembles the crayfish to which it is related. Sowbugs reproduce by means of eggs that hatch into smaller versions of the adults. Since females are able to deposit a number of eggs at one time, sowbugs may become abundant in a compost heap. They are first level consumers, eating decaying vegetation.

SNAILS AND SLUGS

Both snails and slugs are mollusks and have muscular disks on their undersides that are adapted for a creeping movement. Snails have a spirally curved shell, a broad retractable foot, and a distinct head. Slugs, on the other hand, are so undifferentiated in appearance that one species is frequently mistaken for half of a potato. Both snails and slugs lay eggs in capsules or gelatinous masses, and progress through larval stages to adulthood.

Their food is generally living plant material, but they will attack fresh garbage and plant debris and will appear in the compost pile. It is well, therefore, to look for them when you spread your compost, for if they move into your garden, they can do damage to crops.

SPIDERS

Spiders, which are related to mites, are one of the least appreciated animals in the garden. These eight-legged creatures are third level consumers that feed on insects and small invertebrates, and they can help control garden pests.

SPRINGTAILS

Springtails are very small insects, rarely exceeding one-quarter inch in length. They vary in color from white to blue-grey or metallic and are mostly distinguished by their ability to jump when disturbed. They feed by chewing decomposing plants, pollen, grains, and fungi.

BEETLES

The rove beetle, ground beetle, and feather-winged beetle are the most common beetles in compost. Feather-winged beetles feed on fungal spores, while the larger rove and ground beetles prey on other insects as third level consumers.

Beetles are easily visible insects with two pairs of wings, the more forward-placed of these serving as a cover or shield for the folded and thinner back-set ones that are used for flying.

A beetle's immature stage is as a soft-skinned grub that feeds and grows during the warm months. Once grubs are full grown, they pass through a resting or pupal stage and change into hard-bodied, winged adults.

Most adult beetles, like the larval grubs of their species, feed on decaying vegetables, while some, like the rove and ground beetles, prey on snails, insects, and other small animals. The black rove beetle is an acknowledged predator of snails and slugs. Some people import them to their gardens when slugs become a garden problem.

ANTS

Ants feed on a variety of material, including aphid honeydew, fungi, seeds, sweets, scraps, other insects, and sometimes other ants. Compost provides some of these foods, and it also provides shelter for nests and hills. They will remain, however, only while the pile is relatively cool.

Ants prey on first level consumers, and may benefit the composting process by bringing fungi and other organisms into their nests. The work of ants can make compost richer in phosphorus and potassium by moving minerals from one place to another.

FLIES

Many flies, including black fungus gnats, soldier flies, minute flies, and houseflies, spend their larval phase in compost as maggots. Adults can feed upon almost any kind of organic material.

All flies undergo egg, larval, pupal, and adult stages. The eggs are laid in various forms of organic matter. Houseflies are such effective distributors of bacteria that when an individual fly crawls across a sterile plate of lab gelatin, colonies of bacteria later appear in its tracks. You can see how during the early phases of the composting process, flies provide ideal airborne transportation for bacteria on their way to the pile.

If you keep a layer of dry leaves or grass clippings on top of your pile and cover your garbage promptly while building compost, your pile will not provide a breeding place for horseflies, mosquitoes, or houseflies which may become a nuisance to humans. Fly larvae do not survive thermophilic temperatures. Mites and other organisms in the pile also keep fly larvae reduced in number. Though many flies die with the coming of frost, the rate of reproduction is so rapid that a few survivors can repopulate an area before the warm season has progressed very far.

WORMS

Nematodes or eelworms, free-living flatworms, and rotifers all can be found in compost. Nematodes are microscopic creatures that can be classified into three categories: those that live on decaying organic matter; those that are predators on other nematodes, bacteria, algae, protozoa, etc.; and those that can be serious pests in gardens where they attack the roots of plants.

Flatworms, as their name implies, are flattened organisms that are usually quite small in their free-living form. Most flatworms are carnivorous and would live in films of water within the compost structure.

Rotifers are small, multicellular animals that live freely or in tubes attached to a substrate. Their bodies are round and divisible into three parts, a head, trunk, and tail. They are generally found in films of water and many forms are aquatic. The rotifers in compost are found in water which adheres to plant substances where they feed on microorganisms.

EARTHWORMS

If bacteria are the champion microscopic decomposers, then the heavyweight champion is doubtless the earthworm. Pages of praise have been written to the earthworm, ever since it became known that this creature spends most of its time tilling and enriching the soil. The great English naturalist, Charles Darwin, was the first to suggest that all the fertile areas of this planet have at least once passed through the bodies of earthworms.

The earthworm consists mainly of an alimentary canal which ingests, decomposes, and deposits casts continually during the earthworm's active periods. As soil or organic matter is passed through an earthworm's digestive system, it is broken up and neutralized by secretions of calcium carbonate from calciferous glands near the worm's gizzard. Once in the gizzard, material is finely ground prior to digestion. Digestive intestinal juices rich in hormones, enzymes, and other fermenting substances continue the breakdown process. The matter passes out of the worm's body in the form of casts, which are the richest and finest quality of all humus material. Fresh casts are markedly higher in bacteria, organic material, available nitrogen, calcium and magnesium, and available phosphorus and potassium than soil itself. Earthworms thrive on compost and contribute to its quality through both physical and chemical processes.

Both male and female reproductive systems are in one earthworm, but fertilization can only occur between two separate individuals during copulation. The fertilized eggs are deposited and contained in a cocoon, out of which the young worms emerge after eight to ten days.

Since earthworms are willing and able to take on such a large part in compost making, it is the wise gardener who adjusts his composting methods to take full advantage of the earthworm's special talents. For example, he may want to control pH levels, moisture content or change his basic composting methods to a form that includes earthworms as an ingredient. The earthworm's special contributions to the compost heap will be discussed more fully in Chapter 9. It is important here to realize, however, that this creature is the most important of all the larger living beings in a compost pile. Compost and earthworms work together, to the ultimate benefit of growing plants of every kind.

4

Compost and Plant Health

Plants grown in compost-rich soil will be healthier and more resistant to both insects and plant diseases.

All higher plants have, according to C. E. Millar in *Soil Fertility*, the same basic requirements for growth, although their requirements vary widely in amount and degree. The essentials are light, heat, water, air, and certain nutrient elements in reasonable amounts and in suitable balance. Plants obtain needed moisture and nutrients with the exception of carbon dioxide from the soil. The soil also helps to control the temperature in the root zone and, to a lesser extent, in the aerial portions of plants. For a plant to thrive, its soil must be low in toxic substances and disease organisms.

Temperature and Plants

Of the various factors that influence seed germination and plant growth, temperature is one of the most crucial. It seems to take forever for the first planting of peas in early March to be seen above the soil's surface. But in July, beans and new sowings of lettuce seem to germinate overnight by some sort of midsummer night's magic.

The heat necessary for plant growth comes from the sun. Plants were using solar energy long before people got an inkling of its usefulness. But the earth quickly reradiates much of the heat it receives from the sun, particularly when the sun shines on bare, light-colored fields or on the ever-increasing expanses of concrete on this planet's surface. Dark colors absorb heat, however, and the black color of humus helps it retain heat from the sunlight. When you put compost into your garden, you are helping the earth to absorb and store heat for your plants, moderating soil temperatures.

47

Soil that is rich in organic matter will produce lush, healthy plants that yield heavily.

During the growing season, soil temperatures to a depth of several inches vary greatly over a 24-hour period. Low-growing roots must function at temperatures cooler than those for surface roots. The temperature differences exert an influence on the uptake of water and nutrients by plants. Experiments have shown that there is a marked increase in nutrient accumulation in plants as temperatures rise.

The absorption of water by plant roots is retarded by both low and high temperatures. Plants adapted for growth at low temperatures will continue to absorb water in soils under 40°F. (4°C.), but warm-temperature plants will not. Adding compost (and therefore humus) to soil tends to keep it from heating up or cooling down rapidly so water absorption can remain at a relatively constant rate.

Root growth is greatly influenced by soil temperature. In general, growth of roots increases as temperatures rise to a certain point, then decreases rapidly if temperatures rise beyond that point. For example, root growth is most rapid in most plants before midsummer.

Most beneficial soil microorganisms multiply most rapidly at temperatures between 50° and 104°F. (10° and 40°C.). Organic matter in soil decomposes increasingly quickly, due to the work of microorganisms as temperatures rise toward 80.6°F. (27°C.); as the process continues, temperature is less of a factor. Ammonia production is rapid at temperatures of 68° to 104°F. (20° to 40°C.), but nitrate formation is less active at 68° or 95°F. (20° or 35°C.) than it is at 77°F. (25°C.).

Disease organisms are also influenced by temperature. Some do better at high temperatures, especially when such temperatures weaken their plant hosts. Once again, the moderating effects of humus are helpful in controlling disease.

On the whole, growth of most plants is very slow below 40°F. (4°C.). Most higher plants are damaged or killed by temperatures ranging between 110° and 130°F. (43° and 54°C.). Often, disorders such as "sunscald" are produced by rapid change in temperature rather than by the high temperatures themselves. Usually the stem portion of the plant is most affected by these disorders.

Light and Plants

Light is essential to all plants which use chlorophyll to transform solar energy into chemical energy in the form of simple sugars. Light affects germination of seeds, the growth characteristics of plants, the development of plant organs and tissues, blooming, and other plant processes. If you've ever raked over an old compost pile or a pile of garden weeds and discovered a germinating bean seed or a growing weed almost completely cut off from light by the pile, you have noticed how anemic-looking and misshapen it was.

Different plants require different intensities of light. You've probably noticed that some grasses grow better under trees and some in open lawns and, if you're a flower gardener, you know which of your flowers prefer shade and which need lots of sun.

The carbon dioxide of the air and the water of the soil combine in the presence of sunlight to produce glucose in green plants. The carbon dioxide passes through stomata, tiny openings in the leaves. How wide the stomata open to permit carbon dioxide to pass to the assimilating cells is controlled by light. The stronger the light the wider open are the stomata; this is just the reverse of the way the pupils in your eyes enlarge to permit more light to enter in a dark room. Unless plants have too little water, stomata open in response to light and close in dark. A plant needs full sunlight for maximum photosynthesis. When you remember that no single leaf on a plant escapes some shading from

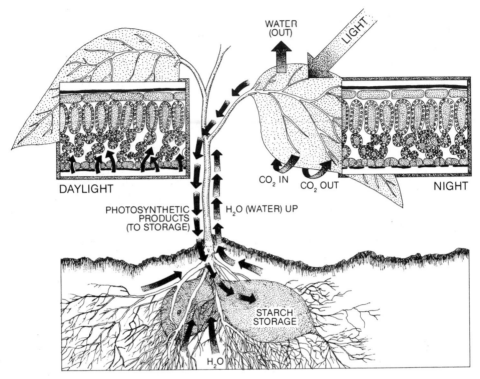

In the process of photosynthesis, carbon dioxide (CO_2) from the air and water (H_2O) from the soil combine in the presence of sunlight to form glucose (starch). Stomata in plant leaves are open during daylight hours to admit CO_2, and closed at night. Excess water and oxygen are transpired through the leaves. The glucose is stored in fleshy roots or tubers to nourish the plant and provide energy for growth.

other leaves in the course of a day, you realize how important sunlight is to plants. Because plants grown in fertile soil have a higher chlorophyll content in their leaves than less well nourished plants, they can manage better in less light.

Water and Plant Growth

All living tissue contains water. Plants need and absorb more water than they do any other element in the soil. Much of the water they take in, they give off again, or transpire, but some is kept in plant tissues and some is broken down to supply the hydrogen and part of the oxygen plants use or store in the form of carbohydrates. Drought is the most common cause of crop failure.

Green tissues of plants contain an average of 75 percent water. Growing tips can run to 93 percent water. Some plants contain more water than others. Tomato leaves are 84 percent water and cabbage leaves 86 percent.

A plant must be turgid—full of water—in order for vital processes to take place within it. Too little water in leaf tissues causes stomata to close, reducing photosynthesis.

Roots are essential for obtaining water and nutrients. One scientist studying four-month-old rye found that the average daily increase in length of the root system was 3.1 miles. Including root hair growth, the figure is 58 miles total growth in 24 hours. Generally, roots grow in response to water need. However, plants differ widely in the amount of root they grow in reaching water. Soils also influence the growth of roots. Tomato roots at 12 weeks reached a depth of 11 inches in loam, but in other soils they were much shallower. Humus increases the potential for deep root penetration and for firm anchorage of root hairs.

The availability of water also affects nutrient uptake. For example, nitrogen can be taken up from low-moisture soils more readily than phosphorus but less so than potassium. This, of course, can affect the growth pattern of the plant. The amount of water in the soil also has an effect on soil bacteria. The helpful nitrogen fixing bacterium azotobacter can resist drying, but many other beneficial soil bacteria cannot. This is one reason why nitrates are produced in smaller quantity in dry soils. On the other hand, too much water in soils leads to anaerobic conditions and cessation of most beneficial bacterial activity. Also, in soils that are too moist, toxic substances form, there is too little oxygen for respiration in the roots, and nitrates do not form. Roots do not develop as quickly as top growth in plants. Very succulent vegetables grown in wet soils are more susceptible to disease than are vegetables grown elsewhere. We have seen how compost added to soil moderates the effects of too much water by preventing hardpans.

Respiration and the Use of Air

Respiration is a process common to all living cells. Most plants need oxygen from the air; a large part of the carbon dioxide used by plants in photosynthesis and other processes also comes from the air. The amount of water vapor in air is an essential factor in plant growth.

Proportions of oxygen, nitrogen, and carbon dioxide do not vary widely in unpolluted air. Air normally contains 0.03 percent CO_2, and 20.96 percent O_2. Most plants thrive on the normal atmospheric percentages.

Soil air, the air involved in the soil and occupying interstices between soil aggregates, contains widely varying amounts of CO_2 and less O_2 than atmospheric air. Roots obtain their oxygen and CO_2 from this soil air.

Compost promotes aeration and there are many benefits to plants. Poorly aerated soils absorb water poorly, and water use by plants in humus-rich soil is more efficient than in unaerated clay. Plants also absorb more nutrients of all kinds in well aerated soils, so long as oxygen and carbon dioxide are in balance. In experiments, forced aeration increased the absorption of nutrients, particularly of potassium and phosphorus.

Humus and Plant Nutrition

The role of humus in plant nutrition has been the subject of much controversy among soil scientists throughout history and it continues to be a subject on which there are varying opinions. Several lines of inquiry are being pursued.

Until quite recently in history, people believed that plants "ate" humus and used its carbon content in their growth. In the 19th century the study of chemistry and the early use of hydroponic techniques—growing plants without soil—led to the opposite thesis, that as long as plants can be fed artificial chemical nutrients, they need no humus. Attempts to isolate and synthesize the organic compounds in humus, mostly humic acids, were for some time unsuccessful. Artificial humic acids did not have the same influence on plants that natural humus did. Only recently with new hydroponic techniques and sophisticated ways of measuring plant uptake of nutrients, such as the use of radioactive carbons, has the plant intake of the nutrients in humus been measured accurately.

In 1936, in *Humus*, Selman A. Waksman wrote of the early investigators of humus nutrients:

Even those investigators that denied the presence of any plant-stimulating substances in soil organic matter had to admit that although green plants grow, remain healthy, and reproduce without any organic matter or bacteria, still certain types of organic substances, especially in the presence of bacteria, may markedly affect the constitution of the plant.

Scientists began to look to humus for vitaminlike substances sometimes called "ausimones," or for "phytamins," which they believed to be in compost and organic manures. Others studied the plant hormones present in organic matter.

According to recent research by W. Flaig of the Institut für Biochemie in Braunschweig, Germany, soil organic matter contains physiologically active fractions of humic substances of low molecular weight which have an effect on the metabolism of plants after their uptake. Some of these substances, which are created in nature by the degradation of lignin (the woody substance found in the walls of plant cells), were synthesized in laboratory experiments. By using carbon 14 in the process, the scientists were able to observe the effect of the lignin-based humic substances in plant roots and to some extent in sprouts when they measured the radioactivity of the carbon 14. The plants exposed to these substances were also found to give off large quantities of CO_2.

W. Flaig also describes experiments in which amino acids (simple proteins) are taken up by plants as intact molecules and utilized in protein metabolism. The mechanism of uptake of humus nutrients by plants is somewhat like the transport of ions in a chemical reaction. It is not, as was earlier believed, always associated with capillarity. In poor environmental conditions such as low levels of moisture and air, humic substances act more rapidly to increase the dry weights of plants. Here we find still another reason for using compost.

V. Hernando Fernandez of Madrid, Spain, has also experimented with humic acids in solution. He found the humic acids derived from manure had even more effect on plants than the substances from peat (or lignin). Manure humic acids fostered nitrogen absorption by plants, but those made from peat did not. An increase in the weight of plants, according to Fernandez, is brought about as the result of the two most important influences of humic substances: their action on respiration, and their action on synthesis and photosynthesis.

One part of humic acid molecules consists of a series of quinonic and phenolic groups in a redox system. A redox, or oxidation-reduction, system is one in which a molecule loses electrons to another molecule.

This part of the molecules helps to liberate oxygen and so increases the rate of respiration in plants.

The other part of the humic acid molecules consists of nitrogen compounds, principally amino acids and proteins. This part exerts an enzymelike effect on photosynthesis.

For a plant to increase in weight, these two influences must be in balance. Hernando Fernandez determined that the effect of humic acids in solution differed markedly from the effect of chemical fertilizers. Increasing the quantities of humic acids used did not bring about corresponding effects in plants the way increasing the amounts of chemical fertilizers would have. This indicated to him that the balance of respiration-connected and photosynthesis-connected acids is all-important when humic acids are provided to plants in solution.

The importance of both the Spanish and German scientists' experiments is that they prove that humus and humus-produced substances do indeed influence plant growth, but that their influence is extremely complex. For example, a plant's ability to assimilate and make use of soil nutrients or to produce carbohydrates through photosynthesis may be influenced by humus even when the humus itself does not provide the nutrients. This provides evidence that the chemical theories of plant growth which contend that all the necessary nutrients can be provided with chemicals and that these alone will assure plant growth and health are indeed oversimplifications. Nature's soil-building processes are incredibly complex.

In addition to these new discoveries about the influence of humic substances, much earlier research bears witness to the benefits of humic materials to plants. In addition to serving as a soil conditioner, humus provides for plant nutrition in a number of ways. Waksman in *Humus* listed the following: (1) Organic compounds can be directly assimilated by plants and can replace nitrates in solution. (2) Leguminous plants obtain nitrogen in the form of organic compounds. (These are the plants with root nodules that play host to nitrogen-fixing bacteria.) (3) Certain sugars in humus can be assimilated by plants; lecithin, which is found in humus, can be used as a source of phosphate; cystine can be used as a source of sulfur. (4) Humus exerts an effect on the availability of inorganic phosphorus in soil. (5) Humus is a source of available iron to plants and microorganisms at reactions which are optimum for the growth of plants. (6) Plants lacking chlorophyll can use organic substances as their entire source of energy. They often do this in association with mycorrhizal fungi. (7) Organic matter and nitrogen have been found to prolong the maturation period of sugar cane plants. (8) Humus may increase the permeability of the protoplasmic membranes of plants, allowing them to assimilate more nutrients. (9) Humus is claimed to have an effect on the vitamins in plants. (10) Humus and decomposing organic matter have a controlling effect on plant pathogens, harmful fungi, nematodes, and harmful bacteria. (11) Humus is an important source of CO_2 for plant growth.

In addition to these specific ways in which humus helps plants, we should bear in mind that a secondary characteristic of humus is that it contains and can make available macro- and micro-nutrients. Though it measures as inefficient when compared to chemical fertilizers, the slow-release nature of humus makes it useful in providing nutrients to plants when and where they need them. Let's go back to the study of plant needs and study the nutrients plants require.

Macronutrients

NITROGEN

Nitrogen is vital for the formation of all new plant protoplasm. Chlorophyll is a nitrogen compound. Without nitrogen in sufficient quantity, plant growth is stunted. When a plant is deficient in nitrogen, it turns pale green or yellow. (It should be remembered, however, that other conditions such as excess or lack of moisture, cold weather, or plant disease can cause the same symptom.)

The demand for nitrogen is particularly strong when new plant tissue is developing; nitrogen is an essential ingredient of protoplasm. In members of the grass family, such as corn, the stems of nitrogen-deficient plants will be slender and the whole plant will lack vigor. If your plants show nitrogen deficiency symptoms, applications of compost may restore them to health. (See the chart on page 61.)

Nitrogen tends to be used more by stems and leaves than in seed production, so plants mature more slowly in soils over-rich in nitrogen. This condition is often seen in plants grown with artificial nitrogen fertilizer. Nitrogen is easily leached from soil when artificially introduced into it.

PHOSPHORUS

Phosphorus is necessary to photosynthesis, for energy transfers within plants, and for good flower and fruit growth. Unlike nitrogen, phosphorus has more to do with plant maturing than with plant growth.

Phosphorus is most frequently present in soil as phosphoric acid. Often this acid is bound up with the oxides of iron or with calcium, but soil bacteria can release it.

Plants exhibit less definite indications of lack of phosphorus than they do if suffering from shortages of nitrogen or potassium. An extreme or early lack of supply may stunt plant growth, but so may other deficiencies. Sometimes, early stunting if caused by lack of phosphorus is followed by a reddish or purple coloration, especially on the underside of the leaves. Fruit tree leaves become bronzed and lose their luster and some, like lemon leaves, show spots. Because the production of seeds is influenced by phosphorus, seed abnormalities may also indicate a lack of this element.

At blossoming time, phosphorous-deficient plants may become yellow. This is especially true of corn and white pea beans. Beets turn yellow in the fall when they need phosphorus.

Phosphorous-deficient plants often respond to applications of compost. Should a general phosphorous deficiency occur in your garden, make it a practice to add bone meal or a high-phosphorous rock powder to your compost or directly to your soil or planting holes.

POTASSIUM

Potassium is used by plants in many life processes, including the manufacture and movement of sugars, and cell division. It is necessary for root development and helps plants to retain water. Potassium or potash in soil is often bound up with silicates. Potassium is not, however, a constituent of the organic compounds within plants.

Symptoms of deficiency appear in older leaves first and take the form of yellowing at the edges. Later, leaf edges turn brown and may crinkle or curl. In the case of corn, streaks appear between the leaf veins and dry brown edges and tips appear on leaves. The brown spreads to the entire leaf. On legumes, yellow spots, turning brown, spread inward from leaf edges. Tomato and potato plants also show yellowing of leaf tips and edges and some curling. Beets, carrots, sweet potatoes, radishes, and similar crops are long and small in diameter when they lack potassium.

Compost made with a formula of 6 inches of green matter to every 2 inches of manure provides adequate potassium for garden needs. When the moisture of the green plants is eliminated and the material is broken down, a sizable percentage of the remaining solid matter consists of potassium. If your soil is extremely low in potassium, add potash rock, granite dust, or wood ashes to the compost heap. Heavy mulching also seems to help maintain soil potassium supplies. In an experiment performed some years ago at Purdue University, Clarence E. Baker found that mulching with manure, straw, and soybean hay eliminated symptoms of potassium deficiency in a peach orchard.

Micronutrients

CALCIUM

A lack of calcium appears to affect growing plants on stems and roots. Plants deficient in calcium are retarded in growth and develop thick woody stems. The lower leaves of cereal crops roll in at the edges and brown spots appear on them. In corn, the leaves sometimes stick together as if glued. Some plants show green veins with yellow tissue between them.

It is difficult to diagnose calcium deficiency because its assimilation is influenced by the quantity of magnesium, manganese, and potassium present in the soil. Calcium is present in sufficient quantities in most soils. But if you do find your soil deficient in calcium, treat it with any good grade of ground natural limestone.

IRON

Almost all soils have sufficient iron for crops. Iron-deficient soils usually have an over-supply of magnesium or lime. Iron deficiency is particularly hard to identify for the symptom—drying up of young leaves—is common to many deficiencies.

Humus serves a crucial function in keeping iron in solution in soils. At neutral or slightly alkaline reactions, inorganic iron is precipitated as hydrate or iron phosphate and becomes unavailable to plants. Humus can form compounds with iron which render it available to plants even under alkaline conditions. Plants also benefit indirectly when iron is supplied to soil microorganisms like azotobacter. Azotobacter needs iron for its synthesis of nitrogen, but humus is necessary before azotobacter can assimilate iron.

Sufficient iron can be added to soil by composting with manure, crop residues, or dried blood. Foxglove stores large quantities of iron in its leaves and is another useful addition to compost piles. Seaweed and many garden and field weeds also contain much iron.

Two examples of the effects of trace element deficiencies: top, normal Sanilac bean leaves (left) compared with bean leaves deficient in manganese; bottom, a corn plant deficient in zinc.

USDA photos

Trace Elements

Agronomists in the 1920s and 1930s discovered that the absence in the soil of a very small quantity of a variety of trace minerals such as magnesium, manganese, boron, silicium, molybdenum, iodine, copper, silicon, zinc, cobalt, chromium, tin, vanadium, nickel, and lithium could severely stunt the growth of crops. For example, a plant's ability to hold water is affected by trace minerals. These same trace minerals, again in minute quantities, have also proved beneficial to the health of animals and humans. Dietary deficiencies of trace elements in plants, animals, and people reflect soil deficiencies in the areas where they live. In 1962, a survey of 41 states revealed soil deficiencies of boron. Thirty had deficiencies of zinc, 25 of iron, 25 of manganese, 21 of molybdenum, and 13 of copper.

An excellent way of getting trace elements in the proper balance back into the soil is to compost with a great variety of organic materials. By applying trace minerals with organic compost rather than in chemical form, you can avoid the risk of toxicity. Many poor soils already have enough trace elements. The problem of these soils is that the minerals are locked into compounds that plants can't use. Earlier we talked about the action of the humic acids that are manufactured in the process of composting. They can pull trace elements out of minerals already in the soil and make them available to plants. We will discuss a few trace minerals in greater detail.

MAGNESIUM

Magnesium deficiency is manifested by discoloration in the tissue between veins, perhaps causing leaves to look streaked. With some plants, a reddish or purplish coloration appears on the leaf, and the leaf margins turn brown or yellow while the veins remain green. Magnesium functions as a carrier for phosphorus and the two deficiencies often go together, though plants require far more phosphorus than magnesium.

MANGANESE

Manganese is believed to be involved with the activity of oxidizing enzymes in plants. It also affects the iron intake of plants. Plants deficient in manganese show a mottling of the tissue between veins. The veins themselves remain green and they are sometimes surrounded by a band of green tissue. Virus diseases, however, can produce the same appearance.

Soybeans, garden beans, and white field beans deprived of manganese show the green veins and mottled tissue in classic form, but potatoes, tomatoes, and fruit trees show less pronounced mottling. Acid soils are most apt to lack manganese.

COPPER

Copper occurs in greatest abundance in the growing parts of plants. Copper deficiency is evidenced in tips and end leaves in plants, especially in fruit trees. The tips of onion leaves die back when deficiency is present and the skins of yellow onions become thin and pale.

ZINC

Zinc deficiency has been reported for citrus fruit, pecans, and corn. The "white bud" of corn is a zinc deficiency. In a number of plants, the older leaves become discolored.

BORON

Plants deficient in boron grow slowly, in severe cases the terminal bud, twig, or leaf dies. Among the conditions caused by boron deficiency are cracked stem in celery, heart rot in sugar beets, internal black spots in table beets, corky spots in apples, and internal browning of cauliflower. A boron deficiency is usually associated with excess acidity.

Plant Diseases

In order for a plant to be healthy, it must not only have suitable nutrition, water, air, heat, and light, but it must be free of disease. Many plant diseases are caused by fungi and bacteria. It is true that these microorganisms are most likely to attack malnourished or weakened plants in preference to healthy ones. Still, microorganisms—including harmful ones—respond favorably to humus just as plants do.

What is the answer to this seeming dilemma? It lies in an as-yet little understood system of nature's checks and balances. Compost and humus promote the growth of both harmful and beneficial microorganisms. In addition, they promote the growth of bacteriophages which destroy harmful bacteria. In the exceedingly complex soil ecosystem, harmful microorganisms—including wilts and smuts—seem to be brought under control when the life of the soil is in balance.

In his book, *Humus*, Dr. Waksman states: "Plant deficiency diseases
(continued on page 69)

NUTRIENT DEFICIENCIES IN PLANTS

Element	Symptoms*	Treatment
Nitrogen (N)	Tomatoes: very slow growth; leaves lighten in color, beginning at top of plant; leaves remain small and thin, veins may become purple. Stems are stunted and brown. Flower buds turn yellow and drop off; yield is reduced. Cucumbers: stunted growth; yellowing of plants. Roots turn brown. Fruits point at blossom end. Radishes: retarded growth. Leaves are small, narrow, thin, yellow in color. Weak, slender stems. Roots small, pale in color, and imperfectly developed. Corn: plants develop yellowish-green color. Fruit trees: older leaves turn yellowish-green, working toward tips; sometimes reddish or reddish-purple discolorations appear. Leaves become very small; twigs are slender and hard.	Apply blood meal, hoofmeal and horn dust, cottonseed meal, fish meal, tankage, bone meal, or legume hay mixed with compost in ample quantities. Apply to soil in fall or very early spring, at least 6 weeks before planting.
Phosphorus (P)	Tomatoes: reddish-purple color develops on underside of leaves; eventually all foliage assumes purplish tinge. Leaves are small; stems are slender and fibrous. Plants are late in setting fruit.	Phosphate rock or bone meal, applied directly to soil or mixed with compost.

Element	Symptoms*	Treatment
	Radishes: leaves develop reddish-purple tinge on undersides.	
	Celery: slender stalks and poor root development.	
	Corn: yellowing of leaves similar to N starvation. Kernels will not fill out all rows or to ends of ears.	
	Fruit trees: young twigs develop ghostly hue; stems show purple coloring. Leaves abnormally small and dark green; old leaves become mottled with light and dark green. Occasionally bronzed leaves will appear on mature branches.	
Potassium (K)	Tomatoes: slow growth and low yield. Young leaves become crinkled. Older leaves turn pale grayish green, developing yellowish-green color along margins. Progresses into bronze spots between longer veins; spots may become bright orange and turn brittle. Leaves turn brown and die. Stems grow hard and woody, and fail to increase in diameter. Roots are brown and not well-developed. Fruit may ripen unevenly and lack solidity. Cabbage, brussels sprouts: leaves become bronzed on border and color spreads inward. Leaf rims parch and brown spots appear on interiors of leaves.	Add potash rock, granite dust, wood ashes, green sand, or seaweed to your compost, or apply these materials directly to the soil.

Element	Symptoms*	Treatment
	Carrots: leaves curl; rims turn brown, and inner portions grayish green and finally, bronzed.	
	Cucumbers: leaves exhibit bronzing and dying of margins. Fruit develops enlarged tips (opposite of N deficiency).	
	Radishes: leaves are dark green in center; edges curl and turn pale yellow to brown. Extreme deficiency indicated by deep yellow leaves and stems. Leaves may grow thick and leathery. Roots are more bulbous than normal.	
	Beets: roots grow long and tapered instead of bulbous.	
	Fruit trees: leaf edges show scorching and purplish discoloration. Dead spots develop on mature, and finally on younger, leaves. Peach foliage often becomes crinkled, and twigs are slender.	
Calcium (Ca)	Tomatoes: upper leaves appear yellow (this distinguishes Ca deficiency from lack of N-P-K, in which lower portion of plant shows diseased leaves, while upper part appears normal). Plants are weak and flabby and lack firmness. Terminal buds die	Apply to soil any good grade of ground natural limestone.

(continued)

Element	Symptoms*	Treatment
	and nearby stem becomes dotted with dead spots. Roots are short and brown in color.	
	Peas: red patches appear on leaves near center and spread out. Healthy green of leaves pales to light green, then white. Growth is slow and plants are dwarfed.	
	Corn: tip ends of leaves stick together as if they'd been glued.	
Iron (Fe)	All vegetables: spotted, colorless areas develop on young leaves; yellow leaves appear on upper parts of plants. Growth of new shoots is affected and plant tissues may die if deficiency is severe.	Avoid over-liming (too much lime can cause Fe deficiency). Add plenty of manure, crop residues, dried blood, and tankage to compost.
	Fruit trees: leaves turn yellow with brown patches; fruit lacks flavor.	
Magnesium (Mg)	Tomatoes: clear leaves turn brittle and curl up; develop yellow color which is deepest further from the veins.	Add a quart of sea water to each 100 pounds of compost, or add dolomite limestone or raw phosphate rock to pile.
	Cabbage: leaves develop mottled, light-colored spots; lower leaves pucker. Edges of leaves may turn pale yellow or white, and leaves may die. If only Mg is deficient, entire leaf becomes mottled with dead areas. If (continued)	

Element	Symptoms*	Treatment
	N is also deficient, entire leaf turns light green, then yellow, then develops mottling of dead spots. K deficiency, sometimes confused with lack of Mg, can be distinguished by bronzing which occurs before dead leaves appear.	
	Turnips: leaves develop brown areas around the rims, light-colored mottling on inner areas.	
	Carrots, cucumbers, squash, lima beans: all develop mottling and browning of foliage.	
	Corn: older leaves develop yellow striping or white streaks.	
	Fruit trees: large, older leaves display patches of dead tissue, not restricted to leaf edges. Watch for dropping of leaves, first on old branches, then on twigs of current season. Defoliation may be so severe that only tufts of thin, small leaves are left.	
Copper (Cu)	Tomatoes: stunted shoot growth; very poor root development. Foliage may be curled and bluish-green. Leaves and stems are flabby, and there is an absence of flower formation.	Apply plenty of compost or well-rotted manure; add raw phosphate rock to heap.

Element	Symptoms*	Treatment
	Lettuce: leaves become bleached-looking. Stems and rims of leaves are affected first.	
	Onions: abnormally thin scale which is pale yellow in color, instead of the usual brilliant brown. Growth may be stunted or fail entirely. Copper deficiency is usually confined to peat or muck soils.	
	Squash, mustard, beans: leaves are abnormally long and narrow, may turn yellow and show mottling of dead spots. These plants usually are first to show signs of Zn deficiency.	
	Corn: older leaves die; yellow striping appears between veins on newer leaves.	
	Fruit trees: rosettes of small leaves (similar to Mg deficiency), but leaves are often crinkled and chlorotic (pale yellow in color). Especially true of peach trees. Citrus trees show very small, smooth fruit, and pointed leaves with striking contrasts in leaf patterns—dark green veins and yellow tissue.	
Boron (B)	Celery: leaves develop brownish mottling; stems turn brittle and show (continued)	Add to compost raw phosphate rock, manure, and acid organic matter such as (continued)

Element	Symptoms*	Treatment
	brown stripes. Crosswise cracks appear in stem, and tissue curls back and turns brown. Roots turn brown and die.	peat moss, sawdust, or ground oak leaves. Do not add lime. Apply plenty of compost to soil.
	Beets, turnips, other root crops: develop brown-heart disease. Dark brown, water-soaked areas appear in centers of roots, some-times resulting in hollow discolored centers. Roots do not grow to full size, and may look rough, un-healthy, and grayish; sur-face may wrinkle or crack. Plants are stunted; leaves are smaller, twisted, and fewer than usual. Leaves may develop yellow and purplish-red blotches; stalks may split.	
	Tomatoes: blackened areas ap-pear at growing points of stems; stems are stunted; terminal shoots curl, turn yellow, then die. Plants ap-pear bushy. Fruit may have dried or darkened areas.	
	Lettuce: exhibits malforma-tion of more rapidly grow-ing leaves; spotting and burning of leaves.	
	Cauliflower: stems develop discolored, water-soaked, or hollow areas. Leaves around curd may be stunted and deformed.	
	Fruit trees: young leaves can become thick and brittle,	

(continued)

Element	Symptoms*	Treatment
	then cause twigs to die back. Some trees may show wrinkled, chlorotic leaves. Apple trees most often suffer boron deficiency, which may show up only in fruit. Early in the season, hard, brown spots with definite margins form inside the fruit. As the season progresses, spots soften, become larger, and lose their definite outline.	
Manganese (Mn)	Tomatoes: leaves show lightening of green color which gradually turns to yellow farthest from major veins. Dead spots appear in center of yellow areas and spread. Growth is stunted; there are few blossoms and no fruit.	Apply plenty of compost and well-rotted manure to soil.
	Spinach: loss of color at growing tips, which spreads in toward center of plant. Normal dark green color gradually changes to golden yellow. White, dead areas eventually appear.	
	Beets: leaves take on deep red to purple color, which gradually turns yellow; dead areas finally appear between veins. Growth of roots and tips is stunted.	
	Snap beans: whole leaves turn golden yellow, and small brown spots appear between the veins.	

Element	Symptoms*	Treatment
	Cucumbers, cabbage, peppers: stems are small, weak, and slender. Leaves turn yellowish white while veins and midribs remain green. Blossom buds may turn yellow.	

*While these are specific examples, they indicate the general symptoms exhibited by most food crops suffering these deficiencies.

---

are usually less severe in soils well supplied with organic matter not only because of the increased vigor of the plants but also because of antagonistic effects of the various soil microorganisms which become more active in the presence of an abundance of organic matter."

Dr. Waksman's statement has been confirmed many times over. The Connecticut Agricultural Experiment Station, in reporting on experiments with fusarium rot of squash seeds, reported,

> It is especially interesting to note that the fungus did not persist as long in the humus-amended soil as it did in ordinary field soil or sand-amended field soil. Either of two theories might explain this behavior. First, the increased microbiological activity of saprophytic organisms might usurp the nitrogen supply and effectively starve the pathogens for this essential element. This is known to occur in the case of certain other soil-borne parasites. Soil analyses run on the various samples, however, refute this theory since they showed a higher available nitrogen content in the humus-amended soil than in either of the other two.

The remaining theory advanced here to explain the relatively short existence of the root rot fusarium in the soil with a high organic matter content is that of antibiosis. Waksman and Horning and other authors have pointed out the omnipresence of soil organisms which produce antibiotic substances. It is quite probable that in the organic-amended soils, such organisms thrived and produced substances toxic to *Fusarium solani f. cucurbitae.* In the field soil and sand-amended soil, the biological activity of such organisms must necessarily have been lower because of the limited nutritive conditions prevailing there.

The theory that compost produces disease-fighting antibiotics is no longer doubted in many scientific circles. The Connecticut Station also reported that root rot fungus that thrived in ordinary soil was unable to survive in compost.

The researcher B. P. Tokine reports, "Today it can be affirmed with certainty that all plant organisms—whether bacteria, birch, mushroom, mold, or pine tree—emit antibiotics which are diffused in the air, in soil, and in waters."

The living organisms in compost can act as antibodies to protect plant roots from disease organisms and nematodes.

As far back as 1944, Sidney J. Gates reported in *Country Gentleman*, "The cure for root rot of cotton consists in nothing more than turning under leguminous organic matter in the fall or spring before the cotton crop is planted. A heavy dose of stable manure will effect the same end."

The University of Florida Agricultural Experiment Station discovered that organic matter kills harmful nematodes. Reported researchers there, "Like practically all forms of animal life, nematodes have their enemies. Among the most common and efficient of these enemies are certain kinds of fungi which live in decaying vegetable matter. This doubtless accounts for much of the importance and advantages of a mulch."

There are many, many more studies, together proving beyond reasonable doubt that compost controls, rather than encourages, the growth of harmful plant disease organisms. As we learn more about the relationships among soil microorganisms—both harmful and beneficial—we will greatly increase our capacity to work with nature in growing healthy, disease-free crops and ornamentals.

Compost and Insect Control

The observations of thousands of organic gardeners and farmers indicate that plants grown in a total organic system, including the copious use of compost, are less likely to sustain insect attack and damage. Further, scientific experiments have borne out these observations.

The chemical approach to insect control has been to discover substances that will eliminate specific insect species, and then to apply them routinely during the growing season. The broad and deleterious ecological effects of this approach are well known. Organic control of insects, on the other hand, is based on manipulating the entire garden or farm ecology in such a way that all life forms are in healthy balance. The predators of harmful insects are allowed to thrive, so that insect damage—although not eliminated completely—causes no serious problem. Compost has a vital place in this total organic system.

Scientists have long known that when organic materials are incorporated into the soil, the rapidly multiplying beneficial microorganisms cause a temporary oxygen shortage which weakens pathogens. Although some pathogens germinate because of the added nutrients of organic matter, they are soon overwhelmed by microbial antibiosis and digestion. Legumes, when grown as green manure crops, are especially valuable for the control of soil pathogens.

In the compost heap, insects are brought under control not only by microorganisms, but also by the intense heat generated inside the heap. Any insect eggs will be destroyed by the heat, and microorganisms will then make short work of the remains. Often, the cool outer edges of the compost heap provide ideal conditions for insect multiplication. If you notice too many flies or sowbugs crawling over your heap, turn it so that the insects and their eggs are thrust into the center of the heap, there to perish by heat and bacterial attack. Any heap which attracts more than a normal number of harmful insects should be covered with a thin layer of soil after each application of organic matter. With a little attention, no compost heap should become a breeding ground for the insects you are attempting to bring into balance.

5

The Frontiers of Composting

Composting's future is bright. At least, it seems brighter today than at any time since before World War II.

It was not until 1945 or so that our nation plunged headlong into a reckless energy binge, of which chemical agriculture was an integral part. After nearly 30 years of that shortsighted policy which Americans accepted without question because it brought prosperity, we woke up and discovered that we were not only running out of fuel, but were despoiling a once-beautiful land in the process.

Agribusiness policy had become so energy-intensive that, for the first time in human history, *we were expending more energy in growing and delivering food than we received from it in terms of calories.* This sobering assessment was delivered to us by energy expert John S. Steinhart, professor of geology, geophysics, and environmental science at the University of Wisconsin. It is an energy deficit we can scarcely afford, and one that we can correct only by correcting our food-growing policies.

One small example of reckless energy use in agriculture will illustrate the point adequately. Nitrogen, a major fertilizer element for plants, can be produced naturally by the growing of leguminous green manure crops. In this process, soil bacteria are attracted to the roots of the crops and form nodules where nitrogen is fixed (made available for use by plants). The three major components of nitrogen fixation are: free nitrogen, hydrogen, and energy. When nitrogen is fixed by growing legumes, the nitrogen is pulled from the air, the hydrogen is provided by photosynthesis in the plant, and the energy used is that of the sun. Our total cost in nonrenewable energy reserves? Very little—only that which is required to plant, cultivate and, later, turn under the crop.

Now, nitrogen can also be produced chemically. The chemical

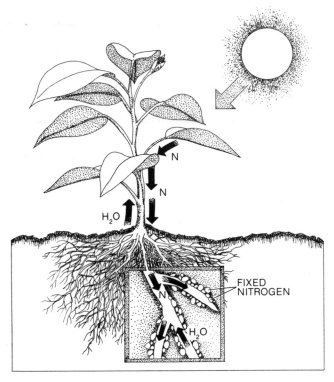

When legumes produce nitrogen (N), soil bacteria form nodules on the roots where N is fixed. The three major components of the process are nitrogen pulled from the air, hydrogen provided by photosynthesis, and energy supplied by sunlight.

process is the same, but the method is different. Nitrogen produced in a fertilizer factory requires tremendous amounts of fossil fuel energy. The free nitrogen must be broken down, and this requires subjecting it to temperatures as high as 900°F. (482°C.) and pressures 200 to 300 times those of the normal atmosphere. Further, the hydrogen used in the industrial production of nitrogen fertilizer comes from *natural gas*. All energy used in the entire process comes from our quickly diminishing reserves of fossil fuels.

Multiply the foregoing example by thousands of similar ones, and you will have some idea of where we went wrong in both energy and agricultural policy. When we step back and look at it, it seems insane to manufacture nitrogen in a factory when we can let soil bacteria, sunshine, and legume crops do the job for us at little cost in fossil fuel. With naturally produced nitrogen fertilizer, there are even further benefits. We do not pollute the air, as fertilizer factories do, and we do not have the cost of bagging the fertilizer, delivering it hundreds of miles by truck and rail, and incorporating it into the ground once it reaches the farm or garden. Soil bacteria manufacture the nitrogen for us, *in place, in the soil,* right where growing crops can use it.

There is such a good case to be made for the wisdom of producing nitrogen fertilizer in the field, rather than in the factory! Increasing numbers of Americans understand that now. They are also seeing the wisdom of returning *all* organic wastes to the soil instead of throwing them away at great costs in money, land, and energy, replacing lost soil nutrients by manufacturing chemicals from fossil fuel at still higher costs.

America has turned energy-conscious because America is growing energy-poor. In our attempts to conserve energy and to find new means of energy production—ones that do not require nonrenewable fuels— we are seeing that compost and composting have a vital role. Compost conserves energy because it supplies soil nutrients without calling on fossil fuel support. It saves energy because it can be made on the farm and in the garden, requiring no transportation from a factory. It saves energy because it is waste recycled in a very short route—as short as the

In some towns and cities, plant debris from city parks and streets is composted and distributed free or at a nominal fee to gardeners.

distance from the kitchen to the backyard compost heap. Even the organic debris of an entire city can be recycled and returned to the land without leaving the metropolitan area. Compare this system to the one we have been following since World War II, and you begin to see not only a major root of our current energy problems, but the answer to those problems as well.

Compost and composting are beginning to be seen as a potentially major part of our new energy policy. In order to recycle organic wastes to the fullest possible extent, we must concentrate on municipal composting, the recycling of industrial wastes, and the intelligent use of sewage sludge. Each is so important that chapters have been devoted to them in this book. They are the boldest lines of composting's new frontier. In this chapter, however, we will look at some new ways of making and using compost that are closer to home, ways that we can effect by ourselves or in small groups. Some of them can be carried out within the family, or even by one person. Others require some community organization and action, or simply a better knowledge of resources already available in the community. All are important in turning around our country's energy policies. But still closer to home, all can provide rich additions to our farms and gardens, usually at no cost.

Compost from City Leaves

Ohio was the first state to make leaf composting a concern of all its citizens. A packet describing the environmental benefits of leaf composting and including how-to-compost information was sent to more than 2,800 municipal executives in Ohio back in 1973.

In Hyde Park, New York, a municipal leaf composting program was set up in 1971. People trucked or carried their raked leaves to a central location where they were composted or shredded, then redistributed for garden use.

Brookhaven, Long Island, tells its citizens to compost their leaves in the backyard, not place them in bags on the curb. Allentown, Pennsylvania; Chico, California; Portland, Oregon; Kirkwood, Missouri; and Maplewood, New Jersey, shred the leaves they collect and hold them in site, in most cases open to the public. Bethlehem, Pennsylvania; Milwaukee, Wisconsin; and Ames, Iowa, will deliver leaves in quantity to city residents. In Arlington County, Virginia, the Transportation Department and the Water Pollution Control Plant are mixing leaves,

Leaves are a widely available raw material for composting, and many cities use them in municipal programs.

sand, and sewage sludge and using the resulting humus on highway right-of-ways.

In May of 1976 the City of Berkeley, California, and the Berkeley Solid Waste Management Commission began a compost and leaf banking program using plant debris from city parks and street sweepings as well as debris from the general public of the city and adjacent area. The public pays fifty cents per cubic yard to dump at the composting site, but receives 2 cubic feet per person of the compost produced at no charge. When compost is in short supply, vouchers to be redeemed later are issued.

The plant debris is ground periodically in a hammermill grinder, and aged in windrows which are turned as necessary with city equipment. The program was originally expected to pay for itself in terms of personnel and equipment and realize a profit of over $10,000 if maximum participation materialized. Although problems have developed in that the single grinder has proven inadequate for the amount of waste generated, the city still hopes to realize other benefits. The sanitary landfill scheduled soon for completion will have its life extended because it will no longer need to accommodate 3,635 tons of plant debris once dumped there annually. The City Parks Department is using compost from the project rather than continuing to buy a commercial product, and it may have enough compost remaining to help in building a new park on the landfill site.

The Berkeley plan involves an educational program of pamphlets and reading materials available to those using the dumping facilities. At present, park and home garden debris are windrowed separately because of possible danger to participating gardeners caused by glass or metal objects in park sweepings.

A proposal has been made, in part in response to recently detected leaching from the rapidly filling Berkeley landfill, that residents of Berkeley separate all glass, cans, and newspapers and place them separately on curbsides for collection. A recycling depot would handle these materials. A pick-up service for retailers collecting beverage cans and bottles has also been proposed. Berkeley's deposit ordinance went into effect on July 28, 1976. The recovery of wood from demolition debris has also been proposed.

Common Sense in Madison

Madison, Wisconsin, keeps landfill space to a minimum by hammering all refuse to sandlike particles. Ferrous materials are first drawn off with huge magnets and are sold as scrap, and city residents are asked to bundle newspapers which are also sold. This, plus Madison's active private recycling efforts, has kept that city's refuse problem under control while recycling some valuable materials. The final landfill product is so close to compost that the Director of Public Works there shows it off by growing his office plants in pure city refuse. Madison city trucks will also deliver pulverized tree trimmings (for mulch) and fall leaves to individual homes at no charge. For the city, it is less expensive—in both time and money—to dump off a truckload of leaves or trimmings at a home in the collection area than to carry it back to the landfill site. Citizens of other cities could doubtless emulate some of Madison's common-sense policies.

The ORE Plan for Garbage Collection and Recycling

Widespread interest has been attracted by the ORE plan which started in Portland, Oregon in 1975. By the following year, it had reduced participants' garbage bills by 20 to 40 percent when compared to fees for standard garbage collection service.

The ORE plan grew out of a user-delivery recycling center, Sunflower Recycling, Inc., which later offered small-scale, hand-cart pick-up service and in 1975 started a trailer vehicle pick-up. ORE is a comprehensive system plan for a low-cost, employment-intensive, and energy-efficient way to recycle household solid waste. Recyclable materials are separated by householders and small-sized vehicles are used to pick up both recyclable wastes and mixed garbage at one visit. Collection fees and the sale of secondary materials and possibly of additional services defray costs, employee wages, and overhead expenses.

On the most basic level is the Neighborhood Recycling Unit (NRU) or pick-up unit. It in turn is served by the Community Recycling Unit (CRU) which is basically a transportation broker, providing transport of recyclable materials to secondary materials markets on either a scheduled or an ad hoc basis. CRU income comes principally from NRUs, but CRU may also do hauling for other concerns.

In May, 1975, Cloudburst Recycling, Inc., of Portland became the first private business enterprise to implement the ORE approach. Refuse collection is weekly and fees average three dollars per month as compared to five dollars per month for standard collection service. Customers are expected to group their recyclable wastes into four categories (see figure 1, page 80). Several alternative kinds of services are available, ranging from weekly collection and recycling to bimonthly collection of recyclable materials only. Cloudburst, by February, 1976, served about 100 households, most of them of middle- to upper-income range and above-average education level. The company uses a small pick-up truck with a trailer for collection and a large van parked in the neighborhood as an intermediate terminal. Income derived from the sale of recyclables is estimated to be between fifty-five and seventy-five cents per household per month.

Figure 1:

FOUR CATEGORIES FOR GROUPING WASTES
AS SPECIFIED BY CLOUDBURST RECYCLING SERVICE

1. **Food Scraps**	Preparation:	We can provide you with an air-tight container in which you store parings, leftovers, etc. No plastic bags please!
	Results:	Composted food scraps become a high-grade organic fertilizer.
2. **Glass** **Aluminum** **Tin Cans**	Preparation:	Rinse. Store in a single card-board box. For cans, remove ends and paper, and flatten. For glass, labels can stay, but re-move any metal.
	Results:	Recycling aluminum requires only 5% of the electrical power needed to produce aluminum from ore.
3. **Newspaper &** **Corrugated** **Boxes**	Preparation:	Stack in a dry place, and bundle. We provide the twine. Flatten corrugated boxes.
	Results:	Each 3-foot stack of newspaper saves a tree.
4. **Everything** **Else**	Preparation:	Put other household wastes in your trash can. (Hauling of yard trimmings, appliances, etc., will be available at additional charge.)
	Results:	Only one-quarter to one-third of your household waste goes to the landfill.

Both Sunflower and Cloudburst composted organic wastes near their shared recycling center until the summer of 1975 when the City Health Department found them in violation of the Sanitation Code. Since then they have landfilled all organic wastes. They are eager to resume composting but lack the necessary capital for equipment, according to Richard C. Duncan, a professor at Portland State University who was the architect of the ORE plan and wrote about ORE and Cloudburst in a January-February, 1976, article in *Compost Science.*

Cloudburst also ran into quasi-political problems with new city ordinances requiring collected materials to be disposed of in designated transfer stations, and other ordinances governing trash disposal franchises and designating given areas to franchises.

Many other communities and organizations—by 1976 there were at least 30—have planned companies similar to Sunflower and Cloudburst. One was designed on the "Vershire" plan developed by Waste Control Systems, Inc., of Hanover, New Hampshire, but unlike ORE it collected no compostable waste.

The states of Oregon, South Dakota, and Vermont have all benefited from increased employment, decreased litter, and energy saving through "bottle bills" banning nonrecyclable bottles. The recycling of empty bottles can be an integral part of a municipal or private recycling service. New bills for national bottle control are almost certain to be introduced in the future.

Another approach to recycling household wastes is being tested in two small cities with federally-sponsored demonstration projects. This is the double home collection service which uses one pick-up operation for recyclable material and a second for mixed wastes. In one city, wastes are grouped into two categories, clear glass and cans, and paper. The other city project specifies three categories: cans and bottles, recyclable paper, and nonrecyclable paper. A set of special compartmented trucks collects recyclable materials once a month. Information on the economic viability and general applicability of the approach should become available soon. There is hope that future study projects will include composting as part of recycling.

The federal government has also committed over $27 million to six demonstration projects to test the effectiveness of large-scale resource-recovery systems. Here there is less hope, for indications are that such large-scale systems will be prohibitively expensive for small cities and will consume energy without producing benefit to the land.

From ORE to NRN

In an article written for *Compost Science* in Summer, 1976, Professor Duncan discusses theoretical possibilities for enlarging the ORE plan toward a National Recycling Network (NRN). "An ongoing task for the

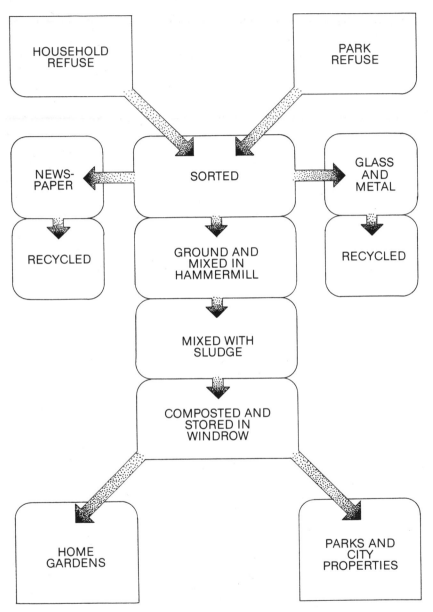

A well-organized community composting system of waste management can make use of refuse from parks and city properties, as well as from the households of community residents.

next decade," he says, "will be to integrate the best of the old and new processes [for handling different kinds of wastes—industrial, agricultural, and municipal] into a total recycling society."

The first step in Duncan's plan toward an NRN has three parts: (1) more efficient return of reusable bottles and metal cans to bottling plants and scrap metal markets. This would relieve retailers of the unrewarding job of handling and sorting empty bottles; (2) combining the pure organic fraction of solid waste with sludge and other wastes for composting; (3) developing Municipal Recycling Networks (MRN).

When foodscraps, yard trimmings, and leaves are kept separate at their household source and collected on a city-wide basis, it is feasible to combine them with municipal sludge. No costly separation equipment is needed for this garbage and debris as it is for mixed municipal refuse. The potential quantity of household organic waste is 6 to 12 times that of sludge, so with a voluntary plan such as ORE a subscribership of only 20

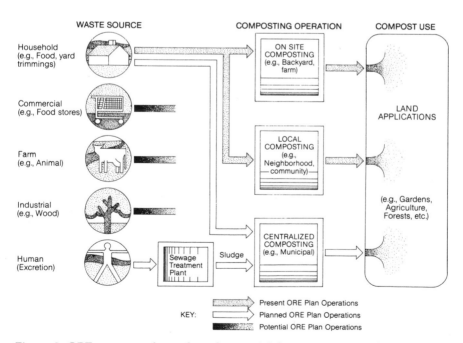

Figure 2: ORE present, planned, and potential future operations for collecting, composting, and utilizing organic wastes.

percent of the city could generate more solid waste than the city's entire population would produce in sludge.

Two municipalities in the Portland area may participate in a test of combined waste composting. Professor Duncan suggests that cities interested in ORE-type planning begin by offering alternative services of recycling along with conventional garbage collection services. This would give citizens a choice, while demonstrating the viability of the plan. When alternative plan subscription reaches 51 percent, a ballot referendum on compulsory MRN can be held.

For further steps toward NRN, see Professor Duncan's diagram of a theoretical total waste management system developed out of the present ORE plan (figure 2).

The Portland Metropolitan Service District has undertaken a valuable energy-use study of nine hypothetical total refuse systems. Energy costs or credits were assumed to have two components: (1) direct energies needed to fuel trucks, power machines, light buildings, etc., and (2) indirect energies necessary to construct and maintain equipment and facilities. The MSD report, summarized in the following table (figure 3), concludes: "Of the so-called energy recovery systems, composting appears to have the highest net yield."

Figure 3:

TOTAL SYSTEM NET ENERGY
FOR NINE HYPOTHETICAL TOTAL REFUSE SYSTEMS
("+" represents net energy gain; "−" represents net energy loss)

Type of System	System Description	Total System Net Energy (per ton of generated waste) $\times 10^3$ BTU
IX (ORE Plan Approach)	Home separation of recyclable materials; truck pickup of all recyclables; separate truck pickup of mixed wastes for landfilling; delivery of all recyclables to market; composting or organics; landfill of mixed refuse.	+17,699.9

Type of System	System Description	Total System Net Energy (per ton of generated waste) × 10³ BTU
VI	Home separation and user delivery of 941 pounds of recoverable components to recycling center; truck pickup of 1,059 pounds for delivery to composting operation; methane generation and piping to user; sludge use as fertilizer; landfill of residue.	+12,865.8
VII	Similar to VI except; truck pickup of 1,059 + 10,191.3 pounds for shredding, air classification, and sale as boiler fuel.	+10,191.3
III	Home separation of the 941 pounds per ton of recoverable recyclable materials; user delivery to Neighborhood Recycling Centers; truck pickup for pyrolysis of 1,059 pounds per ton; landfill of residue.	+ 7,225.2
IV	Truck pickup of all mixed refuse; delivery to processing center; hand-picking of corrugated cardboard; shredding; magnetic separation of ferrous metal; air separation of light combustibles; bailing; sale of combustible 65% for existing boiler firing; landfill of residue.	+ 7,123.8
VIII	Less complete home separation of recyclable material than IX; pickup by separate trucks; delivery of all recyclables to market; landfill of mixed refuse.	+ 5,979.0

Type of System	System Description	Total System Net Energy (per ton of generated waste) × 10³ BTU
V	Truck pickup of all mixed refuse for delivery to fiber recovery plant; steam and electrical generation; recovery of some recyclable materials for processing; landfill of residue.	+ 1,628.3
I	Pickup of all mixed refuse at the home by refuse trucks; delivery of all refuse to landfill for disposal.	− 372.2
II	Home separation and user delivery (as in System III); truck pickup of the remaining 1,059 pounds per ton for central shredding, incineration, and electrical generation; landfill of residue.	−16,591.0

Dateline: Today

Here are a few more current municipal and community projects involving compost and recycling, some of which might serve as models for other communities:

Davis, California: Recycling of all newsprint is now mandatory. If householders persist in mixing newspaper with other refuse, after two notices their rate increases from four to six dollars a month. This is seen as a move toward making people assume the full cost of their waste. They pay for others to separate their waste for them if they are not willing to take the time to do the chore themselves.

San Francisco: On two dozen vacant lots throughout the city, most of them surplus city land, interested residents are encouraged to plant vegetable gardens. The city's organic wastes are composted and the compost delivered to the gardeners on request. The program, which benefits many low income and elderly gardeners, cost the city only $18,000 to launch.

Vancouver, Washington: An operation begun in 1976 uses the Lebo process to mix thickened sludge with sawdust, aerate it, and then compost it in lagoons diked with sawdust walls.

Delaware: Under an Environmental Protection Agency (EPA) grant, the State of Delaware has planned a solid waste treatment plant to produce supplemental fuel for an oil-fired utility boiler and to handle sewage sludge. The planned capacity is 500 tons of municipal solid waste and 230 tons of digested sludge per day. By-products will include composted humus, ferrous aluminum, and glass.

Somerville and Marblehead, Massachusetts: Under EPA grants, these two cities have been testing the feasibility of requiring householders to separate solid wastes. Both cities passed laws under which citizens must separate their refuse into three categories: paper, glass and cans, and miscellaneous. The first two categories are collected weekly by city crews with compartmented trucks. Mixed waste is collected weekly in regular trucks. Extensive public relations and educational work preceded the launching of each project. Recyclable paper, iron, and glass are sold under contract to commercial processors.

Marblehead began its project in January, 1976. By March, 1977, it was recovering 30 percent of its wastes by weight and making a profit. Somerville, which began in December, 1975, and which is a more densely populated community, was recovering 8 percent and breaking even. These community projects will be used by EPA to demonstrate ways to recycle wastes without using complicated technology at high capital cost.

The Flushless Toilet
Joins the Compost Scene

As *New Farm* editor Steve Smyser put it, "To the family that routinely composts its kitchen wastes, recycles its paper, glass, and cans, keeps the thermostat in the 60s, and generally takes pride in maintaining a no-waste organic household, the inconsistency of having to flush away all that clean water can be downright painful—a glaring gap in an otherwise closed loop."

About 41 percent of all water piped into homes is used to flush toilets. At an average of over 5 gallons per flush, this means the typical

A composting toilet recycles both kitchen garbage and human wastes into a safe, effective soil builder.

toilet user contaminates 13,000 gallons of pure water a year to carry away 165 gallons of body waste.

Water is not the only thing wasted, either. Human urine and feces contain nutrients valuable for soil. Human urine can be safely used as a moisture and nitrogen source for compost piles. It won't take the less squeamish and more dedicated composters long to realize that by segregating urine from feces—either by using a special sealable container for urinating, by devising a two-chamber toilet, or by using separate bathrooms, one with a vessel for conserving urine—they can reduce water consumption in toilets considerably.

A new fund of information on water-saving devices and water-conserving toilets is available in *Goodbye to the Flush Toilet: Alternatives to Cesspools, Septic Tanks, and Sewers* by Carol Hupping Stoner. The book contains information on the history of waste water disposal and use, the composting privy, greywater disposal and use, and commercial and owner-built composting toilets as well as on ways to save water.

The decision to go all the way in pursuit of a zero-discharge household and to purchase or to build a composting privy or toilet system is a serious one for the composting gardener. If the composter's main concern is household self-sufficiency, then the compost toilet coupled with a compatible greywater system will end dependence on wasteful municipal sewers, reduce his water consumption and costs—water savings alone are 40,000 to 50,000 gallons a year for the average family—and provide compost periodically. If, however, the goal is food self-sufficiency, the gardener will find he is less able to provide enough compost for the garden if he must divide household garbage and perhaps some garden debris, between the toilet compost and the garden compost. Composting toilets take longer than compost piles to produce humus; their humus is of lower quality in terms of nitrogen content; and the danger of pathogens, though the matter is subject to debate, is still present to a degree whenever feces are used in soil.

As Carol Stoner points out, "The relative risks of composting toilets appear to be less than those associated with either the conventional septic system or the sewers and central treatment plant. . . . the necessary testing on composting toilets and greywater irrigation systems has not been carried out. No definitive conclusions can be made, although there also have not been any serious public health hazards reported due to the use of these alternatives. For final disposal of the contents of a composting toilet, burial in an undisturbed place is recommended for at least two years."

Simple composting privies usually catch urine and feces in an air- and watertight drum or tank. One model uses a drum which is mixed and aerated after removal by being rolled on the ground. Most compost privies are ventilated and aerobic; some use sawdust as high-carbon composting material, while others require additions of other organic matter such as kitchen wastes, leaves, or fresh grass, to maintain the C/N ratio. Material is retained for a period of from two months to a year either in large tank units themselves or in storage vaults. Temperatures

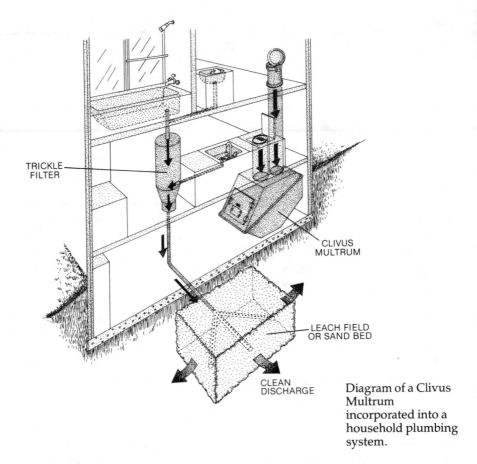

TRICKLE FILTER

CLIVUS MULTRUM

LEACH FIELD OR SAND BED

CLEAN DISCHARGE

Diagram of a Clivus Multrum incorporated into a household plumbing system.

reach near-thermophilic levels. The product, most experts agree, should be treated like digested sludge and either composted further in high-temperature piles or used in the garden after a storage period of from six months to a year. It should be used with caution and never on root crops.

Composting toilets are, unlike composting privies, a recent invention. They are used in the house and resemble ordinary plumbing fixtures. The best-known composting toilet is the Clivus Multrum, developed in Sweden in 1939 by Rikard Lindstrom, an engineer. Almost a dozen kinds of Clivus Multrums are used in North America and 20 to 30 kinds in Sweden. The general principle of the Clivus Multrum and other composting toilets is that "human wastes, when mixed with enough plant matter, like kitchen scraps and garden wastes, and exposed to enough air will, in time, decompose and become nutrient-rich humusy fertilizer."

The Toa Throne, another composting toilet sold on this continent, uses an air staircase for the ventilation which makes for continued aerobic conditions. The staircase is a series of perforated steps slanting downward. Air from holes beneath the steps is mixed with wastes. Semicircular distribution conduits run through the stored wastes down to the emptying hatch to help in aerating the pile and in breaking up incoming wastes. The Toa Throne and other units use long vent stacks to create a ventilating updraft. Some assist the updraft with a fan or a wind-drawn rotary turbine on the top of the stack. The air circulation, however, removes enough of the pile's self-generated heat to slow down the decomposition, and thermophilic temperatures are seldom reached. In fact, temperatures seldom rise above 90°F. (32°C.), though some spot checks have shown temperatures as high as 160°F. (71°C.). Wastes must remain inside the storage chamber for at least two or three years to assure proper decomposition.

The Clivus Multrum uses an impervious fiberglass container to treat wastes. The tank is often located in a basement well below the bathroom, but always directly below the toilet seat. A garbage chute leads directly from a kitchen counter or wall to the tank. A vent pipe is located between the two incoming chutes. The bottom of the holding tank slopes at an angle of 30 degrees to the floor, allowing human waste to accumulate at the top, kitchen waste in the middle, and finished compost at the bottom.

Before use, the bottom of the container must be primed with organic material. A layer of peat 4 to 5 inches deep should cover the entire bottom of the unit, with about 2 inches of good garden soil spread on top of the peat, followed by 2 more inches of cut grass, dead leaves, or garden garbage that normally would go in the compost heap. When the unit is working, the peat soaks up ammonia vapor from the urine. By the time urine and feces reach the garbage heap at middle level, nitrate has been manufactured, and this can be used to break down the cellulose in the garbage.

As garbage and effluent combine and break down, the mass glides slowly down towards the storage area. By the time it arrives in the storage area, it has been reduced in volume by 10 percent of its original bulk. Tests in Sweden have shown that 60 pounds of fertilizer per year are produced for each person using the unit. The N-P-K contents test at 20-12-14.

In contrast, however, you should remember that composting garden debris in piles by the fast method produces humus by the ton in a year. A dedicated composter should also know that it will be four years before he can use any fertilizer from a new composting toilet. This much time is needed for material to accumulate and for pathogens to be destroyed by competition with other organisms over time.

The chief drawbacks to composting toilets, apart from their inefficiency in producing safe compost, is that they are expensive to install in older homes and, though headway is being made, they are still not acceptable under the building codes in some areas.

Meanwhile further research into the presence or absence of pathogens in toilet compost may convince public health officials that regulations can be relaxed. The EPA is beginning to fund studies of alternative waste water disposal systems in rural and suburban areas and is trying out new systems of aerobic septic tanks in West Virginia. For the last word on the controversial subject of the composting toilet, we turn to Clarence Golueke's book *Biological Reclamation of Solid Wastes:*

> The term *composting* here can be applied only in the broad sense of the term; *decomposing* is a more appropriate term. As far as public health is concerned, the saving feature with respect to the use of the "compost" product is the time factor. However, should the unit be loaded such that the retention time is materially shortened, or if short-circuiting should occur, then the "compost" product should be handled with cautions identical to those with nightsoil.

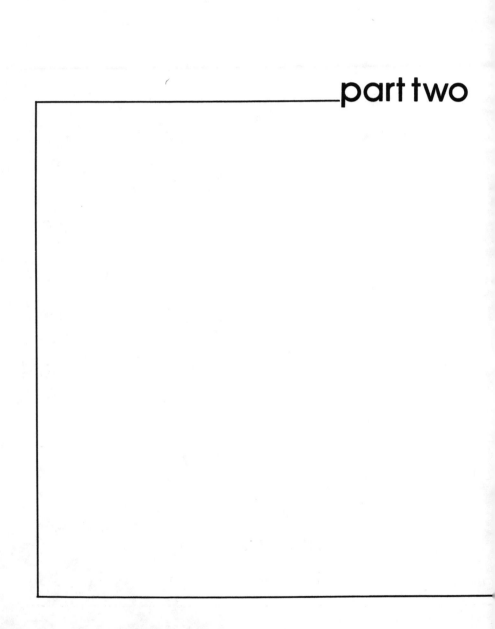

part two

Methods and Practice: Composting in the Garden, on the Farm, in the City

6

Materials for Composting

Materials for composting are all around you. Many gardeners need look no further than the home grounds for a sufficient supply. Kitchen wastes, lawn clippings, weeds and plant debris, dog and cat hair, vacuum cleaner accumulations—nearly anything that once lived (and is thus organic) is a candidate for the compost heap.

After you have exhausted the home supply, and still don't have all the materials you would like, you can begin to plan a series of foraging expeditions, beginning as close to home as possible and ranging out as far as you must in order to fulfill your requirements.

Manure should be the first item on your list, since it is by far the

most important ingredient in any heap. If you try, you can get it free for the hauling or at a token fee at poultry farms, riding stables, feedlots, even zoos and wild game farms—any place that holds large numbers of animals in concentration. Even a friend with one horse and no garden can supply all the manure you'll need for a backyard heap.

Your chances of getting manure at a family farm are not as good, since the farmer will probably use his manure for his own fields. Even if you seem to have all the home materials your compost heap can use, you should try to find a source of manure. Its tremendous bacteria content will bring your heap into biological and chemical balance and aid the rapid reduction of all the other materials.

But you don't have to stop with manure expeditions. In town, you can scavenge at grocery stores, city agencies, factories and mills, restaurants, and many retail operations. Ranging further into the country, you can find materials in fields and along roadsides, streams and ponds, at farms and orchards, at sawmills and canneries. Nearly any organic gardener can find ample composting materials by going no further than five miles from his home. The farmer, of course, must make composting an integral part of his soil management plan, utilizing every scrap of home material and adding green manure crops as necessary. But even the organic farmer—especially if he has few animals or cultivates a small but intensive area—might be called upon to look for supplementary materials. Although this chapter is pointed to gardeners, then, the organic farmer in need of materials can find much of value here.

Where to Begin

Begin, of course, at home. Are you discarding *any* organic matter at all? Newspapers? Tea bags? Clippings from the children's haircuts? Dishwater? With the exception of human and pet excreta (which we shall deal with later in this chapter), you can use everything. Before foraging, be sure that your home recovery program is 100 percent effective.

Your expeditions away from home can begin with a trip through the Yellow Pages. Go through them slowly, listing all possible sources of materials. Your search might end when you find that you can pick up manure at the local riding stable every Saturday morning and vegetable trimmings from the neighborhood supermarket every Tuesday and

Friday afternoon at 3:00 o'clock. After your routine is established, it usually operates like clockwork. No more problems.

Here is a partial list of away-from-home materials. Doubtless, you will come across others in your expeditions—but do consider these for starters.

Farms and orchards

Spoiled hay, corn silage, egg shells, manure of every kind, feathers, barnyard litter, spoiled fruit, spent mushroom soil, whey from dairy operations, and orchard litter.

Factories and mills

Apple pomace from cider mills, cannery wastes of all kinds, shredded bark, sawdust and wood shavings from lumber mills and carpentry shops, botanical drug wastes from pharmaceutical firms, cement dust, cocoa bean hulls (good mulch), coffee chaff from coffee wholesalers, cottonseed meal, excelsior from receiving departments, felt wastes, fly ash from incinerators, agricultural frit from glass factories, grape pomace from wineries, spent hops from breweries, granite dust from cutting operations, leather dust, lignin from paper mills, spoiled meal from flour mills, meat scraps from processing plants, peanut shells, slag from steel plants, spice marc (spent) from spice packers, tanbark from tanneries, tankage from meat processing plants and slaughterhouses. Sources of industrial compost materials are discussed more fully in Chapter 17.

City agencies

Dried sewage sludge, leafmold from parks department leaf depositories, fly ash from municipal incinerators, aquatic weeds, and pulverized wood from tree-trimming operations.

Stables and feedlots

Manure and stable litter of all kinds.

Retail stores

Vegetable trimmings and meat wastes from supermarkets and shops, hair from barbers and salons, pet hair from poodle parlors, food wastes from restaurants, excelsior from gift shops (used for packing breakables), plant wastes from florists, and sawdust from carpentry shops and lumber supply houses.

Roadsides, fields, and waterways

Old leaves, marsh grass from ocean areas, peat moss from bogs, weeds, and water plants from streams, lakes, and ponds.

Regional Materials

Gardeners in certain parts of the country can avail themselves of materials abundant only in their regions. New Englanders can look for wool and felt wastes from mills, leather dust, and maple syrup wastes. Those along seacoasts can find greensand, fish scraps, and seaweed. Southwestern gardeners should look for cannery wastes, mesquite, olive residues, volcanic rock, grape pomace from wineries, and citrus wastes. Southerners might be fortunate in finding cotton gin trash, Spanish moss, peanut shell ashes, snuff wastes, tung oil pomace, sugar cane trash, molasses residue, castor pomace, tobacco stems, rice hulls, and water hyacinth plants.

In collecting materials for your heap, you will not only be adding to your own soil's fertility and structure, but you will also be contributing to the recycling of wastes that might otherwise become pollutants in the environment. Most cities are now more than willing to cooperate in giving organic wastes to gardeners, since it relieves just a little pressure on already crowded landfill sites and obviates much dumping and incinerating of materials. A large poultry farm might be paying to have manure and litter hauled away. Their trash is your treasure! Supermarkets and restaurants will be more than happy to contribute their organic wastes to you, since it lowers their disposal costs. Most important, however, these materials, instead of being dumped, buried, or burned, will find their way back to the soil.

(One note of caution: In gathering materials in fields and wild areas, you will of course have the ecological responsibility to avoid ravaging natural areas of their native plants.)

Materials Not to Use

Although nearly any organic material can contribute to good compost, there are some which should be avoided, and others to be used in limited amounts. First, you want your heap to be balanced among green matter, animal wastes, manure, and soil. If you build your heap of 80 percent tankage from the local meat packing plant, you will not only have a putrid mess, but you will attract every stray dog, cat, and raccoon within a five-mile radius. A truckload of grape pomace, or a ton of wet hops from the brewery, will be equally hard to handle, as will be the neighbors if your heap's odor wafts their way. Strive, then, for a commonsense balance in the materials you select, and be sure to add a layer of soil over the heap every time you add materials that might cause odor or attract varmints.

Human feces and urine should not be used unless they have been properly treated and permitted to age sufficiently, as described in Chapter 5.

Dog droppings may be used in moderation. Certainly, the wastes of one or two dogs will cause no harm if the dogs are not in themselves diseased; their manure is as rich in nutrients as that of farmyard animals. There *is* danger with cat manure, since it is likely to contain a one-celled parasite, *Toxoplasma gondii,* which can cause both brain and eye disease in urborn infants when transmitted by the pregnant mother, and a round worm called *Toxocara cati,* which can cause both brain and eye disease in children. (This is also a good reason to keep cat boxes away from small children.)

Materials which will not decompose readily—large pieces of wood, oyster and clam shells, large quantities of pine needles, rags, brush, corn stalks, heavy cardboard—should not be used in large amounts unless they are shredded first.

Large amounts of highly acid materials—pine needles, oak leaves, etc.,—should not be used without the addition of enough limestone to neutralize the acid. For acid-loving crops, however, you might wish to build acidic compost by the deliberate use of these materials.

Don't use large amounts of grease and oil, since they not only attract varmints but also inhibit the biochemical processes necessary to successful composting. The amount of grease and oil from a normal household will cause no problem. However, carting home tubs of spent grease from the local potato chip factory is unwise. Again, use common sense.

Do not use toxic materials. There is little sense in trying to build an organic soil by including pesticide-treated wastes in the compost heap. Plant debris from roadsides might have been subject to a broad, potent, and persistent herbicide applied by the highway department; or, if the highway is a busy one, plants might be coated with lead emissions from passing motor traffic. Be careful in choosing your materials.

Materials for Enrichment

There are many substances you can buy to increase your compost's N-P-K content or control its pH. Although it is not necessary to add these materials to the heap, many gardeners find it worth the expense to insure a high nutrient level in their compost.

Among the materials and products available at garden centers and through mail order outlets are basalt rock powder, bagged manure, dried blood, bone meal, limestone, cottonseed meal, greensand marl, horn meal, tobacco stems, dried kelp, peatmoss, and other natural products that are valuable to the heap because of their nutrient levels or ability to correct pH. All will be considered in the individual listings that follow.

Rock powders raise the nutrient content of the heap to produce a richer finished product.

The quality of the heap can be boosted considerably by the addition of lime, if needed, although care must be taken to provide plenty of nitrogen-rich materials, as lime's low C/N ratio promotes loss of nitrogen. For compost which is to be used for plants which prefer neutral or slightly alkaline soils, a sprinkling of pulverized limestone should be added to each layer of the heap. The limestone will neutralize the acids and tend to prevent the escape of volatile fermentation products which would otherwise diffuse into the atmosphere. Pulverized dolomite instead of ordinary limestone (a calcium-magnesium lime) may be used in making the heap. Other forms of calcium which are recommended for the compost heap are pulverized oyster and clam shells and egg shells. If an acid compost is wanted, lime should not be added. If a distinctly acid compost is needed for such acid-loving plants as rhododendrons, camellias and blueberries, you may want to use acid peat instead of soil.

If the soil to be treated with compost is known to be low in phosphorus, raw pulverized phosphate rock should be used in alternate layers with the pulverized limestone. Other deficient elements may likewise be added by using different rock powders such as granite dust and potash rock. These rock powders will probably have to be purchased.

Deficient elements can be added in other ways, especially by adding to the compost heap plants which contain them. Seaweeds, such as the kelps, are rich in such elements as iodine, boron, copper, magnesium, calcium, phosphorus and many others and should be used in the compost heap if available locally. The water hyacinths which grow so abundantly in the rivers of the South are especially rich in many of the elements which are apt to be deficient in the soil. Autumn leaves, which will be discussed more thoroughly later, are a teeming source of trace minerals which are not found in upper layers of soil; they should constitute a major part of every compost heap.

Activators

A compost activator is any substance which will stimulate biological decomposition in a compost pile. There are organic activators and artificial activators. Organic activators are materials containing a high amount of nitrogen in various forms, such as proteins, amino acids and urea, among others. Some examples of natural activators are manure, garbage, dried blood, compost, humus-rich soil, etc.

Artificial activators are generally chemically synthesized compounds such as ammonium sulfate or phosphate, urea, ammonia, or any of the common commercial nitrogen fertilizers. These materials are not recommended.

There are two ways in which an activator may influence a compost heap: (1) introducing strains of microorganisms that are effective in breaking down organic matter; and (2) increasing the nitrogen content of the heap, thereby providing extra food for microorganisms.

Claims have sometimes been made that special cultures of bacteria will hasten the breakdown of material in a compost heap, and will also produce a better quality of finished compost. Products are manufactured which are reported to be effective in improving the action of a compost heap.

Most independent tests, however—including those conducted at the Organic Gardening and Farming Research Center—indicate that there is no benefit to be gained from the use of an activator that relies solely on the introduction of microorganisms. It seems that microorganisms will quickly multiply to the limit that their environment will permit. Since all the necessary microorganisms are already present in manure, soil, and other composting materials, there is no benefit to be gained from introducing strains in the form of an activator product.

NITROGEN ACTIVATORS

The cause of most compost heap "failures" is a lack of nitrogen. Almost invariably, a heap that doesn't heat up or decay quickly enough is made from material which is low in nitrogen. Nitrogen is needed by the bacteria and fungi that do the work of composting, to build protoplasm and carry on their life processes.

In experiments conducted at the Organic Gardening and Farming Research Center, it was shown that increasing additions of blood meal (a high-nitrogen activator) produced concomitant increases in the temperature of the pile, indicating increasing bacterial activity. In the tests, 3 pounds of blood meal in a 31-pound pile produced the best results.

Good nitrogen activators include not only blood meal (which is expensive when purchased commercially at garden centers), but tankage, manure, bone meal, and cottonseed meal. Just how much you should add to the heap depends on the nature of the material you are composting. Low-nitrogen materials such as straw, sawdust, corncobs, and old weeds should have at least 2 or 3 pounds of nitrogen supplement added per 100 pounds of raw material. If plenty of manure, grass clippings, fresh weeds, and other high-nitrogen materials are available to be mixed in with the compost, no nitrogen supplement will be necessary.

Materials for Composting

Here is a list of the more common—and some not so common— materials used in composting.

ALFALFA

Alfalfa is a good compost stimulant and activator, especially for composting household garbage. Lyman Wood, who was the head of Garden Way Research in Charlotte, Vermont, relied on alfalfa meal and leaves to aid kitchen refuse composting. The daily collection of garbage was spread out in a small bin and covered liberally with large handfuls of alfalfa meal. Then leaves from the stockpile are placed over the garbage, and they too are sprinkled with alfalfa meal. The layer of leaf-covered garbage is then watered lightly with a hose. Every day the process is repeated until the compost bin is full.

A round "turkey-wire" bin is used to hold the compost heap at the Garden Way Research Center. To control mice and rats, the garbage is kept in the center of the bin, with matted leaves around the outside. For double rodent protection, line your garbage compost bin with a smaller mesh wire. It's also important, when using this system, not to turn the compost for three months or so—until the garbage has a good chance to break down. The nitrogen supplied by the alfalfa meal will make sure that happens.

Dehydrated alfalfa, a common animal feed, can be purchased at feed stores throughout the country. Its cost is moderate, making it a particularly attractive ingredient for any compost heap.

APPLE POMACE

Apple pomace decays readily if mixed with materials that provide for proper aeration. Its value in the wet state is not high, since the nitrogen content is only one-fifth of 1 percent. But when analyzing the ash content of apple skins, it appeared that they had over 3 percent phosphoric acid. Since apple pomace can be had in quantities, a goodly amount of phosphoric acid may be obtained from it at the cost of the hauling. The potash content is, of course, much higher, amounting to about 12 percent of the ash, which corresponds to three-quarters of 1 percent of the pomace. It would seem best to use apple pomace for

Apple pomace is dry
and fragrant, and
looks very much like
cornflakes.

USDA photo

mulching in the orchard whenever feasible, possibly mixed with straw
to permit penetration of air.

In the compost heap, apple pomace should be used in thin layers
because heavy layers tend to become compact and, as a result, fail to
break down. When heavy applications of metallic sprays are used on
apple trees, the apple skins may contain poison residues that will in time
endanger the soil. Care should be taken to prevent the formation of toxic
orchard soils which make future growing of food crops impossible.
Heavily sprayed apple residues should not be used for food crops.

Apple pomace contains large numbers of seeds. Since seeds are
storage organs and contain valuable nutritive substances, especially
phosphorus and nitrogen, the fertilizer value of the seeds is to be
considered, too.

Bagasse, the residue left from the milling of sugarcane, is partially dried, baled, and stacked into huge ricks, and covered with loose sheets of roofing tin for storage at this factory.

USDA photo

BAGASSE

Bagasse is the name of the waste plant residues from sugar cane mills. Gardeners in the Deep South should avail themselves of this resource, which is a valuable addition to the heap. (See also Sugar Wastes.)

BANANA RESIDUE

Analyses have shown that banana skins and stalks are extremely rich in both phosphoric acid and potash, rating from 2.3 to 3.3 percent in phosphoric acid and from 41 to 50 percent in potash, on an ash basis. The nitrogen content, though not given in the literature, must be relatively high, because these residues decompose very readily and must therefore offer an almost complete diet for bacteria. When available in quantity, it would be thoroughly practical to utilize banana residues for gardening purposes. Table cuttings and kitchen refuse containing banana skins are valuable because they contain large amounts of bacteria which effect quick breakdown and act as activators for the rest of the compost material.

BASIC SLAG

An industrial by-product, basic slag results when iron ore is smelted to form pig iron. The ore contains, in addition to iron, small amounts of silicon, aluminum, sulfur, manganese, chromium, titanium, and traces of many other elements. In smelting the iron ore, large amounts of limestone and dolomite are used. The impurities unite with the limestone to form a sludge which rises to the surface of the molten mass and is poured off. In its cold, hard form this sludge is called slag.

The chemical composition of slag varies according to the ore which is used and with variations in the mixtures. The average ranges in the major constituents expressed in terms of the compounds indicated are shown in the accompanying table.

COMPOSITION OF SLAG

Material	Compound	Percent
Lime	CaO	38 to 45
Magnesia	MgO	4 to 9
Silica	SiO_2	33 to 39
Alumina	Al_2O_5	10 to 14
Manganese oxide	MnO	0.2 to 1.5
Iron oxide	FeO	0.2 to 0.7
Sulfur	S	1.0 to 2.0

Spectographic studies of slag indicate that it also contains traces of boron, sodium, molybdenum, tin, vanadium, copper, zinc, titanium, potassium, strontium, chromium and zirconium. Because slag contains so many kinds of essential nutrients, it may be used as a soil builder.

For agricultural purposes, slag must be very finely pulverized. Its efficiency varies directly with its degree of fineness. It is best known as a liming agent, providing crop plants with calcium and magnesium. In comparative studies it has been found to be better than lime, doubtless due to the fact that it contains some of the trace elements which are so important in plant nutrition.

Slag is alkaline in action. It does best on moist clays and loams, and on peaty soils deficient in lime, but can be used in some light soils if a potash mineral is used with it.

It should be applied to the soil in autumn and winter. Slag is especially well suited to the needs of such leguminous crops as beans, peas, clovers, vetches and alfalfa.

Ordinary iron and steel slags contain practically no phosphates but do contain other fertilizer constituents. Before using a slag for agricultural purposes, make sure that it contains soil-building constituents and especially trace elements. Avoid slags which contain excessive amounts of sulfur.

Since slag is made up of finely pulverized but insoluble particles, it can be applied at any time and at any rate without injuring the plants. An average application is from one to several tons per acre.

BEET WASTES

In sugar beet growing regions, wastes are easily available. Whatever cannot be used for ensiling or feeding can be composted, either in a pit or, with manure, as part of a sheet compost. Numerous analyses of beet roots showed that their potash content varied from 0.7 to 4.1 percent; the variation in nitrogen is less pronounced, averaging 0.4 percent, while phosphorus ranges from 0.1 to 0.6 percent. Astonishingly enough, the leaves are not very different in their makeup, although their content in calcium and magnesium far exceeds that of the roots.

BIRD CAGE CLEANINGS

One of the out-of-the-way materials which are often found by alert gardeners is the cleanings from bird cages. Sometimes, you can arrange for a steady supply of this material in exchange for cleaning bird cages in a local pet store. Small amounts of this material will help to activate a compost pile, generating tremendous heat in a short time.

BLOOD MEAL

Blood meal (dried blood) collected from slaughterhouses has a nitrogen content of 12 percent or over. There is often a considerable amount of phosphorus in dried blood, ranging from 1 to 5 percent; while often not indicated on the bag, this may considerably increase the value of the material. There are different grades of blood meal, all of which are used mainly for feeding purposes. Only a small quantity ever finds its way to the fertilizer dealer.

Dried blood can be used directly in the ground or may be composted. Because of its high nitrogen content, a sprinkling suffices to stimulate bacterial growth. It is advisable either to soak the plant matter thoroughly before applying or to apply the dried blood in moist form after a soaking.

Sources of dried blood and similar bagged fertilizers include the mail-order houses, seed dealers, fertilizer plants and dealers, and the feed supply houses.

BONE MEAL

Along with rock phosphate, bone meal is the major source of phosphorus for the garden. Bones have been used for centuries as a fertilizer, their value first recognized in England. They have long been known as an excellent source of phosphorus as well as nitrogen. In the early days of farming in this country, great amounts of buffalo bones were collected for use as fertilizer. Now slaughterhouses are the main source of bone meal.

Bone meal is an excellent source of phosphorus and nitrogen in the compost heap.

The phosphorous and nitrogen content in bone fertilizers depends mainly on the kind and age of the bone. According to Prof. G. H. Collings of Clemson Agricultural College, young bones generally contain less phosphorus and more nitrogen than older bones. The percentage of fluorine in older bones is considerably higher than in younger bones. Raw bone meal generally contains between 2 to 4 percent nitrogen, 20 to 25 percent phosphoric acid. Because of the fatty materials found in raw bone meal, decomposition is somewhat delayed when it is applied to the soil.

Steamed bone meal is more commonly found. It is made from green bones which have been boiled or steamed at high pressure to remove the fats. This causes a slight loss in nitrogen content, but a relative increase in phosphorus. Also, steamed bones can be ground more easily; steamed bone meal is almost always finer than raw bone meal. Steamed bone meal contains 1 to 2 percent nitrogen and up to 30 percent phosphorus.

Another bone fertilizer is bone black, which is charred bone, with a nitrogen content of about 1.5 percent, a phosphoric acid content over 30 percent, and many trace elements.

Although bone meal is often applied alone to soils, best results are obtained when it is applied in conjunction with other organic materials, as in compost. In general, bone meal acts more quickly when applied to well-aerated soils. Because of its lime content, bone meal tends to reduce soil acidity.

BUCKWHEAT HULLS

Buckwheat hulls are seldom used in the compost pile, not because they are not a suitable material, but because they make such an effective and attractive mulch. The hulls are disk-shaped, very light in weight, and after a rain they have the appearance of rich loam. When applied about 1½ inches deep, they will not blow away, but slither into place. After they have served as a mulch, buckwheat hulls can be worked into the soil to provide organic material for sandy soils and to help break up soils of clayey texture.

CASTOR POMACE

Castor Pomace is the residue left after the oil has been extraced from the castor bean. It is widely used as an organic fertilizer in place of cottonseed meal, because the latter is a valuable feed. The nitrogen analysis of castor bean varies from 4 to 6.6 percent, while phosphoric acid and potash analyze from 1 to 2 percent, with greater variation occurring in the phosphorous content.

Where animal matter is unavailable, compost could easily be made with castor pomace and other plant matter. Moisten the pomace and spread over the green matter in semi-liquid form. The finer the plant matter, the quicker the bacterial action.

CITRUS WASTES

Citrus wastes are easily composted. Their oils and resins disintegrate in the composting process. Citrus is generally a heavily-sprayed crop. If residues are present on the peels in only small amounts, they will not likely harm the soil after the material is broken down into compost. But to be absolutely safe, it is best to compost only citrus wastes from organic growers.

Orange skins and citrus skins of all kinds are richer in nitrogen if the skins are thick; their phosphoric acid analysis shows about 3 percent of the valuable element in orange skins, while the potash content of the ash is surpassed only by banana skins; the former analyzing about 27 percent, while banana skins have almost 50 percent in potash. Lemons, as a rule, have a lower potash, but a higher phosphorous content than oranges; grapefruits seem to hold the middle between the extremes: 3.6 percent phosphoric acid and 30 percent potash. Whole fruits, so-called culls, are also useful, though their fertilizer value is necessarily lower than that of the skins, because they contain great amounts of water.

The skins will decompose more quickly if shredded, mixed with other green matter, and inoculated with a nitrogen- and bacteria-rich material.

COAL ASHES

Although coal ashes will lighten heavy soils, there is serious danger of adding toxic quantities of sulfur and iron to the soil by using this material. Some ashes do not contain toxic quantities of these chemicals, but the coals from various sources are so different that no general recommendations can be made. The safest procedure is to regard all coal ashes as injurious to the soil.

An analysis of 32 samples of soft coal ashes showed from 4 to 40 percent iron oxide and from 0.3 to 10 percent sulfur trioxide. When water is added to sulfur trioxide, sulfuric acid is formed. Hard coal ashes have lesser amounts of iron and sulfur, but it is best to play safe and not use them. Use compost or plain sand instead. It is probable that the addition of coal ashes to compost would have similar harmful effects.

COCOA BEAN SHELLS

Coarse cocoa shells are rarely used in the compost heap because they are much better as a mulch. If available in large quantities, however, they make a fine addition to the heap because of their relatively high nutrient value. It must also be remembered that the terms "mulch" and "compost" are not unrelated, and that most mulches, when allowed to remain on the ground surface for some time, will decompose gradually, thus becoming compost.

Cocoa shell dust analyzes rather high in nitrogen for a product of this woody kind, namely 1 percent. The phosphorous content is about 1.5 percent, and the potash content approximately 1.7 percent. Usually theobromine and caffein are first extracted from the shells, and an analysis of the residues shows 2.7 percent nitrogen, 0.7 percent phosphoric acid, and 2.6 percent potash. The raw, untreated shells analyze slightly higher, but must of course be finely ground to be useful as fertilizer. Cocoa pressed cake has also been sold for fertilizing purposes, but the analyses vary according to treatment. As a rule, this cake is rather high in nitrogen, lower than the shells in potash, and with a phosphorous content close to 0.9 percent.

Chocolate factories have begun to market cocoa shell wastes which have been freed of oil and the theobromine. In the extraction process, lime is used. The finished product is useful for mulching soils in acid regions, because the lime content will balance the acidity of the soils while the organic matter of the residue acts as a fine water-storage medium. As an added advantage, it is odor-free and has no weed seeds.

When the shells are spread on the ground about 1 inch in depth, they furnish fine protection against drought. Rain will remove a great deal of the soluble plant food contained in the shells. During the winter months, they afford excellent protection against the damages caused by alternate freezing and thawing of seed beds and roots.

Cocoa bean shells can also be applied on lawns and when used in landscaping, they provide a very colorful, light even-brown color around shrubberies and evergreens as well as flower beds.

COFFEE WASTES

The average gardener usually has access only to coffee grounds. These, like other kitchen wastes, may be applied to the compost heap. They may also be applied directly to plants.

As a seed, the coffee bean has some nitrogen. Coffee grounds have up to 2 percent nitrogen in them, 0.33 percent phosphoric acid, and varying amounts of potash. Drip coffee grounds are richer than grounds that have been boiled, but the potash content is still below 1 percent. They also contain other minerals, trace elements, sugars, carbohydrates, some vitamins and, of course, caffeine. Coffee grounds sour easily because they preserve moisture well and seem to encourage acetic acid-forming bacteria. If mixed with lime and applied to the compost heap or fed to earthworm cultures, they are by no means negligible additions to the fertilizer resources of the average family. Being acid, they are good for blueberries, evergreens, and all acid-loving plants. When using on plants that like lime, mix some ground limestone with the grounds before using as a mulch. They seem to have a remarkable effect on stimulating the growth and health of certain plants.

A waste product from coffee manufacturing, coffee chaff, seems to be an excellent material for use in home gardens as well as farms. Containing over 2 percent nitrogen and potash, chaff also appears very suitable for use as a mulch material, where its dark color is an asset.

CORNCOBS

Corncobs are excellent compost material, but they should first be shredded or it will take years for the material to compost. Corncobs can be left to weather in the open for a few months; they will then break down much finer in the shredder.

Corncobs are a valuable ingredient for the compost heap and should be carefully preserved. Tests show that the cob is equivalent to two-thirds that of the corn kernel in nutrient value.

If gardeners or farmers will contact the mills in their community that shell corn, they will find mountains of cobs free for the taking.

Because of its moisture-holding properties, corncobs are regarded as one of the best mulches available. Used as a mulch, they should be applied to a depth of 3 or 4 inches. In the compost pile, mix the cobs with leaves to prevent the latter from caking and impeding aeration.

COTTONSEED MEAL

An excellent organic fertilizer, cottonseed meal is made from the cotton seed which has been freed from lints and hulls and deprived of its oil. Since cottonseed cake is one of the richest protein foods for animal feeding, relatively little finds its way for use as fertilizer. The special value of cottonseed meal lies in its acidity which makes it a valuable fertilizer for acid-loving specialty crops. The meal is used mainly as a source of nitrogen, of which it contains varying amounts, usually around 7 percent. Phosphoric acid content is between 2 and 3 percent, while potash is usually 1.5 percent.

While cottonseed meal is usually applied directly to the soil, it can be a valuable addition to the compost heap, providing the nitrogen necessary for rapid decomposition.

DOLOMITE

Dolomite, a rock similar to limestone, is interchangeable with limestone for uses in which physical properties are the determining factor. Limestone is composed of the mineral calcite (calcium carbonate) whereas dolomite rock is composed of a mineral which chemically is a *double* carbonate of calcium and magnesium. Theoretically pure dolomite contains 45.73 percent magnesium carbonate, and 54.27 percent calcium carbonate.

EARTHWORMS

The earthworm is a valuable addition to the compost heap. These creatures can help to mix materials, aerate the heap, and hasten decay of organic materials. The addition of earthworms in the heap makes unnecessary the laborious turnings required to mix materials in the Indore composting method. (A comprehensive discussion of the earthworm and its place in composting methods, will be found in Chapters 8 and 9.)

FELT WASTES

Hatteries have a certain amount of hair, felt, and wool wastes which may analyze as high as 14 percent nitrogen. If included in a compost that is teeming with bacteria, hair and feathers as well as felt wastes break down rather easily, provided the heap is kept moist enough. It is always wise to mix some manure or other high-protein material in with dry refuse, such as felt wastes, in order to supply bacterial life from the outset and hasten the decomposition process.

FISH SCRAP

Fish scrap is often available locally; its nitrogen and phosphorous value is high, frequently about 7 percent or above for each, computed on a dry basis. While dried ground fish is free from fats, fish scrap contains much fish oil and may thereby attract fat-eating ants; it also breaks down more slowly. In tropical regions where citrus or banana wastes are easily available or near canneries where refuse is obtainable, composting of fish refuse with plant refuse can be easily undertaken on a large scale, because those plant residues supply good amounts of potash while the fish scrap contains nitrogen and phosphorus besides such minor elements as iodine. In warm regions the outside temperature further hastens the breakdown of the material. But care must be taken to have the heaps well covered with earth and moist enough to secure quick action and absence of odors. The pit method is recommended. By sinking trenches about 3 feet deep, the composter will still supply enough air surface to stimulate aerobic bacterial growth, especially if the plant material is bulky. In the small garden, fish scrap can hardly be used successfully; but on a farm scale, the inclusion of wastes from fish markets or canneries in the compost is by no means impossible, and in the Northeast as well as Northwest, cannery wastes of fish material could profitably be used for making sheet compost.

GARBAGE

Garbage is a neglected source of compost material which is particularly rich in nitrogen and other nutrients essential to soil building and plant growth. You should compost kitchen wastes whether you live in a rural area or a suburb. In either case, use animal-proof bins and if you live in a comparatively densely settled community, consult local statutes.

Commercially built anaerobic bins are also available to the suburban gardener. These are moderately priced and are designed to hold six months' garbage, producing a good quality compost. Homemade bins should be animal-proof. Add garbage daily, covering each layer with a little soil, spoiled hay or straw.

Some gardeners bury their garbage on next year's planting sites, thus rotating their garden and leaving some land "resting" in anticipation of next year's crop. They must, however, take the precaution of burying kitchen waste deep enough to escape detection by rats and other scavenging animals.

Homesteaders can build a cement block enclosure high and strong enough to be animal-proof. This can serve as a garbage dump where kitchen garbage can partially break down. Some of this highly nitrogenous material can be removed from time to time and added to new compost heaps composed mostly of vegetable manures.

The European method of garbage trenching may be used where there is too much garbage to compost or where compost heaps cannot be built, as in some towns. A trench about a foot deep is dug across the

Kitchen wastes are a natural addition to the compost pile. Some gardeners bury kitchen garbage in an unused section of the garden, to decompose underground to enrich the plot used the following year.

garden in spring, and the soil left heaped up beside it. (The trench and heap of soil may both be temporarily covered with mulch, to prevent drying.) The trench is filled with garbage, starting at one end and working toward the other; the garbage covered with soil and again mulched. The row is left unplanted during the entire season to permit bacterial action below ground to be completed.

The relatively recent innovation of municipal composting techniques has returned to the soil much garbage which formerly was incinerated or put in a landfill. This is discussed fully in Chapter 15.

GIN TRASH

The disposal of gin trash (wastes of the cotton plant) had been an expensive burden to the cotton industry until in 1952 the processors stopped burning gin trash and began to compost it. Now, gin trash has joined the growing list of industrial waste materials which are being returned to the soil.

The Texas State Department of Health, in cooperation with commercial bacteria breeders, developed a process of composting everything except the seed and blossoms of the cotton plant. Within 21 days after a pile of gin trash—burs, stems and dust, once destroyed in a bur burner—is injected with a special breed of bacterial culture, a compost equivalent to leaf mold or well-rotted manure is produced.

The significance of the reclaimed organic matter is readily seen. For each bale of cotton harvested from one acre of land, the soil loses about 25 pounds of potash, 2 pounds of phosphate, and 4 pounds of nitrogen, along with varying quantities of trace elements. Portions of those elements go into the seed and fiber of the plant, but the major portions are in the burs and other waste once blown into the bur burners.

Studies observed by the department show that the composted trash exceeds in value both an application of commercial fertilizer and the decomposed residue of a green manure crop. The best effect of applying this humus to the land is the friability which it produces. Normal application rates are 2 to 3 tons per acre. In a comparative per-acre study, 300 pounds of 16-20-0 formula fertilizer supplied only 48 pounds of nitrogen, 60 pounds of available phosphoric acid, no potash and no organic matter. On the other hand, 3 tons of the gin trash compost supplied 60 pounds each of nitrogen, available phosphoric acid, and potash, plus 5,820 pounds of organic matter. The fertilizer effects of the gin trash will be noticeable for several years after the application.

Alert gardeners can obtain composted gin trash for nominal amounts, and can often get uncomposted material free. Both make valuable additions to the compost heap.

GRANITE DUST

Granite dust or granite stone meal is a highly recommended natural source of potash. Its potash content varies between 3 and 5 percent, often more.

The value of using potash rock, such as granite dust, over the chemical form is that it is cheaper and leaves no harmful chemical residues. It also contains valuable trace mineral elements. There are sources of granite and other potash-containing rocks all over the country and these sources are being uncovered gradually to make natural rock powders available to all gardeners.

Granite dust should be used in liberal quantities. It can also be used as a top dressing, worked directly into the soil, or used when establishing a cover crop. In the garden, suggested rates of application are 10 pounds to 100 square feet, 100 pounds to 1,000 square feet; on the farm, the recommended application rate is 2 tons to the acre.

GRAPE WASTES

The prunings of grape vines, when shredded and composted, return much of the organic matter and nutrient content lost by cropping. Vine prunings must be cut into pieces 3 to 6 inches long if they are to pack closely enough for successful composting. The amount of water required depends upon the rate of evaporation and hence upon the local climate. The water content of the mass, if the prunings are to be composted alone, should be from 70 to 80 percent, indicated by the development of fungus mycelium on the surface. Excessive water is harmful, as fermentation cannot proceed in a water-logged medium. Some added nitrogenous fertilizer is desirable to stimulate bacterial activity.

The process should be completed in about six months, and the finished product resembles ordinary garden compost.

Objections have been raised that the compost, because it encourages fungus activity, will predispose the vines to mildew infection. This has not been the case in our experience; in fact, the fungi responsible for forming the compost secrete substances which attack and destroy the vine mildews.

Shredded prunings, of course, are valuable additions of green matter to the ordinary compost heap and should be treated as any other green matter. Although the nutrient content of grape wastes is not very high, the material will add the organic matter necessary to maintain soil health.

GRASS CLIPPINGS

Among the easiest materials to obtain, grass clippings are valuable to the compost heap. Many people, feeling that clippings should not be taken from the lawn, do not use them in compost or as mulch. It is true that clippings are valuable when left on the lawn, but a good lawn doesn't need as much enrichment, added organic matter or mulching as do the more heavily cropped plots. Collecting grass clippings is one way to curtail unwanted weed growth in the lawn, since it helps to remove the weed seeds. Also, periodic collection of clippings promotes better appearance, and aids in keeping a neater lawn.

Grass clippings are a source of extra nitrogen in the compost heap.

We don't recommend that *all* grass clippings be removed. Some can and should be left as occasional replenishment for the lawn itself.

Because freshly cut, green grass clippings are such a wonderful source of nitrogen, they should be utilized to the utmost. There are three excellent ways in which they can be put to work in the garden and flower beds: they may be used as a mulch; they may be turned in as green manure; and they may be used in the compost heap to create the necessary heat for good decomposition.

As a mulch, lawn clippings surpass most others. They are easy to handle, will remain in place nicely, will fit in the smallest spaces with no trouble and, when dried, will give your rows and beds a very neat appearance. Of course you will not have enough clippings to mulch your entire garden from the first cutting; mulch as much as you can each week, first mulching vegetables that mature early, then working on the others.

Because they are so finely chopped, clippings disappear completely into the soil by fall. The mulch may be replenished in late summer, but it is not necessary. For some reason, grass does not grow well in areas covered with decayed clippings.

Green mulch such as this may temporarily rob the soil of available nitrogen, including both ammonia and nitrates. But this condition is so short-lived that it cannot stunt the rapid growth of the plants.

Later in the season, if there is a surplus of grass clippings on hand, scatter a few inches of the green clippings over an unused area in your garden. Turn these in immediately as green manure, along with any previously applied mulch. Work a small plot at a time. Later, you can remulch the entire area until the following spring.

When green vegetation is mixed with the soil under favorable conditions of temperature and moisture, decomposition immediately begins. This rapid decomposition is brought about by many species of bacteria and fungi found in the earth. These microorganisms require a source of energy such as nitrogen, which green grass supplies in abundance. The hungry bacteria and fungi draw nitrogen from the grass instead of robbing the soil of its necessary supply. The grass is soon digested into humus, and soil nitrogen increased. When used as green manure, grass clippings greatly improve the physical condition of heavy-textured soils. If acidity is a factor, a small amount of limestone may be applied with the clippings.

If you care to turn in green grass clippings as green manure before planting a second crop in a vacant plot, you may do so. Give the section a week or ten days to rest, then plant.

When using grass clippings in the compost heap, use two-thirds grass clippings and one-third stable manure.

GREENSAND

Glauconite greensand or greensand marl is an iron-potassium-silicate that imparts a green color to the minerals in which it occurs. Being an undersea deposit, greensand contains traces of many (if not all) the elements which occur in sea water. Greensand has been used successfully for soil-building for more than 100 years. It is a fine source of potash.

Greensand contains from 6 to 7 percent of plant-available potash. The best deposits also contain 50 percent silica, 18 to 23 percent iron oxides, 3 to 7.5 percent magnesia, small amounts of lime and phosphoric acid, and traces of 30 or more other elements, most of which are important in the nutrition of higher plants.

HAIR

Hair, in common with wool and silk, has a high nitrogen content. Six to 7 pounds of hair contain a pound of nitrogen or as much as 100 to 200 pounds of manure. If kept in a well-moistened heap, hair will disintegrate as easily as feathers. Perhaps a local barber will give you the sweepings from his shop.

HOOF AND HORN MEAL

There are many grades of hoof and horn meal. The granular form breaks down with some difficulty unless kept moist and well covered; it also tends to encourage the growth of maggots because it attracts flies. Finely ground horn dust, which gardeners use for potting mixtures, is quite easily dissolved. The nitrogen content is from 10 to 16 pounds per 100 pound bag or as much as a ton or more of manure, while the phosphoric acid value is usually around 2 percent. If available, this is a very handy source of nitrogen for flower growers and gardeners with small compost heaps, because it can be easily stored, is pleasant to handle, and is relatively less costly than other forms of bagged organic nitrogen.

HOPS

Spent hops (the residue after hops have been extracted with water in the brewery) is another industrial by-product valuable to the gardener. In their wet state, hops contain 75 percent water, 0.6 percent nitrogen, and 0.2 percent phosphorus. Moisture content varies considerably, and the analysis expressed on the dry matter is the most satisfactory figure. On this basis the nitrogen ranges from 2.5 to 3.5 percent and the phosphoric acid about 1 percent.

Spent hops in their natural condition are to be regarded mainly as a source of nitrogen. In many areas, people have been successfully spreading wet hops in the same way as farmyard manure. Others have been composting the hops before applying to the soil.

Spent hops have been used as a mulch with excellent success. For the small gardener, however, they have one disadvantage—a very strong odor—which disappears in a short time. Used in larger areas where the odor is not seriously objectionable, spent hops prove to be a very effective mulch. It does not blow away when dry and does not burn if a lighted match or cigarette butt is thrown into it. Many other mulch materials burn easily.

Hop vines and manure are the basis of a successful compost for one farmer. The two ingredients are loaded into a mixing machine which blends them and deposits the material in piles measuring 7 feet at the base and 5 feet in height.

Compost Science *photo*

Like other mulches, spent hops conserve soil moisture, raise the soil temperature in the late fall and early spring, and aid bacteria in their work in the soil. Spent hops direct from the brewery are very wet and have a pH of about 4.5. One 6-inch application about a plant will last at least three years, sometimes longer. Stirring the material once or twice during the growing season aids in keeping down any of the weeds that may have grown up through it.

Because of their tremendous water content, fresh hops heat very readily in the compost pile, serving as an activator for other materials. This same property may be harmful to young plants, however, if fresh hops are used as a mulch; it is best to keep them at least 6 inches away from any young stems.

Another brewery waste often available is the grain material left over from the mashing process. This wet brewer's grain, which decays readily, has been found to contain almost 1 percent of nitrogen.

INCINERATOR ASH

Incinerator ash, if available, is a fine source of phosphorus and potash for the compost heap. Its phosphorous content depends upon what was burned, but runs around 5 or 6 percent; its potassium content is from 2 to 3 percent. It often can be obtained from municipal incinerators or from large apartment dwellings.

LEATHER DUST

Leather dust makes an excellent high-nitrogen fertilizer material. The nitrogen content varies from 5.5 to 12 percent, and the material also contains considerable amounts of phosphorus. Leather dust may be added to the compost pile or may be applied directly to the soil. It is available commercially, but may often be secured from leather processing plants.

LEAVES

Since most trees are deep-rooted, they absorb minerals from deep in the soil; a good portion of these minerals go to the leaves. Pound for pound, the leaves of most trees contain twice as many minerals as does manure. For example, the mineral content of a sugar maple leaf is over 5

Leaves are a valuable compost ingredient. Pound for pound they contain twice the minerals of manure, and if properly handled, they will produce a beautiful compost.

percent, while even pine needles have 2.5 percent of their weight in calcium, magnesium, nitrogen, and phosphorus, plus other trace elements. (See the accompanying chart for an analysis of the nutrient elements in some common leaves.) Actually, though, leaves are most valuable for the large amounts of fibrous organic matter they supply.

Some people complain that they have no luck composting leaves. This does seem to be a common complaint. There are two things you can do that will guarantee success in composting leaves:

1. Add extra nitrogen to your leaf compost since leaves alone don't contain enough nitrogen to provide sufficient food for bacteria. Manure is the best nitrogen supplement, and a mixture of five parts leaves to one part manure will break down quickly. If you don't have manure, nitrogen supplements like dried blood, cottonseed meal, and bone meal will work almost as well. In general, add two cups of dried blood or other natural nitrogen supplement to each wheelbarrow load of leaves.
2. Grind or shred your leaves. A compost pile made of shredded material is easily controlled and easy to handle.

If you don't have a shredder, there are various other devices you can adapt to leaf shredding. Many people use a rotary mower for shredding. A mower that is not self-propelled is best and easiest to control. Two people can work together very nicely, one piling up leaves in front of the mower and the other running it back and forth over the pile. A leaf-mulching attachment attached to the blade will cut the leaves finer, but sometimes it is not necessary. You will be surprised how many leaves you can shred this way in a half-hour or so, even working alone.

Of course, some people use a mower with a mulching attachment to cut up leaves right on the lawn. This does not make them available for compost or mulch somewhere else—like the garden—where they are more essential.

If you have so many leaves on your place that you can't compost all of them—or if you don't have the time to make compost—you can make leaf mold. Leaf mold is not as rich a fertilizer as composted leaves, but it's easier to make and is especially useful as mulch.

A length of snow fencing or wood or stones placed in a circle make the best kind of enclosure for making leaf mold. Gather leaves in the fall and wet them thoroughly; then tamp them down in the enclosure. Leaves are slightly acid. If your plants don't need an acid mulch, add

Leaf mold, the end product of leaf decomposition, is a rich, black, crumbly humus that can be worked into the soil or used as a fine mulch.

some ground limestone to the leaves before tamping them down.

These leaves will not break down over the winter into the kind of black powdery leaf mold found on the forest floor. By spring or summer they will be broken up enough to serve as a fine mulch. Some people including nursery men who require fine potting soil keep leaves "in cold storage" for several years. When they come for their leaves, they find black, crumbly humus.

Leaf mold is ordinarily found in the forest in a layer just above the mineral soil. It has the merit of decomposing slowly, furnishing plant nutrients gradually and improving the structure of the soil as it does so. The ability of leaf mold to retain moisture is amazing. Subsoil can hold a mere 20 percent of its weight in water; good, rich topsoil will hold 60 percent, but leaf mold can retain 300 to 500 percent of its weight.

Freshly fallen leaves pass through several stages from surface litter to well-decomposed humus partly mixed with mineral soil. Leaf mold from deciduous trees is somewhat richer in such mineral foods as potash and phosphorus than that from conifers. The nitrogen content varies from 0.2 to 5 percent.

If you keep poultry or livestock, use your supply of leaves for litter or bedding along with straw or hay. Leaf mold thus enriched with extra nitrogen may later be mixed directly with soil or added to the compost pile.

A lawn sweeper is a good tool to use for collecting leaves. It is easier than raking and often does a better job.

NUTRIENT ELEMENTS IN FALLEN LEAVES

Name	Cal-cium	Magne-sium	Potas-sium	Phos-phorus	Nitro-gen	Ash	pH
Red maple	1.29	0.40	0.40	0.09	0.52	10.97	4.70
Sugar maple	1.81	0.24	0.75	0.11	0.67	11.85	4.30
American beech	0.99	0.22	0.65	0.10	0.67	7.37	5.08
White ash	2.37	0.27	0.54	0.15	0.63	10.26	6.80
White oak	1.36	0.24	0.52	0.13	0.65	5.71	4.40
Eastern hemlock	0.68	0.14	0.27	0.07	1.05	....	5.50
Balsam fir	1.12	0.16	0.12	0.09	1.25	3.08	5.50

LIMESTONE

The best way to apply limestone to your soil is to use ground limestone. This allows the lime to be available over a long period of time. The limestone should be fine enough to sift through a 100-mesh screen. In this form the lime will be exposed to water in the soil in sufficient quantities to dissolve slowly, but the entire application will not dissolve for several years. Lime is particularly valuable in the compost heap, as it will neutralize many acidic materials.

Lime is seldom used as a fertilizer, although its calcium content is as important to plant life as it is to animals. Most soils contain enough calcium in one form or another to supply all that plants need.

The primary use for lime in the garden or on the farm is as an alkalizer, to raise the pH of soil or compost. But it is important that certain acid-loving plants do not receive too much lime, and that alkaline-loving plants receive enough. Both the soil and compost pile should be tested annually for pH (as well as for N-P-K).

The following garden plants prefer soils which are approximately neutral: abelia, alyssum, anemone, arborvitae, aster, barberry, begonia, clematis, columbine, coreopsis, cosmos, dahlia, deutzia, forsythia, larkspur, lilac, mock orange, narcissus, pansy, peony, poppy, bell flower, box, bittersweet, butterfly bush, calendula, canna, carnation, chrysanthemum, geranium, gladiolus, hibiscus, honeysuckle, hyacinth, hydrangea, iris, ivy, primrose, privet, rose, spirea, tulip, violet, wisteria and zinnia.

Some plants which prefer slight to medium acidity are: some varieties of aster, bunchflower, fir, heather, holly, huckleberry, juniper, lily, lily-of-the-valley, magnolia, red oak, phlox, pine, spruce, creeping willow and wintergreen.

Medium to strongly acid soils are required by the following: arethusa, arnica, azalea, most varieties of ferns, galax, gardenia, orchid, ladyslipper, pitcher plant, rhododendron, rose pogonia, sand myrtle, sundew, trailing arbutus, and wild calla.

Most vegetables prefer lime, and dislike acidity. Carrots and tomatoes are only slightly affected by acidity, but only potatoes, radishes, and watermelons positively dislike lime. Fruits which prefer acid soil are blackberry, blackcap raspberry, blueberry, cranberry, huckleberry and strawberry.

The only field crops which prefer acid soil are flax and velvet bean, while flint corn, millet and rye are only slightly affected by it. All others prefer limed soils.

Leguminous crops—peas, beans, vetch, clover—increase their yield remarkably in the presence of sufficient lime. Beans sown in the open field have been known to yield ten times as much after the field was limed. The reason for this is that the nitrogen-fixing bacteria which live on root nodules of legumes, thrive in alkaline soils.

Lime has a physical as well as a chemical effect upon soil. When spread upon clay soils, lime flocculates the clay (i.e., it causes particles to gather in groups, making larger physical units in the soil). Water and air penetrate more easily than they do a soil composed of fine clay particles. In a sandy soil lime has the effect of holding the particles more closely together so that water is held for a longer period.

Lime also releases some of the phosphorus and potash from their insoluble compounds, making them available for plant use. Thus, though lime is not itself a fertilizer, it effectively increases soil fertility.

Lime may be applied either to the compost heap or, more commonly, directly to the soil. Generally, apply one ton of ground limestone per acre every three or four years. This rate will be effective, on most soils, although soil testing is always advised to avoid unnecessary liming. Since ground limestone becomes available slowly, dangers of overliming are lessened. For the garden, apply about 50 pounds for 1,000 square feet every three or four years, unless tests indicate differently. Lime freshly cultivated soil in fall or early spring, preferably on a windless day. Spread the lime evenly and thoroughly to avoid skipping areas. Unlike fertilizers, lime does not spread itself over adjacent areas, but works itself down into the soil.

TONS OF GROUND LIMESTONE NEEDED TO RAISE pH

	pH range		
Soils of warm-temperate and tropical regions:	3.5 to 4.5	4.5 to 5.5	5.5 to 6.5
Sandy and loamy sand	0.3	0.3	0.4
Sandy loam	...	0.5	0.7
Loam	...	0.8	1.0
Silt loam	...	1.2	1.4
Clay loam	...	1.5	2.0
Muck	2.5	3.3	3.8
Soils of cool-temperate and temperate regions:			
Sandy and loamy sand	0.4	0.5	0.6
Sandy loam	...	·0.8	1.3
Loam	...	1.2	1.7
Silt loam	...	1.5	2.0
Clay loam	...	1.9	2.3
Muck	2.9	3.8	4.3

MANURE

Manure is the most valuable ingredient in the compost pile. For a full discussion of using manure in composting, see Chapter 7.

MOLASSES RESIDUES

Molasses residues are a valuable addition to the compost heap. Molasses is high in fermentable sugars and also contains essential elements. Yeasts in the compost heap will ferment the sugars in the molasses.

OLIVE RESIDUES

Olive pomace analyzed at 1.15 nitrogen, 0.78 phosphoric acid and 1.26 potash, while some olive refuse showed 1.22 nitrogen, 0.18 phosphoric acid and 0.32 potash. The analysis of olive pits is unavailable but they not only contain phosphorus and nitrogen but lignin as well. Olive residues should be thoroughly composted and mixed with other materials before using. If the residue contains many pits, they should be ground.

PEA WASTES

Pea wastes of several kinds are mainly available near canneries. The best use for pea residues is if pea shells and vines can be fed to animals and the animals' manure composted. If not, they should be returned to the land in some form. If they are diseased, they can be burned and the ashes used for fertilizing (pea pod ash contains almost 3 percent phosphoric acid and 27 percent potash). They can be easily composted since the high nitrogen content in green pods and vines tends to produce a quick breakdown.

PEAT MOSS

Peat moss is the partially decomposed remains of plants accumulated over centuries under relatively airless conditions. It is a highly valuable organic material for soil building. Peat moss loosens heavy soils, binds light soils, holds vast amounts of water, increases aeration, aids root development, and stops nutrients from leaching away. It can be added to the soil, used as a mulch, or added to compost.

When dry, it will absorb up to 15 times its weight in water. Soil-held moisture is not only vital in preventing drought damage, but it carries the nutrients the plant must have to grow in solution (for every pound of actual plant solids, the plant uses ¼ to ½ ton of water from the soil). Proper amounts of moisture also aid the soil organisms to break up the organic compounds into usable forms.

Peat moss has a very open, fibrous texture, permitting free development of tiny hair roots. It improves aeration, too, letting the soil "breathe deeply." The ground is kept loose and friable, without crusting or compacting. Drainage is also improved in heavy clay soils and, in light, sandy ones, plant nutrients are prevented from leaching away. Peat moss is biologically sterile—it contains no weed seeds, no plant disease organisms, no insect eggs or larvae.

Finally, its effects last many years. Tests at Pennsylvania State Agricultural College showed that 70 percent of its organic content was still in the soil after ten years.

For all its good points, peat moss should not be regarded as a miracle soil amendment. While some sedge peats do contain as high as 3 percent nitrogen, this is released slowly over many years. Compost, or materials like leaf mold, are preferable to peat moss if easily procurable, because they have more nutrients in a more readily available form.

Because of its low nutrient content, and because peat often is rather expensive to purchase, it is not generally used in compost. If, however, you want a distinctly acid compost for certain plants, substitute peat for soil and omit the lime. (See Soil in this chapter.) Peat compost is used for camellia, rhododendron, azalea, blueberries, sweet potatoes, watermelons, eggplant, potatoes, tomatoes, many perennial herbs and most shrubs and trees—all acid-loving plants.

PET LITTER

Moderate amounts of pet litter may be used without concern in the compost heap. The manure of household pets is generally on a par with that of barnyard animals.

As mentioned earlier, however, there is a danger in using cat droppings. Harold S. Perlmutter, M.D., of Newton, New Jersey, says, "Cat droppings harbor two extremely dangerous organisms, both of which are prominent causes of blindness, especially in children.

"The most common cause of retinal inflammation in this country is due to the one-celled parasite, *Toxoplasma gondii*, which is carried by the cat and excreted in its droppings. This organism can form cysts which are extremely resistant to adverse conditions such as cold, heat, and drying. It causes a flu-like illness in pregnant women and can be transmitted to the unborn fetus, causing both brain and eye disease.

"The second organism is *Toxocara cati*, which is a nematode (round worm) of extremely common occurrence in cats. The eggs of this worm, when finding their way to the mouths of children, enter the blood stream and cause infection of many organs, including the eye.

"I, therefore, urge that cat droppings and litter material be handled with extreme caution, if at all. In our attempt to recycle waste materials, we must be sure that we are not also perpetuating disease organisms which can lead to blindness and other severe physical defects."

PHOSPHATE ROCK

Phosphate rock is an excellent natural source of phosphorus for fertilizer use. Phosphate rock varies somewhat in its composition depending upon its source. However, calcium phosphate or bone phosphate of lime composes 65 percent of the total. Phosphate rock contains other compounds and mineral elements, many of which are essential for plant growth; included are calcium carbonate, calcium fluoride, iron oxide, iron sulfide, alumina, silica, manganese dioxide, titanium oxide, sodium, copper, chromium, magnesium, strontium, barium, lead, zinc, vanadium, boron, silver and iodine.

Superphosphate. The difference between superphosphate and rock phosphate is that superphosphate has been treated with an equal amount of sulfuric acid to make it more soluble. This results in mono-calcium-phosphate, a slowly water-soluble phosphate and calcium sulphate, a highly soluble neutral salt. It also results in a product that has lost many of the minor elements of phosphate rock: such as boron, zinc, nickel, iodine, and others.

Rock phosphate, on the other hand, is not highly water soluble and is lost in the soil only through cropping. The beneficial effects of rock phosphate far outlast those of super-phosphate. Finely ground rock phosphate is available as plants need it. Plant roots give off carbon dioxide and certain organic acids which make rock phosphate in the soil available for plant use. Rock phosphate remains unchanged in the soil until roots develop in its vicinity.

Phosphate rock is often added to the compost pile. A light sprinkling applied with each series of layers (in the Indore heap) will be sufficient to supply phosphate to maintain a healthy soil. For vegetable and flower gardens, phosphate rock may be applied alone; generally, 1 pound for 10 square feet is enough for three to five years. The same application is usually recommended for lawns. The other major source of phosphorus for the garden is bone meal.

PINE NEEDLES

Pine needles are compostible, although they will break down rather slowly because of their thick outer coating of a waxy substance called cutin. Pine needles are also acid in nature and for this reason should not be used in large quantities. For best results, shred the needles before adding them to the heap.

POTASH ROCK

Potash rock, a naturally occurring rock containing a high percentage of potassium, is the material most often added as a potash source in the compost heap. It is readily available in most parts of the country and is inexpensive.

Potash rock may also be used alone. Usually, ½ ton per acre, or 2⅓ pounds per 100 square feet, is the recommended application. It may be used on most soils, contributing a wide variety of minerals without danger of overdosage.

POTATO WASTES

The potash content of tubers is usually around 2.5 percent. Since tubers are storage organs, they abound with trace minerals. Dry potato

Potato peels are rich in trace minerals, and should always be used in the compost pile.

vines contain approximately 1.6 percent potash, 4.0 percent calcium, 1.1 percent magnesium, and considerable amounts of sulfur and other minerals. Potato skins are usually put on the compost with other kitchen wastes. Their nitrogen content has been found to be 0.6 percent, even when the skins were reduced to ashes.

RICE HULLS

Often considered a waste product, rice hulls have been found to be very rich in potash and decompose readily, increasing humus content, when worked into the soil. The hulls make an excellent soil conditioner and a worthwhile addition to the compost heap. They also make a good, long-lasting mulch that does not blow away.

Gardeners in the Texas-Louisiana Gulf Coast area can often get ample amounts of this material from rice mills; occasionally it is free. Some mills make a practice of burning the hulls, and the residue from this operation contains a high percentage of potash, making it especially valuable as a composting material.

SAWDUST

Sawdust is often useful in the compost heap, although it is better used as a mulch. Some gardeners who have access to large quantities use it for both with equally fine results. In most areas, lumber yards will occasionally give sawdust free for the hauling. Sawdust is very low in nitrogen. One of the objections against using sawdust is that it may cause a nitrogen deficiency. However, many gardeners report fine results applying sawdust as a mulch to the soil surface without adding

Sawdust is especially valuable as a surface mulch; its low nitrogen content makes it less valuable as a compost ingredient.

USDA photo

any supplementary nitrogen fertilizer. If your soil is of low fertility, watch plants carefully during the growing season. If they become light green or yellowish in color, side-dress with an organic nitrogen fertilizer such as cottonseed meal, blood meal, compost, manure, or tankage.

Some people are afraid that the continued application of sawdust will sour their soil; that is, make it too acid. A very comprehensive study made from 1949 to 1954 by the Connecticut Experiment Station of sawdust and wood chips reported no instance of sawdust making the soil more acid. It is possible, though, that sawdust used on the highly alkaline soils of the western United States would help to make the soil neutral, a welcome effect.

SEAWEED

Seaweed has been in use as a fertilizer in England, Scotland and Wales for many years. Wherever it can be collected easily, it makes an ideal material for composting. There are different types of seaweed, but the most important are *Laminaria,* also called driftwood or kelp. This plant has a stem and a broad flat lamina or leaf and grows immediately below low-water mark. It is collected on shores. Its stems are high in

Gardeners in coastal areas should be sure to take advantage of nutrient-rich seaweed in their composting efforts.

moisture and have a high percentage of potash; the leaves are somewhat drier and have a lower percentage of potash. The dry stems contain about 10 to 12 percent potash, the dry leaves or fronds, 5 percent. Another seaweed sometimes used as fertilizer is fucus, also known as bladder wrack or cutweed. It grows between tide marks in sheltered inlets where not so many *Laminaria* can be found. It can be cut from the rocks at low tide. Its potash content is low; when dried it does not contain more than 2 to 4 percent. Ulva, also called sea lettuce, is washed ashore in great quantities in quiet bays and inlets. This weed is very rich in nitrates. Ulva, grown in bays and inlets where sweet water rivers carry a lot of mud, is much higher in nitrogen than one grown in pure sea water.

Seaweed in general (that is a mixture of all of those which can easily be found on the shore) contains on the average 7 pounds of nitrogen compounds, 2 pounds of phosphoric acid, 22 pounds of potash, 36 pounds of sodium chloride, and about 400 pounds of organic matter per ton. Fresh seaweed is similar to barnyard manure in its content of organic matter. It is, however, poorer in nitrogen and poorer in phosphate, but much richer in potash. In the Old World seaweed was used to condition the soil for growing potatoes, broccoli, lettuce, peas and cabbage; it was also used for root crops and mangels. Barley responds well to seaweed, particularly on light, sandy soils. For cabbage and root crops, use well-rotted seaweed; for potatoes, plow the seaweed under in November or December. (This is more easily done when the seaweed is well rotted.) However, if you can't wait, plow it under immediately after collecting; that is, while it is still wet and green, and early enough so that the salt which adheres to it can be washed out by rain and does not poison the soil.

The difficulty with drying seaweed is that it deteriorates. If it is rained on, many of the minerals, particularly the easily-soluble potassium salts, are washed out and lost. It should be dried on a platform or a floor through which the moisture cannot run away, and should also be protected from rain. It is better to dry it relatively quickly and spread in the dried state.

To save as much of the mineral content as possible, compost seaweed when green. Composting also helps take care of the salt content which might be a problem otherwise. If composted with manure that is very rich in litter, seaweed aids the speedy decay of the straw; very little nitrogen is lost and all the other elements are preserved. Decay is very rapid.

Where there is a shortage of potassium, seaweed is a very good substance to use for balancing compost. For this reason seaweed is excellent for potatoes, which need a lot of potassium.

SEWAGE SLUDGE

The use of sewage sludge by gardeners and farmers throughout the United States has been climbing in recent years. The fertilizer value of the sludge produced depends largely on the processing method used.

Activated sludge is produced when the sewage is agitated by air rapidly bubbling through it. Certain types of very active bacteria coagulate the organic matter, which settles out, leaving a clear liquid that can be discharged into streams and rivers with a minimum amount of pollution.

Activated sludge is generally heat-treated before being made available to gardeners and farmers; its nitrogen content is between 5 and 6 percent, phosphorus from 3 to 6 percent. It is highly recommended organic fertilizer and a good material for the compost heap.

Digested sludge is formed when the sewage is allowed to settle (and

Liquid sludge is sprayed on a field. The sludge may either be left on the surface, or plowed under after it has dried.

liquid to drain off) by gravity without being agitated by air, and is then subjected to anaerobic fermentation. The conventional anaerobic digestion system takes about 15 to 30 days at 37°C (99°F) from the time the sewage reaches the sedimentation tank until the digested solids are pumped into filter beds for drying. The final step is removal of the dry material, either to be incinerated or used for soil improvement.

Digested sludge has about the same fertilizer value as barnyard manure. Nitrogen varies from 2 to 3 percent, phosphorus averaging about 2 percent.

When putting sludge into a compost heap, break it up thoroughly or it will not be able to aerate itself. Apply in very thin layers, not more than one inch at any one place. Complete breakdown can be assured through the use of manure, good soil and earthworms in the heap.

SOIL

Soil is an important ingredient in the compost heap. The heap itself should be built directly on freshly dug earth. The site of the heap should be leveled and the soil loosened. Each layer of an Indore heap includes 6 inches of plant material, 2 inches of fresh manure, and about ⅛-inch of soil. It won't be possible to get this layer perfect, of course; estimate as best you can. You can also sprinkle lime on these earth layers. Any kind of soil except sterile sand can be used in a compost pile.

The soil in the compost heap acts as a base for absorbing volatile substances produced in fermentation and prevents them from being lost to the air. Fertile soil also contains billions of soil organisms which do the work of breaking down the plant and animal residues and converting them into compost. Soil also contains the minerals necessary for the life processes of the soil organisms which grow and reproduce rapidly in the compost heap.

After the heap has reached 5 feet in height, it is covered with an outer layer of soil about 2 inches thick to prevent excessive evaporation of water and to conserve heat in the heap. The outer layer of soil on the side of the heap can be dispensed with if a suitable enclosure is used. Compost may be made in a pit dug in the ground in which case the earthen walls of the pit form the enclosure. In some cases the sides of the pit are lined with bricks or cement blocks; but the bottom must never be anything but the soil.

One need not hesitate to take top soil from the garden or field for building a compost heap as it will be returned again and in manifold measure. When the heap is turned, the outer layer of soil can be carefully removed and used over the rebuilt heap.

To hasten composting, add old compost to the new heap in place of soil. When this is done, the composting may be completed in approximately one-third of the time that is ordinarily required.

For making peat compost, replace the soil with peat in making the successive layers of the heap; also, use peat for the outside casing of the heap. Peat compost is especially recommended for blueberries, azaleas, camellias, and other acid-loving plants.

Many gardeners consider soil as the compost ingredient hardest to obtain in sufficient quantities. Those with small gardens may have trouble finding enough soil unless they can haul it away from a building excavation or they can purchase topsoil from a local nursery.

Mud from ponds, lakes or streams that are not chemically contaminated should be mixed with straw, hay and leaves and spread out for aeration in flat heaps not over 6 or 7 inches in height, before using in the compost pile. Add plenty of ground limestone or wood ashes, as the mud will probably be quite acid. Don't apply this mud directly to the land; it causes the same problems experienced when raw manure or a green manure cover crop is plowed under.

The overflow from the River Nile in Egypt contains a fine sediment that makes the application of other fertilizers unnecessary. The Chinese also use the sediment of streams, but include it in compost heaps instead of directly adding such sediment to the land. River bottoms and soil washed down from floods and overflows provide excellent composting material.

SPANISH MOSS

Spanish moss can be profitably used in the compost heap. It is not a real moss, but a seed plant belonging to the pineapple family of flowering plants. Spanish moss is harvested, cleaned, and sold to furniture, mattress, and upholstery makers. The cleanings outside moss gins accumulate like the sawdust around a sawmill. There are hundreds of moss gins in Louisiana alone. Composted moss gin wastes are now being sold under the name "Gro-Mulch."

STRAW

Although straw will add few nutrients to the compost heap, it is widely used because it is readily available and adds considerable organic material. Most farmers can offer bales of spoiled hay to gardeners at nominal costs.

The fertilizer value of straw is, like that of all organic matter, twofold; it adds carbon material and plant food to the compost. The carbon serves the soil bacteria as energy food, while the plant food becomes released for growing crops. Where much straw is used, incorporate considerable amounts of nitrogen (preferably in the form of manures) so that the bacteria which break down the straw into humus do not deplete the soil of the nitrogen needed by growing plants.

If used in quantity, cut up the straw. Long pieces of straw mixed with other materials that hold water or composted with ample amounts of barnyard manure offer no trouble, though heaps cannot be turned easily. Straw compost must therefore be allowed to stand longer. For quicker compost, weigh down the material with a thicker layer of earth. This also preserves the moisture inside the heap.

If a large straw pile is allowed to stay outside in the field it will eventually decay at the bottom into a crumbly substance. Such material is excellent for compost-making and mulching. Some of the fungi it

Straw that has been used for animal bedding adds bulk and nutrients to the compost heap. Because straw breaks down very slowly, it should be shredded for best results.

contains are of the types that form mycorrhizal relations with the roots of fruit trees, evergreens, grapes, roses, etc., and a straw mulch will therefore benefit these plants not only as a moisture preserver but as an inoculant for mycorrhizae.

The nitrogen value of straw is so small that it need not be accounted for in composting. The mineral value of straw depends on the soils where the crops were grown. Typical analyses of straws, computed by Kenneth C. Beeson of the U.S. Department of Agriculture, are here given in percent:

	Calcium	Potash	Magne- sium	Phos- phorus	Sulfur
Barley	0.4	1.0	0.1	0.1–0.5	0.1
Buckwheat	2.0	2.0	0.3	0.4	?
Corn stover	0.3	0.8	0.2	0.2	0.2
Millet	1.0	3.2	0.4	0.2	0.2
Oats	0.2	1.5	0.2	0.1	0.2
Rye	0.3	1.0	0.07	0.1	0.1
Sorghum	0.2	1.0	0.1	0.1	0.2
Wheat	0.2	0.8	0.1	0.08	0.1

SUGAR WASTES

In sugar manufacturing, several wastes accumulate; the greatest quantity is the filter material, often made of bone charcoal, which when filled with sugar residues is sold as bone black. Its phosphorous content is above 30 percent, its nitrogen value around 2 percent; its potassium content varies. Raw sugar wastes show a content of over 1 percent nitrogen and over 8 percent phosphoric acid.

TANBARK

Tanbark is the residue resulting from the process of tanning leather. In past years, it was made up of hemlock, oak, and chestnut bark. For the most part, this tanbark was piled in huge mounds near the tanneries, similar to the large waste piles near coal mines.

The tanbark being used today represents the waste materials from plants used in modern tanning methods, wattle, mangrove, myrobalans and valonia, imported from South America, Africa, India and Asia Minor. A high pressure steam process extracts the tannins which are used to tan the leather. The resulting wastes are ground, piled and inoculated with four different types of bacteria. After the bacteria has worked on the material for two weeks, it is turned over by a bulldozer and allowed to work for another week or ten days.

At the end of three weeks, the material looks and smells like virgin soil. It is packaged in several sized bags and is sold in bulk.

Laboratory tests have given the following analysis of the material: nitrogen 1.7 percent; phosphorus 0.9 percent; potash 0.2 percent and trace minerals of aluminum, calcium, cobalt, copper, iron, lead, magnesium, manganese, molybdenum, zinc and boron.

TANKAGE

Tankage is the refuse from slaughterhouses and butcher shops, except blood freed from the fats by processing. Depending on the amount of bone present, the phosphorous content varies greatly. The nitrogen content varies usually between 5 and 12.5 percent; the phosphoric acid content is usually around 2 percent, but may be much higher.

Tankage, because it is usually rich in nutrient value, is especially valuable to the compost pile. It is one of the few sources of animal matter available. However, it is available only sporadically and each slaughterhouse handles tankage differently.

TEA GROUNDS

Useful as a mulch or for adding to compost heap, one analysis of tea leaves showed the relatively high content of 4.15 percent nitrogen, which seems exceptional. Both phosphorus and potash were present in amounts below 1 percent.

TOBACCO WASTES

Tobacco stems, leaf waste and dust are good organic fertilizer, especially high in potash. The nutrients contained in 100 pounds of tobacco wastes are 2.5 to 3.7 pounds of nitrogen, almost a pound of phosphoric acid, and from 4.5 to 7 pounds of potassium.

Tobacco leaves are "stripped" for market in late fall, leaving thousands of stalks. Some farmers use their stalks to fertilize their own fields, chopping up the stalks and disking them into the soil. Some stalks are available for gardeners, however, and tobacco processing plants bale further wastes for home use.

These wastes can be used anywhere barnyard manure is recommended, except on tobacco, tomatoes and other members of the tobacco or potato family, because they may carry some of the virus diseases of these crops, especially tobacco mosaid virus.

Compost tobacco wastes, or use them in moderation in mulching or sheet composting mixed with other organic materials. They should not be applied alone in concentrated amounts as a mulch—the nicotine will eliminate beneficial insects, earthworms and other soil organisms as well as harmful ones.

WATER HYACINTH

Southerners who lack sufficient green matter for compost can often find quantities of the water hyacinth *(Eichhornia crassipes)* growing in profusion in southern streams. This plant is considered a serious menace to agriculture, fisheries, sanitation and health in the South and other parts of the world where it grows with remarkable rankness. For best results, shred and mix with partially decomposed "starter material" such as soil or manure.

WEEDS

Weeds can be put to use in the compost pile. Their nitrogen, phosphorous and potash content is similar to other plant residues, and large quantities can provide much humus for the soil. Weed seeds will be killed by the high temperatures in the compost pile, and any weeds which sprout from the top of the heap can be turned under. Weeds can even be used for green manure as long as they will not be stealing needed plant food and moisture. Some produce creditable amounts of humus, help make minerals available, and conserve nitrogen.

WINERY WASTES

Residues from wineries are highly recommended for the compost heap. The roots of the grape vine drive deeply into the subsoil, bringing up valuable minerals and trace elements. You can recapture these nutrients by adding fruit residues to the compost heap. Other important fruit wastes include apple pomace, peach and plum pits, spoiled citrus fruits, and similar residues that may become available.

WOOD ASHES

Wood ashes are a valuable source of potash for the compost heap. Hardwood ashes generally contain from 1 to 10 percent potash, in addition to 1.5 percent phosphorus. Wood ashes should never be allowed to stand in the rain, as the potash would leach away. They can be mixed with other fertilizing materials, side-dressed around growing plants, or used as a mulch. Apply about 5 to 10 pounds per 100 square feet. Avoid contact between freshly spread ashes and germinating seeds or new plant roots by spreading ashes a few inches from plants. It is not recommended to use wood ashes around blueberries or other acid-loving plants, since they are alkaline. Added directly to the compost heap, wood ashes lend potash and can take the place of lime as an acid neutralizer.

WOOD CHIPS

Like sawdust and other wood wastes, wood chips are useful in the garden. In some ways wood chips are superior to sawdust. They contain a much greater percentage of bark, and have a higher nutrient content. They do a fine job of aerating the soil and increasing its moisture-holding capacity, and also make a fine mulch for ornamentals.

Generally the incorporation of fresh chips has no detrimental effect on the crop if sufficient nitrogen is present or provided. Better yet, apply the chips ahead of a green manure crop, preferably a legume; allow

Wood chips can be used as a mulch, added to the compost pile, or worked into the soil before a green manure crop is sown.

about a year interval between application and seeding or planting of the main crop. Other good ways to use wood fragments are: (1) as bedding in the barn, followed by field application of the manure; (2) as a mulch on row crops, eventually working the partially decomposed material into the soil; or (3) after adequately composting the chips with other organic materials. Well-rotted chips or sawdust is safe material to use under almost any condition.

WOOL WASTES

Wool wastes, also known as shoddy, have been used by British farmers living in the vicinity of wool textile mills since the industrial revolution in the early 19th century. The wool fiber decomposes when in contact with moisture in the soil, and in the process, produces available nitrogen for plant growth. Generally, the moisture content of the wool wastes is between 15 and 20 percent. It analyzes from 3.5 to 6 percent nitrogen, 2 to 4 percent phosphoric acid, and 1 to 3.5 percent potash.

NATURAL SOURCES OF POTASH

Miscellaneous	Percent Potash
Wood ashes (broad leaf)	10.0
Wood ashes (coniferous)	6.0
Molasses wastes (curbay)	3.0 to 4.0
Fly ash	12.0
Tobacco stems	4.5 to 7.0
Garbage (NYC analysis)	2.3 to 4.3
Water lily stems	3.4
Cocoa shell residues	2.6
Potato tubers	2.5
Dry potato vines	1.6
Vegetable wastes	1.4
Castor pomace	1.0 to 2.0
Rapeseed meal	1.0 to 3.0
Cottonseed meal	1.8
Olive pomace	1.3
Beet wastes	0.7 to 4.1
Silk mill wastes	1.0
Wool wastes	1.0 to 3.5

Hay Materials	Percent Potash
Vetch hay	2.3
Alfalfa hay	2.1
Kentucky blue grass hay	2.0
Red clover hay	2.1
Cowpea hay	2.3
Timothy hay	1.4
Soybean hay	1.2 to 2.3
Salt hay	0.6
Pea forage	1.4
Winter rye	1.0

Immature grass	1.2
Garden pea vines	0.7
Weeds	0.7

Leaves	Percent Potash
Apple leaves	0.4
Peach leaves	0.6
Pear leaves	0.4
Cherry leaves	0.7
Raspberry leaves	0.6
Grape leaves	0.4
Oak leaves	0.2

Natural Minerals	Percent Potash
Granite dust	3.0 to 5.5
Greensand marl	7.0
Basalt rock	1.5

Straw	Percent Potash
Millet	3.2
Buckwheat	2.0
Oats	1.5
Barley	1.0
Rye	1.0
Sorghum	1.0
Wheat	0.8
Corn stover	0.8

Manure	Percent Potash
Cow	
(fresh excrement)	0.1
(dried excrement)	1.5
(fresh urine)	0.5
Horse	
(fresh excrement)	0.3
(dried excrement)	1.6
(fresh urine)	1.5
Hog	
(fresh excrement)	0.5
(fresh urine)	0.8
Goat and Sheep	
(fresh excrement)	0.3
(dried excrement)	3.0
(fresh urine)	2.3
Chicken	
(fresh)	0.6 to 1.0
(dried)	1.2
Pigeon (fresh)	1.0
Duck (fresh)	0.6
Goose (fresh)	0.6
Dog (fresh)	0.3

Ashed Material	Percent Potash
Banana residues (ash)	41.0 to 50.0
Pea pods (ash)	27.0
Cantaloupe rinds (ash)	12.0

NATURAL SOURCES OF NITROGEN

The following is a list of representative classifications of organic matter and typical analyses with respect to their nitrogen content:

Meal	Percent Nitrogen
Bone black bone meal	1.5
Raw bone meal	3.3 to 4.1
Steamed bone meal	1.6 to 2.5
Cottonseed meal	7.0
Corn fodder	0.41
Oats, green fodder	0.49
Corn silage	0.42
Gluten meal	6.4
Wheat bran	2.36
Wheat middlings	2.75
Meat meal	9 to 11
Bone tankage	3 to 10

Manures	Percent Nitrogen
Cattle manure (fresh excrement)	0.29
Cattle manure (fresh urine)	0.58
Hen manure (fresh)	1.63
Dog manure	2.0
Horse manure (solid fresh excrement)	0.44
Horse manure (fresh urine)	1.55
Human excrement (solid)	1.00
Human urine	0.60
Night soil	0.80
Sheep manure (solid fresh excrement)	0.55
Sheep (fresh urine)	1.95
Stable manure mixed	0.50
Swine manure (solid fresh excrement)	0.60
Swine (fresh urine)	0.43
Sewage sludge	1.7 to 2.26

Animal Wastes (Other than manures)	Percent Nitrogen
Eggshells	1.00+
Dried blood	10 to 14
Feathers	15.3
Dried jellyfish	4.6
Fresh crabs	5
Dried ground crabs	10
Dried shrimp heads	7.8
Lobster wastes	2.9
Shrimp wastes	2.9
Mussels	1
Dried ground fish	8
Acid fish scrap	4.0 to 6.5
Oyster shells	0.36
Milk	0.5
Wool wastes	3.5 to 6.0
Silkworm cocoons	10
Silk wastes	8
Felt wastes	14

Plant Wastes	Percent Nitrogen
Beet wastes	0.4

Brewery wastes	1.0
Castor pomace	4.0 to 6.6
Cattail reeds	2.0
Cocoa shell dust	1.0
Cocoa wastes	2.7
Coffee wastes	2.0
Grape pomace	1.0
Green cowpeas	0.4
Nut shells	2.5
Olive residues	1.15
Peanut shells	3.6
Peanut shell ashes	0.8
Pine needles	0.5
Potato skins	0.6
Sugar wastes	2.0
Tea grounds	4.1
Tobacco stems	2.5 to 3.7
Tung oil pomace	6.1

Leaves	Percent Nitrogen
Peach leaves	0.9
Oak leaves	0.8
Grape leaves	0.45
Pear leaves	0.7
Apple leaves	1.0
Cherry leaves	0.6
Raspberry leaves	1.35
Garden pea vines	0.25

Grasses	Percent Nitrogen
Clover	2.0
Red clover	0.55
Vetch hay	2.8
Corn stalks	0.75
Alfalfa	2.4
Immature grass	1.0
Blue grass hay	1.2
Cowpea hay	3.0
Pea hay	1.5 to 2.5
Soybean hay	1.5 to 3.0
Timothy hay	1.19
Salt hay	1.06
Millet hay	1.22

Seaweed	Percent Nitrogen
Fresh seaweed	0.2 to 0.38
Dry seaweed	1.1 to 1.5

NATURAL SOURCES OF PHOSPHATE

(Other than Phosphate Rock or Bone Meal)

Material	Percent Phosphoric Acid
Marine products	
Shrimp waste (dried)	10
Dried ground fish	7
Lobster refuse	3.5
Dried blood	1 to 5
Tankage	2
Hoof and horn meal	2
Wool wastes	2 to 4
Cottonseed meal	2 to 3
Raw sugar wastes	8
Rapeseed meal	1 to 2
Cocoa wastes	1.5
Castor pomace	1 to 2
Silk mill wastes	1.14
Activated sludge	2.5 to 4.0
Manure	
Poultry, fresh	1 to 1.5
Poultry, dried	1.5 to 2.0
Goat and sheep, fresh	0.6
Goat and sheep, dried	1.0 to 1.9
Hog, fresh	0.45
Horse, fresh	0.35
Horse, dried	1.0
Cow, fresh	0.25
Cow, dried	1.0
Wood ashes	1 to 2
Pea pod wastes (ashed)	3
Banana residue (ashed)	2.3 to 3.3
Apple pomace (ashed skin)	3
Citrus wastes (orange skins, ashed)	3

PERCENTAGE COMPOSITION OF VARIOUS MATERIALS

Material	Nitrogen	Phosphoric Acid	Potash
Alfalfa hay	2.45	0.50	2.10
Apple, fruit	0.05	0.02	0.10
Apple, leaves	1.00	0.15	0.35
Apple pomace	0.20	0.02	0.15
Apple skins (ash)	....	3.08	11.74
Ash from Cana tree	....	....	15.65
Banana skins (ash)	....	3.25	41.76
Banana stalk (ash)	....	2.34	49.40
Barley (grain)	1.75	0.75	0.50
Bat guano	6.00	9.00	....
Beet wastes	0.40	0.40	3.00
Beet wastes (roots)	0.25	0.10	0.50
Blood meal	15.00	1.30	0.70
Bone meal	4.00	21.00	0.20
Brewer's grains (wet)	0.90	0.50	0.05
Brigham tea (ash)	....	....	5.94
Ground bone, burned	....	34.70	....
By-product from silk mills	8.37	1.14	0.12
Cantaloupe rinds (ash)	....	9.77	12.21
Castor-bean pomace	5.50	2.25	1.13
Cattail reed and stems of water lily	2.02	0.81	3.43
Cattail seed	0.98	0.39	1.71
*Cattle manure (fresh)	0.29	0.17	0.10
Coal ash (anthracite)	....	0.125	0.125
Coal ash (bituminous)	....	0.45	0.45
Cocoa shell dust	1.04	1.49	2.71
Coffee grounds	2.08	0.32	0.28
Coffee grounds (dried)	1.99	0.36	0.67
Common crab	1.95	3.60	0.20
Corn (grain)	1.65	0.65	0.40
Corn (green forage)	0.30	0.13	0.33
Corncobs (ground, charred)	....	....	2.01
Corncob ash	....	....	50.00

Material	Nitrogen	Phosphoric Acid	Potash
Cotton seed	3.15	1.25	1.15
Cottonseed meal	7.00	2.50	1.50
Cottonseed-hull ashes	....	8.70	23.93
Cotton waste from factory	1.32	0.45	0.36
Cowpeas, green forage	0.45	0.12	0.45
Cowpeas, seed	3.10	1.00	1.20
Crabgrass (green)	0.66	0.19	0.71
Cucumber skins (ash)	....	11.28	27.20
Dog manure	1.97	9.95	0.30
Dried jellyfish	4.60	....	....
Dried mussel mud	0.72	0.35	....
*Duck manure (fresh)	1.12	1.44	0.49
Eggs	2.25	0.40	0.15
Eggshells (burned)	....	0.43	0.29
Eggshells	1.19	0.38	0.14
Feathers	15.30	....	....
Field bean (seed)	4.00	1.20	1.30
Field bean (shells)	1.70	0.30	1.30
Fire-pit ashes from smokehouses	....	....	4.96
Fish scrap (red snapper and grouper)	7.76	13.00	0.38
Fish scrap (fresh)	6.50	3.75	....
Fresh water mud	1.37	0.26	0.22
Garbage rubbage (New York City)	3.50	0.80	3.25
Garbage tankage	1.50	0.75	0.75
Greasewood ashes	....	....	12.61
Garden beans, beans and pods	0.25	0.08	0.30
Gluten feed	4.50	....	....
Greensand	....	1.50	5.00
Grape leaves	0.45	0.10	0.35
Grapes (fruit)	0.15	0.07	0.30
Grapefruit skins (ash)	....	3.58	30.60
Hair	14.00	....	....
Harbor mud	0.99	0.77	0.05
*Hen manure (fresh)	1.63	1.54	0.85
Hoof meal and horn dust	12.50	1.75	....

Material	Nitrogen	Phosphoric Acid	Potash
*Horse manure (fresh)	0.44	0.17	0.35
Incinerator ash	0.24	5.15	2.33
Kentucky bluegrass (green)	0.66	0.19	0.71
Kentucky bluegrass (hay)	1.20	0.40	1.55
King crab (dried and ground)	10.00	0.25	0.06
King crab (fresh)	2.30	. . . .	. . . .
Leather (acidulated)	7.50	. . . .	. . . .
Leather (ground)	11.00	. . . .	. . . .
Leather, scrap (ash)	. . . .	2.16	0.35
Lemon culls (California)	0.15	0.06	0.26
Lemon skins (ash)	. . . .	6.30	31.00
Lobster refuse	4.50	3.50	. . . .
Lobster shells	4.60	3.52	. . . .
Milk	0.50	0.30	0.18
Mussels	0.90	0.12	0.13
Molasses residue in manufacture of alcohol	0.70	. . . .	5.32
Oak leaves	0.80	0.35	0.15
Oats, grain	2.00	0.80	0.60
Olive pomace	1.15	0.78	1.26
Olive refuse	1.22	0.18	0.32
Orange culls	0.20	0.13	0.21
Orange skins (ash)	. . . .	2.90	27.00
Pea pods (ash)	. . . .	1.79	9.00
Peach leaves	0.90	0.15	0.60
Peanuts (seed or kernels)	3.60	0.70	0.45
Peanut shells	0.80	0.15	0.50
Peanut shells (ash)	. . . .	1.23	6.45
*Pigeon manure (fresh)	4.19	2.24	1.41
Pigweed (rough)	0.60	0.16	. . . .
Pine needles	0.46	0.12	0.03
Potatoes (tubers)	0.35	0.15	0.50
Potatoes (leaves and stalks)	0.60	0.15	0.45
Potato skins, raw (ash)	. . . .	5.18	27.50
Poudrette	1.46	3.68	0.48
Powderworks waste	2.50	. . . .	17.00
Prune refuse	0.18	0.07	0.31

Material	Nitrogen	Phosphoric Acid	Potash
Pumpkins, fresh	0.16	0.07	0.26
Pumpkin seeds	0.87	0.50	0.45
Rabbit brush ashes	. . . .	. . . .	13.04
Ragweed	0.76	0.26	. . . .
Red clover, hay	2.10	0.50	2.00
Redtop hay	1.20	0.35	1.00
Residues from raw sugar	1.14	8.33	. . . .
Rhubarb stems	0.10	0.04	0.35
Rockweed	1.90	0.25	3.68
Roses (flower)	0.30	0.10	0.40
Rock and mussel deposits from sea	0.22	0.09	1.78
Salt-marsh hay	1.10	0.25	0.75
Salt mud	0.40	. . . .	. . . .
Sardine scrap	7.97	7.11	. . . .
Seawood (Atlantic City)	1.68	0.75	4.93
Sewage sludge from sewer beds	0.74	0.33	0.24
*Sheep manure (fresh)	0.55	0.31	0.15
Shoddy and felt	8.00	. . . .	. . . .
Shrimp heads (dried)	7.82	4.20	. . . .
Shrimp waste	2.87	9.95	. . . .
Siftings from oyster shell mound	0.36	10.38	0.09
Silk worm cocoons	9.42	1.82	1.08
Sludge	2.00	1.90	0.30
Sludge (activated)	5.00	3.25	0.60
Soot from chimney flues	5.25	1.05	0.35
Spanish moss	0.60	0.10	0.55
Starfish	1.80	0.20	0.25
String bean strings and stems (ash)	. . . .	4.99	18.03
Sunflower seeds	2.25	1.25	0.79
Sweet potato skins, boiled (ash)	. . . .	3.29	13.89
Sweet potatoes	0.25	0.10	0.50
*Swine manure (fresh)	0.60	0.41	0.13
Tanbark (ash)	. . . .	0.34	3.80
Tanbark ash (spent)	. . . .	1.75	2.00
Tankage	6.00	5.00	. . . .

Material	Nitrogen	Phosphoric Acid	Potash
Tea grounds	4.15	0.62	0.40
Tea leaves (ash)	....	1.60	0.44
Timothy hay	1.25	0.55	1.00
Tobacco leaves	4.00	0.50	6.00
Tobacco stalks	3.70	0.65	4.50
Tobacco stems	2.50	0.90	7.00
Tomatoes, fruit	0.20	0.07	0.35
Tomatoes, leaves	0.35	0.10	0.40
Tomatoes, stalks	0.35	0.10	0.50
Waste from hares and rabbits	7.00	2.40	0.60
Waste from felt hat factory	3.80	....	0.98
Waste product from paint manufacturer	0.02	39.50	....
Waste silt	9.50	....	....
Wheat, bran	2.65	2.90	1.60
Wheat, grain	2.00	0.85	0.50
Wheat, straw	0.50	0.15	0.60
White clover (green)	0.50	0.20	0.30
White sage (ashes)	....	....	13.77
Wood ashes (leached)	....	1.25	2.00
Wood ashes (unleached)	....	1.50	7.00
Wool waste	5.50	3.00	2.00

*Dried manures contain amounts up to 5 times higher in nitrogen, phosphoric acid and potash.

7

Using Manure

Manure, the dung and urine of animals, is the most important single ingredient in the compost heap. It is difficult, although not impossible, to make a good compost pile without it.

On a broader scale, manure is a great national resource that we have been wasting at a fearsome rate. Some observers have estimated that, between mismanagement and misuse, less than 20 percent of the nutrients in manure ever find their way back to agricultural lands. Considering that there are more than 200 million farm animals in the country, and that a single hog, for example, will produce more than 3,000 pounds of manure annually, the aggregate waste is horrendous. Composting is the best way to reclaim the nutrients and organic matter in manure.

The most common domestic sources of manure are horses, cattle, goats, sheep, pigs, rabbits, and poultry. The dung consists of undigested portions of foods ground into fine bits and saturated with digestive juices in the alimentary tract. Dung contains, as a rule, one-third of the total nitrogen, one-fifth of the total potash, and nearly all of the phosphoric acid voided by the animals. But it is because of the large bacterial population—as much as 30 percent of its mass—that manure is so valuable in the compost heap. The addition of manure provides the necessary bacteria which will quickly break down other materials.

The urine contains compounds from the digested portion of the foods and secretions from the animal body. The urine usually contains about two-thirds of the total nitrogen, four-fifths of the total potash, but very little of the phosphoric acid voided by the animal. Because they are in solution, the elements in the urine become available much more quickly than the constituents found in the dung. Urines are especially

155

The manure of farm animals is a great national resource which we have sadly wasted. It is estimated that less than 20 percent of the nutrients in the manure produced by animals in this country ever find their way back into our soil.

valuable as activators in converting crop residues into humus.

The value of animal manure varies with the food eaten by the animal, the age of the animal, the products yielded (for example, milk, wool, or meat), and the physical condition and health of the animal. The richer the animals' food is in elements essential to plant growth, the more valuable the manure. The manure of animals fed on wheat bran, gluten meal, and cottonseed meal, for instance, will be richer than that from animals fed straw or hay without grains. Likewise, the manure of young animals which are forming bones and muscles from their foods will be poorer in nutrients than the manure of mature animals.

Sometimes cattle are first grazed on grasslands with mineral-rich soils and then fattened in regions where grains are abundant and cheap. The manure from mature animals which are being fattened is relatively rich in minerals, as fat production requires little or no minerals from the feed.

The Real Value of Manure

The value of the manure varies also according to the products the animal produces, such as milk which contains considerable amounts of nitrogen, phosphorus, and potassium; or wool which contains a large amount of nitrogen. In areas with highly alkaline soils (like the Southwest), urine may add to the salt problem. Manure should also be used with caution on salt-sensitive plants.

In addition, the value of the manure depends on the way it is handled. In rotting, manure loses some of its nitrogen. Half its fertilizing value can be lost within four days if it's allowed to lie in a thin pile on the ground, recent EPA studies have found. Bedding should be composted when fresh for best results. Even short-term storage wastes nutrients.

Unfortunately the values of manure and fertilizers in general have been, in the past, based on the relative amount of nitrogen, phosphoric acid, and potash they contain. While these are major elements and doubtless affect the values of manure to a greater extent than the proportion of any other constituents, it is misleading to make a direct comparison between farm manures and chemical fertilizers on the basis of the relative amounts of N-P-K. Soil needs continual replenishment of its organic matter to convert into humus, and humus plays an important role in making nutrients available to the higher plants.

There is a difference between fresh manure and rotted manure. Assuming that fresh manure is a normal mixture of urine and feces, fresh manure differs from rotted manure in several ways:

1. Rotted manure is richer in plant nutrients, largely a result of the loss in dry weight of the manure. One ton of fresh manure may lose half its weight in the rotting process.
2. The nitrogen in the composted manure has been fixed by microorganisms while nitrogen in fresh manure is mostly soluble.
3. The solubility of the phosphorus and potash is greater in the composted manure. If leaching during composting can be prevented, there is no change in the total amount of phosphorus and potassium. Precautions must be taken to prevent the loss of nitrogen in the composting process, however.

Manure in the compost heap decomposes in definite stages. These may be briefly outlined as follows:

1. Decomposition of urinary nitrogen. Ammonia in the urine is lost unless the manure is kept moist and compact.
2. Decomposition of insoluble nitrogen. Next, the insoluble nitrogen contained in the solid parts of the excrement breaks down with the formation of ammonia.
3. Conversion of soluble into insoluble nitrogen. The ammonia and other soluble compounds of nitrogen are used in considerable amounts as food for the bacteria in the manure and are stored in their bodies in insoluble form. This nitrogen becomes available when the bacteria die and undergo decomposition themselves.
4. Formation of free nitrogen. Under certain conditions ammonia and nitrates are decomposed. Free nitrogen is formed and escapes into the atmosphere, becoming permanently lost.
5. Decomposition of nitrogen-free compounds. The fibrous parts of the manure which are made up largely of cellulose, lignin, and other complex carbohydrates are eventually broken down. Carbon in the form of carbon dioxide, and hydrogen in the form of water escape into the atmosphere. These elements escape in such amounts that from a quarter to a half of the original dry matter in the manure is lost, the pile shrinking in bulk.

PERCENTAGES OF NITROGEN, PHOSPHATE AND POTASH IN DIFFERENT MANURES

Kind of Animal Manure	Percent Nitrogen	Percent Phosphate	Percent Potash
Rabbit	2.4	1.4	0.6
Hen	1.1	0.8	0.5
Sheep	0.7	0.3	0.9
Steer	0.7	0.3	0.4
Horse	0.7	0.3	0.6
Duck	0.6	1.4	0.5
Cow	0.6	0.2	0.5
Pig	0.5	0.3	0.5

Manure Shortage,
or Distribution Problem?

It has been estimated that enough animal and poultry manure is produced in the United States each year to cover the yards of all 40-plus million single-family dwellings to a depth of 3 feet. The total figure comes to two billion tons annually.

The greatest virtue of the traditional family farm in America is that it is a self-contained unit with a balanced complement of crops and livestock. Livestock eat farm-produced grain and grass, and the land on which these crops are raised is enriched with the animals' manure. A farmer who manages his animal manure wisely can return to the soil 70 percent of the nitrogen, 75 percent of the phosphorus, and 80 percent of the potash which was taken out by the home-grown plants his animals ate.

The operation of one-crop farms, containing no livestock, used to be virtually unknown in this country, except in the South where the land

A dairy manure stockpile in California. Farmers who use their animal manures to fertilize their fields can return to the soil 70 percent of the nitrogen, 75 percent of the phosphorus, and 80 percent of the potash removed by the crops grown to feed the animals.

Compost Science *photo*

was soon worn out. Now, although more animals are raised in this country than at any time in history, they are mostly raised on huge tracts of ranch and pasture land and fattened in feedlots where their nitrogen-rich manure causes ecological imbalance instead of contributing to agriculture. More than a million tons of manure are produced annually in the United States. Unfortunately, much of it falls on grassland, on ranges, and in poorly managed feedlots where it is lost to agriculture. Even farmers who do attempt to return manure to their fields lose much of its value through misunderstanding and mismanagement.

Using Manure to Advantage

Animal manure by itself is not a completely balanced fertilizer, either chemically or biologically. There may be too much urine and too little cellulose, or vice versa. When manure is added directly to the soil, the instability of its C/N ratio usually has an adverse effect on crops. When first composted, manure's imbalances can be rectified and the manure itself can be digested and used more quickly than if added alone.

The use of urine-soaked bedding or litter in the compost pile is an especially wise practice. The litter catches urine which would otherwise be lost. Urine has a high-nitrogen content, and so extra high-carbon material (in addition to the bedding) should be used. In other words, compost manure and bedding with plenty of fresh green matter—weeds, plant debris, etc. Freshly cut material retains more nutrients. Also, by covering your compost pile with black plastic, you can prevent nutrients from being leached out by rain.

Manure is full of weed seeds which can be killed by the high temperatures in composting. The high temperatures will also kill many pathogens which may be present in the manure of sick animals. Even so, this manure lacks the quality of manure from healthy animals, and it is wise to avoid it when you can. This is another advantage to composting manure.

CHICKEN MANURE

Chicken manure is the richest animal manure in N-P-K; fowls do not excrete urine separately, as mammals do. Chicken droppings *must* be composted before use or they will burn any plants with which they come into contact. Some chicken farmers use pits partially filled with soil, rotted steer manure, finished compost, green matter, or leaves

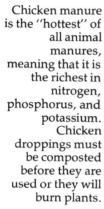

Chicken manure is the "hottest" of all animal manures, meaning that it is the richest in nitrogen, phosphorus, and potassium. Chicken droppings must be composted before they are used or they will burn plants.

under the roosts in the henhouse to catch droppings. This method controls odors which can cause respiratory problems in chickens as well as discomfort to people. It also provides a rich humus. Other poultry-men use leaves, shredded straw, ground corncobs, or ground corn stalks for litter and then compost these.

HORSE MANURE

Horse manure is richer in nitrogen than cow or hog manure and, like chicken droppings, is called a "hot" manure. It is also much more prone to fermentation or "fire-fanging," a fairly rapid oxidation which destroys nutrients. Some farmers water horse manure to prevent fire-fanging, but leaching can occur if too much water is added. When using horse manure in the compost pile, mix it with other manures or with large quantities of high-carbon materials, and add moisture. Horse manure also prevents the harmful action of denitrifying bacteria.

PIG MANURE

Pig and hog manure is also highly concentrated, but less rich in nitrogen than horse manure. It is best used when mixed with other manures or with large quantities of green or dried vegetation. It ferments relatively slowly.

SHEEP MANURE

Sheep manure is another hot manure. Like horse manure, it is quite dry and very rich.

COW MANURE

Cow manure is moister and less concentrated than that of other large animals. Because of its high water and low nitrogen contents, it ferments slowly and is commonly called a cold manure.

RABBIT MANURE

Rabbit manure is even higher in nitrogen than some poultry manures and it also contains a large percentage of phosphates. It decomposes easily and requires no shredding. Because the nitrogen level is so high, however, it should be used in small quantities. Rabbit droppings can be sprinkled over layers of green matter in the compost pile. Some composters use litter in their rabbit cages and add this to the compost pile to conserve the rabbits' urine. Earthworm pits set directly under wire rabbit cages offer another sensible use of rabbit manure. The worms quickly turn the raw manure into fully composted castings, and the rabbit raiser can have an extra source of income through earthworm sales. This method will be discussed in greater detail in the chapter devoted to earthworms.

Finding Manure

The best places for the home gardener or homesteader to get manure are those where there are high concentrations of animals and no fields to fertilize. These include riding academies and stables, feedlots, dairies, and poultry farms. Some gardeners go so far as to contact zoos or to visit local fairgrounds or circus grounds after the animals have left town. Sometimes, one will be asked to pay a modest sum for manure but often it comes free for the hauling. The urban gardener with a very small plot can probably afford to buy commercially prepared manure, already composted, screened, and bagged. The small-scale homesteader might raise a few chickens, a pony, ducks, geese, or a few pens of rabbits, and will certainly use every scrap of manure produced by these animals. He may, however, still wish to supplement this supply by making some arrangement to haul manure away from a nearby dairy or poultry farm.

When you buy or haul away manure from those who have no use for it, you are not only helping your own garden, but you are also helping to solve what is becoming a major ecological problem caused by the concentration of stock and poultry in areas with little or no ground available for the disposal of wastes. Operators of large livestock production units are interested in disposing of much waste at minimal expense, and often dumping wastes on small parcels of land where high concentrations of salts result in nutrient imbalance in soil, excessive nitrate accumulation in plants, and leaching to ground water. Some poultry growers may produce as much as 12 tons of manure a day from 60,000 laying hens per acre; often there is no arrangement for handling their manure. In the long run, it would be in our best interests to deconcentrate stock and poultry production—break up the animal factories—to regain the ecological balance that was ours when farms were small and diversified. In the meantime, any manure you can remove from these concentrated lots and use in home composting is all to the good.

However, feedlots, stockyards, and other large commercial stock facilities are gradually finding manure a usable, even profitable, by-product of their enterprise. They process bagged, dried manure and manure compost for gardeners. These products are frequently available at garden and hardware stores. The Chicago stockyards were one of the first to sell their manure, at one time processing 20 tons of manure and bedding per load in huge digesters that used injected air to fuel and speed bacterial activity. The digesters produced compost every 24 hours.

Manure Tea

Another use for manure, apart from composting, is for manure tea or liquid manure. One economical method for making this valuable substance is to fill 100-pound burlap feed sacks with a mixture of equal parts of fresh cow, horse, and chicken manure. Suspend the sacks, one each, in 55-gallon steel drums, and fill the drums with warm water, making sure the sacks are submerged. Let the manure steep for 30 to 45 days. You can make different quantities of liquid manure, but try to keep the proportions at one-fourth manure to three-fourths water.

This tea solution is especially favored for use on house plants and around flower and vegetable plants, but it is also useful to the composter who lacks large quantities of manure. A strong brew of manure tea poured over the layers of green and dried material in a compost pile not only provides needed moisture, but distributes bacteria and nitrogen to

Manure tea can be made by suspending a burlap sack containing livestock manure in a drum of water.

all parts of the pile. Manure tea can be saved longer than fresh manure and requires less storage space.

Those who compost by the earthworm pit method find manure to be an essential ingredient. It is also important to any rapid composting method which requires a high-nitrogen, high-bacteria heat-up material.

Substitutes

If you absolutely can't find or afford manure for your pile, be sure to use a high-nitrogen substitute. Among the best of these are blood meal; cottonseed meal; tankage; activated sludge; shoddy; hoof meal or horn dust; fish and shellfish scraps; hair (if time for decomposition is allowed); ground leather or leather dust; or wool wastes. Freshly cut weeds, grass, or other plants or their leaves or stems are high in nitrogen, but this nitrogen is released quickly and they cannot be depended upon for all the nitrogen source material in a pile. Check Chapter 6 for more information on these materials.

8

Methods

There are quite a few ways to let nature make compost for you—under the ground, above the ground, in bins, boxes, pits, bags, and barrels, in strips, in sheets, in trenches, in 14 months or 14 days, indoors or outdoors. They all stem from the famous Indore method developed by Sir Albert Howard and they all (except for anaerobic methods) have the same basic requirements. For a pile to heat up properly, it requires air, moisture, nitrogen, bacteria, heat, sufficient size, and plenty of organic matter.

Special ingredients like succulent green matter, methods like shredding, or equipment like tumblers help to raise the pile's temperature more quickly, but are not essentials. Let's first examine those essential requirements, for a lack of any one of them can limit the heap's temperature, slowing the reactions that conserve nutrients, killing weed seeds and disease organisms, and producing the substances that make compost the superb growing medium that it is.

AIR

Sunflower stalks build air channels into Warren Pierce's compost at the Community Environmental Council's Mesa Project, an urban gardening experiment in Santa Barbara, California. Air is essential for the aerobic bacteria whose furious proliferation and action within the pile cause the intense heat.

"Sunflowers have stalks with soft centers which rot out quickly," Warren says. "The stalks themselves rot through and bring air right to the middle of the pile."

"Place numerous stalks of this type as the bottom 2- to 4-inch layer of your pile. Then put the first 12-inch layer of moistened compostable

165

Turning the heap regularly aerates the compost and insures that all the materials are exposed to the heat of the pile's interior.

materials on top of the stalks followed by ¼ inch of soil. Now place a few stalks on top of the soil layer, followed by another 12-inch layer of moistened compostables and ¼ inch of soil on top. This layering process goes on until the pile is 4 feet high. The last layer should be 2 inches of soil," he says.

Jerusalem artichoke stalks are also effective, but cornstalks do not rot out easily and cannot be used for air channeling.

The usual way to be sure your pile has enough air is to turn it every week or so. This aerates the pile and speeds up the decomposition process. Another time-honored trick for good aeration involves layering poles into the heap and withdrawing a few every day or so during the major heat buildup. You can also stick the pile with the tines of a pitchfork to open air channels.

Another method of aerating a pile is to layer several long poles into the heap as you build it, and withdraw a few every day during the period when the pile is at its hottest.

One of the main benefits of a compost tumbler is the aeration that tumbling provides.

One commercially produced model of the tumbler-style composter stands on a tube-steel base and holds 14 bushels of material. A crank on the end turns the tumbler and screened vents allow air into the composting mass. You only have to rotate the drum for five complete turns to achieve finished compost in 14 days. Because of the amount of air it lets in, you'll have to water the pile almost daily. A similar tumbler could be constructed at home using a 55-gallon drum with holes punched in it, mounted on an axle. (Compost tumblers are discussed more fully in Chapter 10.)

Another method for aeration involves building the pile on chicken wire or hardware cloth about a foot off the ground, allowing air to enter from the bottom. Stretch the wire tightly so it holds the weight of the pile, which can reach several tons in a large heap. You can lay plastic sheets under the mass to catch any liquids that drain out, returning them to the top of the pile for double action.

MOISTURE

Good compost will be about as damp as a moist sponge, says Professor James R. Love, a soil scientist at the University of Wisconsin in Madison. "Grab a handful and squeeze it. No drops of moisture should come out." Too little moisture slows down decomposition, and prevents the pile from heating up. The microorganisms need a steamy environment. Too much moisture drives out air, drowns the pile and washes away nutrients.

A pile containing a great deal of hay can also be a problem. Country folks know how a haystack sheds water—a well-made haystack keeps the bulk of the hay dry through winter rains. If you are using hay, counter this water-resistant tendency by keeping the hay layers to 6 or 8 inches, and wetting each layer thoroughly as you build the pile. To control the moisture in an exposed heap, cover it with a few inches of hay which should help shed rain. Some gardeners cover their compost with black plastic and remove it during selected rains.

Be especially careful to check the moisture content when turning the pile.

NITROGEN

Lack of nitrogen seems to be the main reason why composts fail to heat up. Scientists talk of specific carbon-to-nitrogen ratios, but the home composter doesn't need numbers.

Manure should comprise about a quarter to a fifth of the pile, the rest being plant wastes. Using chicken droppings, the highest in nitrogen of any commonly available manure, just about guarantees that the pile will get hot.

Fresh horse manure, kitchen garbage, and materials like blood meal, guano, and cottonseed meal are also rich in nitrogen. Fresh cow or pig manure is good, but not so good as the others, so use a little more. Hay that has been used for animal bedding is an added nitrogen source, although you'll need more manure to get the pile cooking.

Additionally, some hays or grasses contain more nitrogen than others: alfalfa has a high nitrogen content, timothy hay a low one. Grass clippings are high in nitrogen, but leaves are low.

BACTERIA

Bacteria exist in the raw ingredients of a compost heap, but they might not be the right mix of the right types for best composting. Most composters seed their piles by finishing each layer with a thin covering of good garden soil, which contains just the right kinds of micro-organisms—bacteria, fungi, and actinomycetes. The soil also improves the texture of the pile.

HEAT

It will be next to impossible to get a pile working during the cold months, but the warmer temperatures of spring through fall provide enough ambient heat to allow the pile to work. A fall-built pile can be insulated to work into the winter, however. It is better to compost while it's still warm enough; cover the pile from winter rains, and use the finished product in the spring.

SUFFICIENT SIZE

The larger the pile, the easier it is to get it to heat up to its optimum 140°F. (60°C.). Below a minimum size (a cube of material 3 feet on each

FINISHED COMPOST

FRESH INGREDIENTS

Spohn's wandering compost pile.

dimension) the pile may get warm, but it's unlikely to get hot enough to kill weed seeds or pathogens. For best heating, try for a heap 4 or 5 feet square on the bottom, rising to 4 feet high. Dr. Clarence Golueke, author of *Biological Reclamation of Solid Wastes*, says that in a pile this size, less than half the material (that part right in the middle) is exposed to the highest temperatures. Temperature decreases toward the outside of the pile. When turning, shovel the undigested materials from the outside portions of the pile into the middle. This often causes a second heating as this material gets a chance to decompose in the heart of the heap.

Dr. Eberhard Spohn, a consultant in waste recycling and soil health in Heidelberg, Germany, uses what he calls a "wandering compost pile." Fresh ingredients, such as kitchen refuse (minus meat or animal fat), are tossed on the sloping front face of the heap, which is at least 3 feet wide and high and at least 3 feet long. Finished compost is sliced from the back, which means the pile creeps forward about 6 inches a week. Dr. Spohn screens the finished compost, and uses the large particles left in the screen to cover additions to the front face, thus seeding them with bacteria. This method continuously composts household, yard and garden waste in a pile the right size for suburban and small-scale composters.

ORGANIC MATTER

Any plant material will compost, but some types do have drawbacks. Leaves, for instance, unless finely shredded, tend to mat into tough layers that thwart intense heating. All tough, stalky matter, wood chips and other refuse high in lignin resist rapid breakdown. Use leaves and tough plant matter in limited quantities and strive for a good balance in your selection and use of organic matter.

Choosing a Method

The choice of a method of composting is an important decision for the gardener, one that must take into account many factors: the space and constructions available, the total need for compost reckoned in terms of the area under cultivation and the rate of use, the time to be given to the project, the human and mechanical energy available, the equipment owned or obtainable, the materials at hand or easily procurable, and special crop needs. No matter which method you choose, however, it is really a modification of Howard's Indore method.

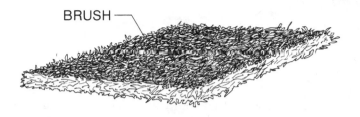

BRUSH

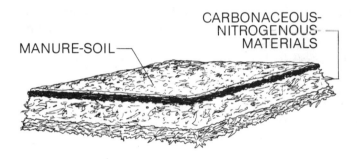

CARBONACEOUS-
NITROGENOUS
MATERIALS

MANURE-SOIL

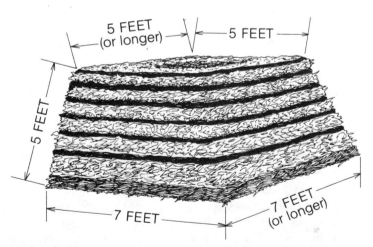

5 FEET
(or longer)   5 FEET

5 FEET

7 FEET

7 FEET
(or longer)

In the Indore method, a layer of brush forms the base of the pile.
It is followed by a layer of green or dry vegetable matter, then a layer of manure
and a sprinkling of soil.
The layers are repeated until the pile is 5 feet high.

The Indore Method

HISTORY

The Indore process, named for the locale in India where it was first practiced, was developed by a British government agronomist, Sir Albert Howard, who is now generally acknowledged to be the father of the organic method. Sir Albert Howard was in India between 1905 and 1934 and realized the necessity of improving the quality of the depleted soil and the crops in the region.

In his research, also carried out in the West Indies and in England, Sir Albert concluded that the secret of animal and plant health lay in the soil, and that the secret to soil fertility was abundant humus. Shortage of fuel in India had led to burning dried animal dung for cooking fuel, a practice which reduced the quantity of manure returned to the soil. To compensate for this loss, Howard advocated using plant remains with manure to increase the bulk of the manure. He learned from Chinese farmers the importance of using all organic remains to fortify the land.

In 1931, in cooperation with Mr. Y. D. Yad, Howard published *The Utilization of Agricultural Wastes*, the book in which he made his greatest contribution as a scientist. His later books reemphasized the importance of humus, and refined the process of composting he had developed at Indore.

METHOD

The Indore process consists of a systematic use of traditional procedures. When Howard first put the system into practice he used only animal manures, brush, leaves, straw or hay, and sprinklings of chalk or earth. The material was piled in alternating layers to make a 5-foot-high stack, or placed in a pit 2 or 3 feet deep. The original procedure was to use a layer of brush as a base and to heap green or dry vegetable material over it in a 6-inch layer, followed by a 2-inch layer of manure and a sprinkling of soil. The order of layers was repeated until the desired height of 5 feet was reached.

The general proportions were three to four parts by volume of vegetable matter to one part of animal manure. Howard advised spreading limestone or chalk between layers along with earth. In his work with village or large farm-scale projects, he suggested 5-foot high piles measuring 10 by 5 feet, or windrows of any practical length, 10 feet wide.

(continued on page 176)

How to build an Indore heap:

Put down
a layer of
manure,

followed by a layer
of straw, brush, or
leaves,

and a sprinkling of chalk or lime.

Lay down some poles to aerate the pile,

then repeat all the layers, adding moisture as necessary,

until the pile is about 5 feet high.

Later in the history of the Indore method, composting with night-soil (mixed human urine and feces), garbage, and sewage sludge was done. These materials were layered with high-carbon organic material such as straw, leaves, animal litter, and municipal trash.

The piles were turned, usually after 6 weeks, and again, usually after 12 weeks. Two turnings were the general practice, but the exact timing of these turnings varied. Occasionally additional turnings were given to control flies, though the more common practice was to cover the pile with a 2-inch layer of compacted soil when flies or odors were a problem. The liquor draining from the composting mass was, in some variations of the early Indore process, recirculated to moisten the pile.

Harold B. Gotaas in *Composting: Sanitary Disposal and Reclamation of Organic Wastes* suggests that the early Indore process stacks were aerobic for a short period after piling and after each turn, but anaerobic otherwise.

The chief advantage to the Indore method as originally practiced is that it can be practiced on a fairly large scale without the need for either mechanization or a great amount of labor.

According to Clarence Golueke, although many successful large-

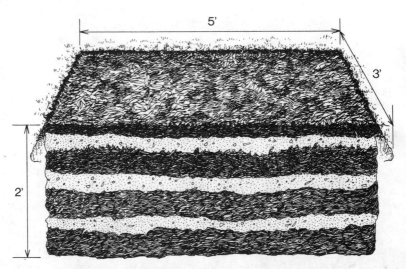

In a variation of the Indore method, a 5-foot by 3-foot pit, 2 feet deep, is dug and filled with alternating layers of green matter and soil.

scale modified Indore composting efforts use windrows, composting of garden and kitchen waste by the Indore method is done best in bins or pits. A 5-foot by 3-foot pit, 2 feet deep, he says, can be dug in the garden area and filled with alternating layers of green matter and soil. After filling, the pit may be left until the following year when the humus resulting from decomposition will be ready to use. A 5-foot high screen-covered bin may also be used with this method.

MODIFICATIONS

The Indore process has been used widely in India where it is most frequently seen today in a modification called the Bengalore method. The process is also employed in Malaya, China, Ceylon, South Africa, Costa Rica, East Africa, and other parts of the world. In general, Indore modifications have emphasized the use of nightsoil, sewage sludge, garbage, or green matter as substitutes for manure. They have also sought higher temperatures through increased frequency of turning and by substituting turning for covering as a means to fly control. Mechanized Indore windrows are now used in some countries.

Another adaptation of the Indore method uses only animal bedding and fresh green plant matter. A sheet of black plastic covers and confines the pile to increase heat and reduce leaching. The total process takes about three weeks and no turning is necessary.

The University of California Method
HISTORY

The composting method developed at the University of California in the early 1950s is probably the best known and the most clearly articulated of the rapid-return or quick methods.

In 1951 the University of California received a grant of $5,000 from the State of California to investigate the feasibility of using composting methods to reclaim municipal refuse. Work on the project began at the University's Sanitary Engineering Research Laboratory, Richmond Field Station. In 1952 Clarence G. Golueke was put in charge of it, but by that time funds had been exhausted and much of the pioneering work was done with minimal equipment and personnel.

The first materials used by Golueke were vegetable trimmings discarded by grocery stores and, for dry material, dry bones, straw, and sawdust. Later in the project, paper was used in the place of these dry materials.

The study concentrated on moisture content, temperature, aeration, pH, and nutrient availability. Various inoculums were also tested for their contribution to the process through experiments using control piles. Inoculums proved ineffective in themselves and unnecessary.

The experiment began with bench-scale samples in 5-gallon jars. Through these it was learned that a material must be neither too wet nor too finely ground. A range of moisture content between 70 to 85 percent was found to be most conducive to rapid composting when straw, leaves, or sawdust was the absorbent.

Two bins measuring 40 by 40 feet and 60 inches high were used in the next phase of the experiment. Autumn leaves became the absorbent in fall and manure the chief nitrogen source. The larger quantity of material allowed for self-insulation which permitted temperatures to rise to measureable thermophilic levels. The piles were turned at varying intervals and heat was measured before and after turning. The C/N ratio was also adjusted and results were measured at different ratios. Different quantities of lime were added to acid material to test the function of the pH factor in composting.

In the final phase of the experimental project, work was done at the City of Berkeley landfill site. Here the researchers learned a great deal about the nature and the economic-level sources of municipal refuse. Sewage sludge, both raw and digested, and cannery wastes became subjects of experiment. C/N ratios were adjusted at this phase of the experiment by adding varying quantities of paper, and by selecting refuse materials from certain parts of the city. The site experiments confirmed laboratory findings.

Among the findings of the study were: (1) no test to determine the point at which compost is finished is more reliable than the measurement of the final drop in temperature, after which further decomposition will be slow and without appreciable odor; (2) the maximum allowable moisture content when paper is used as the principal absorbent is 55 to 60 percent, because paper compacts easily and reduces pore spaces, but to compost most effectively with non-paper dry materials, a moisture content of 70 to 85 percent is required; (3) acidity and alkalinity are not major factors in composting, because an initial drop in pH is corrected during the process and finished compost is usually slightly alkaline; (4) speed of composting is a function of aeration, but every-other-day turning intervals are most efficient and more frequent ones are unnecessary unless moisture content is too high; (5) compost can be made within two weeks by turning garden debris compost materials every other day for four turnings; (6) the nose, eyes, and thermometer are the most effective measuring devices for home composters (improper aeration leads to foul odors, and failure of temperatures to rise during the initial period indicates that some factor is out of balance); (7) composting is a natural, biological process, not magic, and all we can do is to provide the best possible conditions for the process.

METHOD

The method developed from the California experiments is similar to earlier methods recommended by modifiers of the Indore method, as well as to those practiced in mechanical digester units in Europe and America, and to those described and advocated by Harold B. Gotaas of the World Health Organization in his 1935 book, *Composting*. The California method has been used in the windrow composting of municipal wastes where shredding of materials, planned adjustment of the C/N

The California method requires the use of wooden bins.

ratio, regular and frequent turning for aeration, and control of moisture content are practiced. Municipal composting differs from garden composting in the nature of its materials and in the quantity of its product. Paper and ash that are present in municipal compost require specific adjustments and so do factors resulting from the bulk of the material, such as compaction and overheating due to self-insulation.

The California method as it applies to the home gardener's individual needs may be summarized this way: (1) raw material of proper composition and in a suitable condition must be provided and the pile should be built all at one time; (2) a bin is needed to contain the material; (3) a set procedure must be followed in setting up the contents of the bin.

According to Golueke, "Appropriate materials for composting are garden debris, manures, garbage, vegetable trimmings, unprinted paper and cardboard, and various absorbent materials. In other words, any decomposable organic material is suitable."

According to Golueke, the C/N ratio of the material should be 25 to 30 parts of carbon to 1 of nitrogen. The home gardener may achieve this by using green garden debris or garbage for the nitrogen and dry garden debris for the carbon matter. A high C/N ratio can be lowered (in favor of nitrogen) through the use of manures. "Meat scraps," says Golueke, "are [also] rich in nitrogen—but who can afford to have meat scraps?"

For the home gardener who wishes to adjust the C/N ratio of his pile, Golueke recommends "trial and error, coupled with good judgment." He suggests layering dry and green materials in 2-to-4-inch deep layers. Paper, he says, is an ineffective absorbent, while high-cellulose or woody materials offer carbon in a resistant form and therefore require additional nitrogen material to balance them at the early stages of the process. High-carbon material acts as an absorbent in the pile and gives it structure.

A minimum volume of 1 cubic yard will usually assure self-insulation, but greater volume may be required in cold weather. The minimum floor dimensions of the bin should be 3 feet square, and the height of material inside the bin should not exceed 6 feet or be less than 4 feet. A bin may be constructed from wood and hardware cloth, wood alone, or concrete. It may be covered with a screen to discourage flies. (Bins are discussed in more detail in Chapter 10.)

Material to be composted should be reduced in size to pieces of 6 to 8 inches, though in garden composting all you really need to do is chop

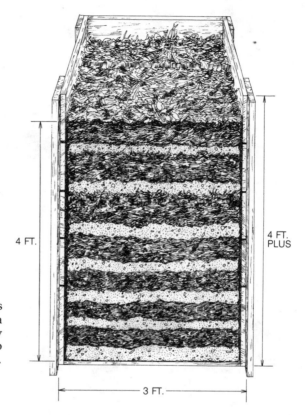

The minimum dimensions of a bin for the California method should be 3 feet by 3 feet, with a height of 4 to 6 feet.

any thick flower stalks and vegetable vines. Shredding with a power shredder is ideal but not essential. Ground material composts faster than coarse, high-cellulose material.

Compost is wet enough if the particles glisten. Failure of the pile to heat up may indicate that too little moisture is present, while too much moisture may be signaled by foul odors and a drop in temperatures. Turning the pile frequently reduces moisture.

Turning is essential to the California method, for it provides aeration and prevents the development of anaerobic conditions. The more frequent the turning (so long as it is not done more than once a day), the more rapidly the method works. To turn the pile, remove the front of the bin and fork out the contents, beginning with the top layer and keeping track of the original location of the material. When you return the contents, make sure that the material from the outer layers

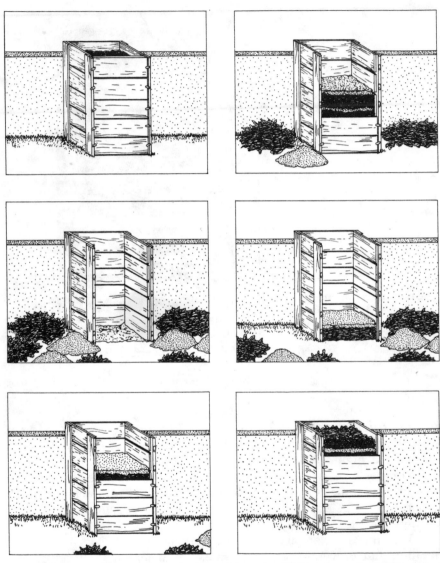

Turning the compost properly is essential to the California method. You must keep track of every layer of compost you fork out of the bin, so the outer layers are moved to the middle of the heap after turning.

(top and sides) of the pile end up in the interior of the new pile. The material should be fluffed as it is forked and it should be so thoroughly mixed that the original layers are indistinguishable. In the course of the composting process, every particle of the pile should at one time or another have been exposed to the interior heat of the pile.

Turning schedules are not absolute, and by varying the turning frequency the compost-making process may be extended to a month or even more, or reduced to as little as 12 days. The suggested schedule for 12-day compost is: (1) turn on the third day after starting the pile; (2) turn again on the third day after the first turning (skip a day); (3) make the third and final turn on the ninth day afer setting up the pile.

On the 12th day, following this schedule, the compost will be complete and ready for use, though it can benefit from further ripening.

If moisture is needed, add it to the pile during turning. Remember that frequent turning causes some loss of nitrogen, so if a high-nitrogen compost is your goal, less rapid methods or modifications of this method will give you better results.

The best way to monitor the decomposition process is by noting the course of the temperature changes in the heap. This may be done with a hotbed thermometer placed inside the pile about 12 inches from the surface. (A string on the end of it will aid in retrieval, for if the pile is working it will be too hot to dig around in.) The temperature will rise from 110° to 120°F. (43° to 49°C.) within 24 to 48 hours after the process begins, and to 130°F. (54°C.) or higher within three to four days. When the temperature sinks back to 110°F. (43°C.), the compost is ready for use.

Over the years, we have found that home composters tend to be either too casual or too compulsively pseudo-scientific and precise in their composting operations. The most important human ingredient in the process is good judgment and common sense. Use your nose and eyes to determine the cause of any failures you have, and be intelligent about making adjustments of C/N ratio, moisture, and aeration until you achieve satisfactory results.

MODIFICATIONS

Most of the common modifications of the California system are easily anticipated within the system itself. Schedules, as we have noted, can be adjusted. An experiment performed at the Organic Gardening and Farming Research Center, for example, followed a 14-day schedule with turnings on the 4th, 7th, and 14th days. This experiment started with proportioned but thoroughly mixed ingredients (the mixing was done during the grinding). All material was ground. Sprinklings of dried blood or cottonseed meal were used for nitrogen when manure was scarce or absent.

One variation of the California method, developed by Peter Tonge, emphasizes a second shredding after the second week in a two-week process, when a thorough turning has been given after one week. The second shredding is followed by sifting. Residue is removed to be used as mulch.

Another, more substantial, modification of the California method is becoming increasingly popular. As might be anticipated, it is the work of the California method with its frequent back-straining turnings that many gardeners object to. Modifications have focused on reducing or eliminating the need for turning. F. W. Bassett and others claim to have successfully substituted bottom aeration for turning. Bassett's raised compost pile was constructed with the bottom 1 foot above the ground to make maximum use of convection currents. One composter claims to have reduced composting time to six days, through use of the Bassett method and by grinding materials thoroughly. This method, also called the "no-turn" method, will be discussed in more detail later in this chapter.

The Bio-Dynamic Method
HISTORY

The bio-dynamic method of farming and gardening was developed by a group of people surrounding or influenced by Rudolph Steiner, an Austrian social philosopher who died in 1925. Steiner, in turn, was influenced by the German poet and dramatist Johann von Goethe. The bio-dynamic method is part of a wider philosophical world view called anthroposophy, a world view with both scientific and humanistic roots, which aims at the creation of a new culture based on the unity of all life processes. The bio-dynamic method of gardening is practiced on all continents, but is especially associated, through Steiner, with Germany and England.

Bio-dynamic gardeners share many attitudes with other organic gardeners. Like all those who practice natural, rather than chemical, methods of fertilization and pest control, adherents of bio-dynamics are concerned with the health of the soil—its natural limits and the processes employed by nature to improve it. Bio-dynamic gardeners go beyond other organic gardeners in seeing their husbandry of the land as part of a philosophical or quasi-religious expression. Mental, or "inner" attitude is considered of prime importance in bio-dynamics. The rhythms of nature, while studied scientifically, are endowed with an almost mystical significance, and those who practice bio-dynamic farming and gardening guard secrets of land care, particularly in the area of composting, much as a cult guards its sacred symbols.

METHOD

In his book, *Bio-Dynamic Farming and Gardening*, Ehrenfried Pfeiffer, who served as the director of the Biochemical Research Laboratory at the Goetheanum Dornach, Switzerland, and who was a disciple of Rudolph Steiner, explains the bio-dynamic composting system: "The setting up of the compost heap is carried out as follows: The first step is to dig a pit for the pile from 5 to 10 inches deep. . . . This should be covered, when possible, with a thin layer of manure or compost already rotted. . . . The structure and consistency of the compost should be moist, but not wet."

The bio-dynamic compost pile is trapezoidal in shape with a base width of 13 to 15 feet and a top width of 6 feet. It is 5 to 6 feet high. Alternate layers of compost material (any organic material) and earth are

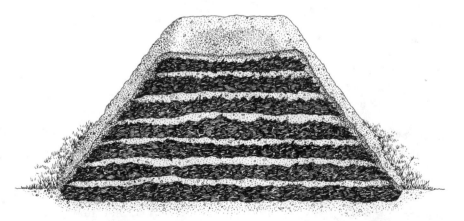

A cross section of a bio-dynamic heap, in which layers of compost materials are alternated with layers of soil. Each layer is sprinkled with lime, and the completed pile is covered with dirt.

used with lime sprinkled between layers. When complete, the pile is entirely covered with dirt.

When manure is composted, bedding straw, leaves, or sawdust are layered with it. Piles are moistened with sprinkled or pumped liquid manure or rainwater. Brushwood or drainage tiles in the bottom of the shallow pit provide drainage. Only freshly fallen leaves, those that have not dried or "washed out," are used. When garbage is used, it can be covered temporarily with matting or evergreen branches.

So far, the bio-dynamic method is not much different from the Indore method or any partly anaerobic slow-acting method of composting. The "trademark" of the bio-dynamic method comes with the next step.

When the pile is about a yard high, special bio-dynamic "preparations" are added to the pile. These preparations are known by numbers and are obtainable only from specially designated and certified bio-dynamic farmers of standing who alone know how to make them. These preparations are not to be sold for profit.

The preparations are made from various plants which have traditionally been employed as medicinal herbs. Among them are camomile, valerian, nettle, yarrow, dandelion, and horsetail. These plants are themselves composted by the farmers and given a long fermentation process. They are buried at certain depths in the earth in contact with certain parts of animal organs. The bio-dynamic farmers believe that the scientific basis for the changes that occur in the course of the fermentation of compost have to do with hormone influence. They believe they can direct the composting process in the garden through predetermined use of these plant preparations. The humus-like mass resulting from the composting of the special herbs is distributed as a compost activator or inoculum. Different preparations have different uses.

In three to five months, the bio-dynamic pile is turned and mixed. More preparations are added at this time, if necessary. The turning is important for aeration and to expose all weed seeds to the inner part of the pile. Pfeiffer says that it is the lack of air in the middle of the pile which, coupled with the conditions of fermentation, destroys the seeds.

Bio-dynamic gardeners believe that everything in nature is there for a purpose. All substances are related dynamically. Weather and the phases of the moon, they say, should be studied so that the farmer can work in harmony with them by intention, just as the early peasant once used them through instinct or superstitious tradition.

Through experiment and observation, a bio-dynamic gardener finds the chemical substance most required by each plant for protection and growth. He or she then locates the best natural organic source of this chemical and uses it in custom-blending compost for each particular plant. Tomatoes, for example, do well in compost made from their own discarded leaves and vines; while sugar beets need a boron-rich compost made with such substances as seaweed; and potatoes do well in a calcium-rich horseradish compost. Stinging nettles aid in the rapid decomposition of other weeds and organic matter and are an essential ingredient of bio-dynamic compost.

The problem in evaluating the bio-dynamic method is that it is at once more related to philosophical intangibles and, at the same time, is purported by its adherents to be more scientifically precise than other methods. The experiments carried on by Pfeiffer's laboratory and at other centers show that seeds and plants treated with bio-dynamic preparations grow faster and are healthier than those grown in control experiments. However, most of the reasons used to explain this phenomenon are still speculative.

Some modern composting experts, such as those who developed the California method, have found that activating preparations neither aid nor hinder the properly managed composting operation. It is possible that the bio-dynamic preparations, all made from plants rich in trace minerals or natural acids, bring anaerobic processes closer to the chemical state of aerobic processes than they would otherwise be, but this has not been proven conclusively. Modern scientific composters cannot, of course, measure the effects of inner attitudes on composting. These remain an article of faith to the followers of the bio-dynamic method and anthroposophy.

On one point at least, evidence indicates that the early bio-dynamic theory is in error. It is high temperatures, not lack of air, that causes weed seeds to be destroyed in the center of the heap. Turning the pile more often than is called for in the bio-dynamic method is required for the destruction of weed seeds.

However, gardeners who wish to create special composts for the needs of particular plants may learn much from the writings of bio-dynamic farmers and scientists. Modern rapid-method composting, because it was developed using municipal refuse, is less precise in its techniques than is bio-dynamic composting and is therefore less adaptable to the custom-mixing of composts. Its corresponding advantage, however, is that it requires no guarded secrets or preparations which may or may not be scientifically useful or necessary.

Ruth Stout's "No-Work" Mulching System

In one of the collected articles in *The Ruth Stout No-Work Garden Book* by Ruth Stout and Richard Clemence, Mrs. Stout refers to an article in *Organic Gardening and Farming* magazine about a man who made a ton of compost:

> The man is pictured, too, and he looks far from young, and I'm wondering how he'll make out when he gets really too old to be able to handle all that work. I can only hope that when that time comes, he will have found out it's quite unnecessary. All you need to do is put the leaves and hay and refuse wherever you want them, all over your garden and around your trees—for keeps.

Ruth Stout, now in her nineties, insists with common sense, charm, and stubborn logic that permanent, year-round *mulch* is the only answer to managing all garden chores. Compost-making, she declares, although "fine," is "hard and cumbersome work for a woman."

Actually, Ruth Stout admits that she is using compost of a sort, for mulch when left on the ground from year to year decomposes slowly and adds nutrients and bulk to the soil in much the same way that applications of finished compost do. The Stout system, once established on relatively fertile ground, transfers the work of tilling, hoeing, cultivating, weeding, and fertilizing from the gardener to natural processes. Ruth Stout does fertilize with high-nitrogen broadcast cottonseed meal occasionally, and she used manure in her plot prior to beginning her mulching program almost 30 years ago.

The main functions of the mulch are to retain moisture in the soil, moderate soil temperatures, and prevent the growth of weed seedlings by reducing light. Mulch, by providing insulation and adding humus to the soil as it rots, encourages earthworms and beneficial soil organisms and microorganisms.

Many of the advantages that come from the use of compost are shared by mulch. The chief economic and human argument for mulching as a substitute for composting when composting is coupled with conventional tilling methods, is that mulching saves labor. Ruth Stout puts it this way:

> I am not a particularly vigorous woman, but I do all the work in a garden 40 by 60 feet, raising enough vegetables for my husband, my sister, myself, and many guests. I freeze every variety, from early asparagus to late turnips. We never buy a vegetable. I also do my housework, raise quite a few flowers, rarely do any work after 1:00 P.M. I'm scarcely ever more than just pleasantly tired.

It would be hard to find a more convincing testimony to the labor-saving advantages of mulch than Ruth Stout's description of her own good life. If you are a city gardener, however, you may find that the time you save in hoeing is spent in traffic jams as you chase all over the county looking for hay for sale, or spent vacuuming the messy hay residue out of the back seat of your car once the hay has been found. Labor economy is not the only kind of saving, either, and when you add the price of hay or straw to the cost of the gasoline used in looking for it, you may be fully ready to return to the cheap old hoe.

When compared to composting, mulching is a slow method of adding nutrients to the soil. The process is at least partly anaerobic, for air is sealed off from underlying materials by the top layers. High-nitrogen materials such as partly rotted manure and garbage decay rapidly when applied in mulch. High-carbon materials like hay and straw serve better to retain water and retard weeds. Since mulch sits on top of the earth and is not mixed with soil, this high-carbon, decay-resistant material will not call upon large quantities of soil nitrogen all at once like it would if plowed under. However, it will add bulk and nutrients to the soil very slowly; it may be that your soil needs only these slow additions. If so, mulching alone may suffice to keep your garden in shape for several years.

Almost all compostable wastes can be used for mulching. However, it is almost impossible to layer and mix correct proportions of ingredients in mulch form. Rapid decomposition of mulch is impossible because of the lack of self-insulating mass, but even if you could put a 5-foot layer of mulch on your garden and aerate it regularly, the temperatures generated would burn or wilt anything growing there and do damage to the soil and its organisms.

If you need to add large quantities of humus to your garden for building the soil's texture and increasing its productivity, or for modifying the pH level, many experts agree that you would do well to combine the labor-saving advantages of mulch with a seasonal composting program.

The Lyle Some-Work Mulching System

A Texas gardener named Hank Lyle wrote an article for *Organic Gardening and Farming* in 1972, entitled "Have Your Mulch and Compost It, Too." The system he described is a modification of the Ruth Stout method. It is much like a home version of the sheet method of composting used by farmers (see page 205).

Mr. Lyle, unlike Ruth Stout, started with, ". . . red clay, baked by the sun. What wasn't clay was a very hard soil that looked lifeless."

Lyle plowed under his first poor early crop of fungus-attacked pea plants and other vegetables and devoted the remainder of his first growing season to gathering materials. He writes:

> Our next-door neighbor had a 6-acre patch of grass and weeds. Many of these weeds were knee-high when the neighbor had them cut. When we asked for permission to use them on our garden, the neighbor said (with an amused look), "Sure, use all you want. But I can tell you right now that all that ever grew in that garden was weeds."

The sheet compost Hank Lyle made with these weeds and other materials covered his 150-by-50-foot patch 4 inches deep. After dampening it with a hose, he broadcast 35 pounds of cottonseed meal by hand (he says a lawn fertilizer spreader would have worked better). The cottonseed meal acted as a high-nitrogen layer in the compost.

The next layer consisted of 3 inches of leaf mold. This layer was dampened and an additional 40 pounds of cottonseed meal was applied over it. The sheet compost settled to a height of 6 inches. Lyle continues the account:

> What we had now was a giant compost pile which was also a mulch. After three days we used a tiller (with the two inside rows of tines removed) to stir and fluff the mulch and mix in what soil the tines could pick up. . . . We dampened the heap again with the spray nozzle.

By the evening of the fourth day, Lyle reported, the material had begun to heat up under the top layer. More material (leaves, grass clippings) was added with 15 pounds of cottonseed meal being sprinkled over each inch of material. Every fourth day the tiller was used to mix the material.

By the 20th day, the material had shrunk considerably. We noticed that the soil beneath the compost was beginning to soften and turn dark brown. There were earthworms too. Before we had started the compost, hardly a worm was to be found.

Lyle began to scour his whole area for material to add to the pile and in the course of one foraging expedition, he found a free source of cottonseed hulls at an abandoned gin. He continues:

Much of the lower part of the stack had turned dark from weathering and nearness to the ground. This we used first. We hauled 28 loads in our 6-by-8-foot trailer, which is 4 feet high, and made an 8-inch layer over the garden which we did not mix with the rest. By this time it was September and we added no other material.

Through the winter the compost weathered and absorbed moisture from rains which would formerly have run off, until by spring all that remained was a 3-inch layer of cottonseed hulls. This layer was kept for a year-round mulch.

Lyle used a garden fork to clear 8-inch-wide planting row spaces at intervals in the mulch and later, when his plants emerged, he pulled the cottonseed hull mulch back closer and filled in to the plants with grass clippings. The earth in Hank Lyle's garden was brown and dark by planting time. He continues:

Well, that small plot of ground produced three bushels of beans and four bushels of peas at a market value of $150 a bushel, plus 100 pounds of okra . . . Many of the corn stalks bore two ears. The tomato plants formed a solid mass . . . the carrots [yielded] 60 pounds . . . one day's picking yielded 40 pounds of squash. . . . We ate fresh squash, put squash in the freezer—about 80 pounds—and sold squash—200 pounds of it . . . There are only three rules to follow. Use the greatest variety of material available, add plenty of organic nitrogen, and mix thoroughly. Your back may ache some at the beginning, but you will soon forget about that when you see the results of this method of gardening.

When compared with rapid bin composting, Hank Lyle's novel type of sheet composting shows much similarity to the conventional method. It provides moisture through hosing, aeration through tiller turning, a C/N balance of materials through the use of pre-mixing layering techniques and thorough sprinklings of high-nitrogen cottonseed meal, and it allows for an aging period (winter) after the initial temperature rise. It would probably be classified as a long-term method, although in its particulars it is most similar to the California method and it is mostly aerobic. Unlike the California method of bin or windrow composting, it involves a maximum "pile" depth of less than 10 inches, so the mass cannot insulate itself enough to achieve thermophilic temperatures long enough to kill weed seeds. No potentially pathogenic raw material was used, so the absence of high temperatures is not a serious drawback to this method.

The important difference between Hank Lyle's and Ruth Stout's methods is that in his no crop growing went on during the mulch composting period, so the temporary nitrogen drain caused by rapid decomposition didn't threaten crops. The whole plot was used like an oversize compost pile. The chief aim of the process was soil fertility and soil tilth. Weed reduction and water retention were only secondary. At this point, Hank Lyle probably won't have to repeat the initial fallowing and enriching of his plot for many years. He can now make compost in a bin or pit, using the finished compost in the rows he makes in his replenished year-round mulch of hulls.

The City People's Method

Helga and Bill Olkowski, coauthors of *The City People's Book of Raising Food*, produce much of their own vegetable supply on a comparatively small plot of land in a city.

They say that the energy some people put into fertilizing and weeding they put into composting. They also find composting "an ideal way of handling the organic wastes that accumulate around an ordinary household—kitchen garbage, weeds, grass clippings, ashes, bits of paper, dust from the vacuum cleaner, etc."

The method they practice and recommend to the urban gardener is a "fast" aerobic process. One reason for their recommendation comes from the special need city people have to avoid giving offense to neighbors through foul smells and the nuisances such as stray dogs, rats, and flies which these smells may bring. By maintaining an aerobic pile through frequent turnings, smells are avoided.

In a time of increased incidence of often expensive litigation resulting from neighborhood friction, gardeners must be careful to keep composting operations inoffensive. Many modern city dwellers, not understanding the need for or importance of composting, associate it with offenses to public health like leaving garbage exposed on the street. Public education about composting is needed; so are definitive court rulings on the side of careful composters and sound municipal ordinances.

The Olkowskis, in outlining their method, suggest putting a sturdy, covered bin in a shady place such as the north side of a garage so that the contents will not dry out too rapidly. Three bins are ideal to facilitate turning.

In writing of use and timing they say:

> Usually it takes us about a week or so to use up the compost once it is made, as we don't have much time to devote to gardening generally. Since it takes about three weeks for a batch to be ready for use, this means we end up making one every month or so. However there are times during the summer when both our garden needs and garden wastes demand a more rigorous attention to the system.

During this period, they explain, they make compost every two weeks, using a three-bin "assembly line" that has one batch cooking and one being used at all times.

One fairly unique feature of the Olkowski system is the provision for storing kitchen garbage between compost makings. They do this in 5-gallon covered cans where garbage is layered with sawdust to absorb odors. Ashes, soil, or dry leaves, they say, would work as well.

While living on a city street on property with no lawn and no trees, they have had to be clever and even stealthy in acquiring the important compost ingredients, grass and leaves: "In the summer and fall, we make trips out across the town with a broom, flat shovel, and plastic garbage can to sweep up leaves from the curbsides of more fortunate folks."

City people, the Olkowskis remind us, have an additional reason to balance high-nitrogen and high-carbon materials in their piles. If materials like chicken manure which are high in nitrogen are added to the pile "in such quantity that there is more than one part of nitrogen to approximately 30 parts carbon, the excess nitrogen will be respired by the microorganisms as ammonia." Ammonia odor, though less distressing than the odors of putrefaction found in an anaerobic pile which has not heated up, still upsets neighbors.

The Olkowskis recommend human urine as an excellent nitrogen source. Urine, since it is liquid, is easy to apply and can be substituted for some or all of the moisture added to the pile.

Recent studies at the Organic Gardening and Farming Research Center have concluded that human urine contains enough nitrogen to be effective as a compost activator. It is relatively disease-free and is less likely to lose potency than some animal manures because it is easier to apply soon after it is excreted. As a liquid, it can be stored in a closed container.

According to Clarence Golueke, human urine is a "minimal health risk entity. That is, the chances of catching anything from it are small." Urine may be collected directly in storage containers or by use of a special toilet such as the one designed 20 years ago in Japan, which collects urine in a separate airtight section.

Urine should be poured directly onto the heap. In order to do this it is necessary to modify the Olkowskis' methods (and the California method on which it is based) of building compost all at once, unless you provide airtight storage for urine until you are ready to build the pile. If you are adding urine daily to a maturing pile, begin the pile with a supplementary nitrogen source, preferably one that releases its nitrogen quickly. Daily additions of urine replenish the nitrogen as the pile heats up. The urine of sick people should be used only in fast thermophilic methods of compost making.

Helga and Bill Olkowski recommend using a layering technique to build the pile. They use sawdust as a bottom layer and then alternately layer green and dry material, sprinkling urine or another easily-sprinkled nitrogen source, like dried blood or cottonseed meal, over each layer as they build. Although they abandoned the use of a grinder because of its fuel consumption, they still chop large or tough dry materials with a cleaver. "After the pile is built," they continue, "you may need to water it. If you have been adding urine every other layer or so, it may be wet enough."

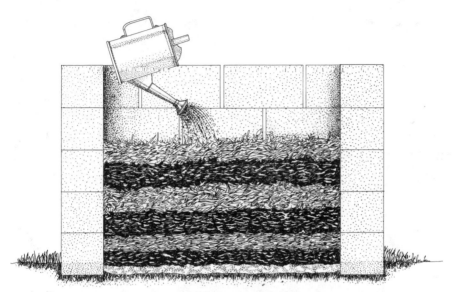

The Olkowskis' method of layering compost ingredients calls for a base layer of sawdust topped with alternating layers of green and dry materials. Each layer is sprinkled with a high-nitrogen material, and the completed pile is watered if necessary.

They turn the pile after a day or so by forking it into an adjacent bin. The same procedure is followed in subsequent turnings every three days. As city dwellers, the Olkowskis particularly wish to avoid the odors of an improperly aerated pile which has gone anaerobic. On the other hand, they advise against using side vents in a bin because, they claim, it will increase the heat loss and encourage fly breeding around the cover edges. City neighbors object to flies as much as they do to offensive odors.

The Olkowskis either turn their finished compost into the soil with a spading fork or let the earthworms in loose humus do the turning for them. They use compost around plants or on top of beds as a mulch, spread it on newly harvested beds and turn it under, or sift it and use it in seed beds, sometimes mixing in equal parts of sand and sifted dirt.

Ogden's Step-by-Step Method

Sam Ogden in his book *Step-by-Step to Organic Vegetable Growing* gives detailed instructions on how to start a compost pile using his method:

> I started in the spring by laying out on a level piece of well-drained ground a rectangle about 5 feet by 12 feet, marking the corners with stakes. Then I lay up an outside wall of one or two thicknesses of sod or cement blocks. My system requires the maintenance of two compost piles, one of which ages for a year while the other one is being built, so in preparing for current use the pile which has stood a year, I strip off all outside material, much of which is only partly decomposed, and place it within the borders of my sod strips as the first layer in my new compost pile. From now on, all decomposable garbage from our house, and from our neighbors' as well, if I can get them to sort their waste, is spread on the pile and covered with a thin layer of topsoil before it has a chance to become nasty.

Sam Ogden builds his piles gradually through the spring and summer, adding garden refuse and weeds when he has them. As he adds to the pile he keeps building up the sides with sod or other heavy material, and he keeps sprinkling each layer with topsoil or manure.

In the fall, Sam Ogden puts on all the material he gets from the garden clean-up. Then he covers the pile with sod placed root side up, or with manure, and he doesn't touch it again until a year from the next spring. "By that time," he says, "the pile is 2 years old . . . having taken 6 months to build and 18 months to cure."

Early in the spring when the pile is ready for use, Ogden strips his old pile and puts all undecomposed material on a new pile. What remains is crumbly, nearly odorless humus, ready to use in planting.

Although Ogden refers to his method as the "lazy man's method," the outstanding characteristic of both the system and its developer is that they are sensible, sure, methodical, and steady, rather than flashy and quick. Gardeners will recognize the Ogden method as being closely akin to the Indore method of Sir Albert Howard. It is largely anaerobic and depends on layers of dirt or sod to retain heat of decomposition over a long period of time.

Ogden produces about three-quarters of a cord (96 cubic feet) of compost each year. He uses an additional four cords of manure to keep his large garden fertilized. He does not turn or water his piles.

The drawbacks of this method, according to Mr. Ogden, are: it

Sam Ogden's method of making compost:

(1) Lay out rectangle 5 feet by 12 feet.

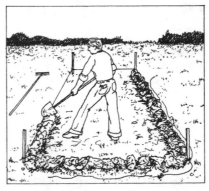

(2) Lay up sods for outside wall.

(3) Garbage goes in daily. Cover lightly with earth or manure.

(4) Add garden wastes throughout the summer. Build sod walls higher.

(5) At season's end, the pile is roofed over with inverted sods or manure.

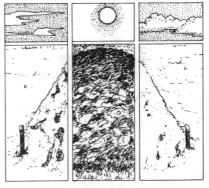

(6) Leave pile alone for 1½ years. Let nature do the work.

requires at least two piles and space for a third; it takes over a year to get started; it won't handle materials that are hard to decompose, unless they are chopped up; and it is not foolproof. Sometimes garbage added to such piles in large quantities putrifies without oxygen and turns into a black, slimy mess instead of crumbly compost. Ogden avoids the problem by spreading garbage thinly and covering it with soil.

Sam Ogden is frank about the shortcomings of his method, but feels its near-effortlessness compensates for them. He suggests using a rapid method like the California method to supplement his system during the first year when it is getting started. Ogden now uses three concrete pits that look a little like the Olkowskis' bins.

In a few particulars Sam Ogden's advice differs markedly with that of other composters. He writes:

> Unless you give them special treatment, keep dry leaves and lawn clippings out of your compost pile. . . . If you are going to use autumn leaves, they must be specially treated, either put through a chopper before being put in the pile, or . . . composted in a special pile of their own which will require a considerable time to produce leaf mold, and that will be only at the bottom of the pile. Of all the trouble which the composter may have to face, undecomposed leaves are the worst, and this you must expect if you carelessly dump dried leaves in your compost. Green lawn clippings should be piled separately and cured before introducing them into the compost pile. Unless this is done, the raw grass will heat too hot and decompose into a slimy mess which will eventually harden into a substance far removed from compost.

In our experience, the first advice is well taken. Leaf matting, even in frequently turned compost, can be a real problem. On the other hand, we would not avoid leaves altogether, for they offer a unique source of trace minerals and a bulk-giving high-carbon ingredient. If dried leaves are thoroughly mixed with other compost materials, a good product may be obtained.

Grass clippings, an excellent nitrogen source when fresh, cause more problems in Mr. Ogden's partly anaerobic system than in a fast method where plentiful oxygen allows for their fast breakdown. We feel that grass clippings should not be banned from a fast-acting pile.

Mr. Ogden's sensible step-by-step method is particularly recommended: (1) where large quantities of compost are not needed to

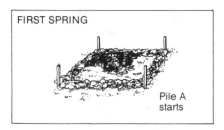

FIRST SPRING

Pile A
starts

FIRST SUMMER

Pile A
builds

FIRST WINTER

Pile A
complete

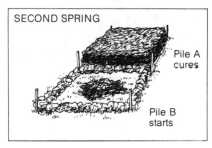

SECOND SPRING

Pile A
cures

Pile B
starts

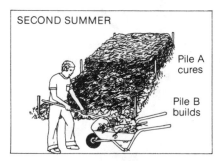

SECOND SUMMER

Pile A
cures

Pile B
builds

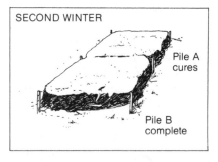

SECOND WINTER

Pile A
cures

Pile B
complete

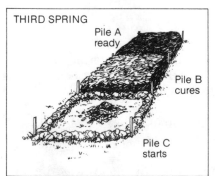

THIRD SPRING

Pile A
ready

Pile B
cures

Pile C
starts

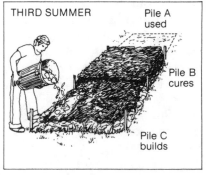

THIRD SUMMER

Pile A
used

Pile B
cures

Pile C
builds

Gardeners with extra space may consider building two or three Ogden-method
piles for continuous use over successive years.

replenish the land and there is no need for haste; (2) where human energy and machines for grinding are lacking; (3) where supplemental materials for fertilizing and enriching the soil can be used (that is, animal manures, quick-method compost, or broadcast cottonseed, soy, or blood meal); (4) where winters are severe and compost is needed early in the spring.

It is quite easy to have two of Mr. Ogden's piles going for early season use in successive years, while at the same time practicing quick methods for making compost to use during the growing season and for fall enrichment.

The Movable Compost Pile for Raised Beds

Recently there has been much interest in the raised bed method of intensive gardening, a method commonly used in France and in Japan. In this country, the system has been practiced for many years on the West Coast, and is now being accepted by gardeners with small plots all over the United States.

In raised bed gardening, plants are tightly grouped in small beds. Since more nutrient demand is made on soil by closely grouped plants, beds are dug about 24 inches deep and the soil in the beds is carefully prepared and contains large quantities of compost and/or manure. Root systems develop vertically instead of horizontally in the beds, which reduces the need for watering and heavy fertilization during the growing season. Mulch is not needed, for the plants themselves shade the soil and form a living mulch.

Beds in the raised system are about a foot higher than ground level. In such enriched and carefully drained beds, crops can be planted at intervals closer than normal, and complete accessibility allows for staggered spacing and interesting and beneficial interplantings. Interplanting not only conserves space, but promotes growth and guards against pests. Rock powders are also frequently used in preparing raised beds.

One gardener has devised a special composting system for use with intensive raised beds. He writes:

> My aim was to take the compost pile with its lively earthworm colony out of its isolated site away from the garden, and make it instead a part of the garden where it is most needed—in my raised

In the hopscotch method, cement-block bins are built right in the garden and moved as batches of compost are finished and used. This method works especially well for people who garden intensively, because the compost is made right where it's needed—in the garden's raised beds.

beds. . . . The beds are 6 feet wide by 50 long and two cement blocks or 16 inches high, while the soil level in the beds is about 8 inches high.

This raised-bed gardener scooped out the soil at one end of the raised garden bed and built a three-sided structure with cement blocks. Grass clippings, hedge cuttings, and the remains of an old compost heap were placed in the structure. Grass, soil, manure and ashes were layered until the pile reached 4 feet in height. When the compost was finished, it was shoveled down to the level of the bed, for use in other parts of the garden. The top and left-hand blocks were moved down the line to form another bin alongside the first, hopscotching up the row with a minimum of work.

To anyone who has discovered that no plant or weed grows better than the one accidentally "planted" where an open-bottomed compost pile once stood, this on-site method makes good sense. Its chief advantage is its handiness for use, both as a receptacle for weeds and debris and, later, as a source of finished compost. Even in intensive gardening, where every inch of land counts, enough room for a bin can generally be found, and in fast-method composting you only need spare the space for 14 days. The land repays its use by allowing even more intensive planting of the next crops. This hopscotch method would work well in the short-term California method.

The "No Turn" Method

"Turning a compost pile can be a tedious job," says F. W. Bassett, "especially if you are a retirement gardener." Bassett's complaints about the hard work of fast composting echo those of Ruth Stout, but his solution to the problem is different from hers.

Bassett's solution is the open-hearth-bottom bin sitting on a cement slab. A grill made of three lengths of 1-inch pipe 1 foot long sets 1 foot

In the forced-air method, compost is made in a bottom-aerated bin. As the pile heats up, it pulls up cooler air from the ground, drawing it through the mass by convection currents. Thus, the need for turning the pile is eliminated.

above the slab. The grill, says Bassett, allows air into the center of the heap for complete composting. Bassett's bin itself is made of wood salvaged from an old barn door. Another gardener has found that hollow concrete blocks lying on their sides, with pipes thrust through the center of the blocks that are set 10 inches above the ground, also works well.

The first experimental raised bases were made by U. S. Public Health Service researchers who found that one ton of rapidly decomposing compost uses up 18,000 to 20,000 cubic feet of air daily.

The theory behind the forced air method is that as the pile heats up it pulls up the cooler air from the ground. This air percolates through the mass, aerating it as it passes upward. It is believed that forced aeration by convection currents (cool air pulled in by heat) is more thorough than aeration through turning.

Mr. Bassett speaks of his bin with pride:

> My bin has definitely put an end to laborious turning. . . . I made a planter of scrap wood, wrapped some chicken wire around the bin, and set in a few plugs of wild grapevine. Very soon the vines, aided by some morning glories, surrounded the bin and required repeated pruning.

Compost experts are not unanimously agreed, in spite of Mr. Bassett's success, that the elevated bin is such a miracle worker. Some insist convincingly that in looking for relief from compost turning, there is simply no place to turn.

Golueke, in *Composting*, states that the major difficulty of aeration such as that achieved in elevated piles is that it is difficult to diffuse the air through the pile so that all parts of the pile are uniformly aerated. Air channels form and air flow is short-circuited through these channels, causing materials near the channels to dry out—a particular problem when this method is used in municipal composting. There is less of a problem in small-scale operations that don't use high-pathogen materials like sewage sludge and night soil. Weed seeds, however, require high temperatures for destruction, and dryness can be a problem in any compost operation.

It is easy enough for curious composters to experiment with raised-bottom bins. As a cautionary measure, use no raw sewage or other potential pathogen sources with this method.

Windrows and Piles

Piles and windrows are both heaps for open composting. The systems are used in the open, on the ground, with no confining structure like a bin, pit, or pen. Windrows are elongated piles which require periodic turning to expose all particles of the mass to similar conditions within the windrows. They are often used in large-scale agricultural or municipal composting operations.

In all but the far northern parts of the United States, windrowing can be practiced on any drained land. Some people set shed-type roofs over windrows to protect them from heavy rains. In severe weather, shed sides may also be added to protect active piles. Windrows may be of any convenient length. As to their height, Clarence G. Golueke in *Composting* explains, in speaking of municipal composting, that height is critical because too shallow a pile loses heat too rapidly and too high a

In dry weather, windrows generally have a trapezoidal cross section (rear); in wet climates they should be semicircular to shed water (front).

pile can become compressed by its own weight, with a resulting loss of pore space which can lead to anaerobic conditions. Golueke writes of both height and width:

> Although experience quickly demonstrates the most suitable height of pile for any particular refuse, a maximum of 5 or 6 feet is recommended for freshly ground municipal refuse. As the material loses volume during decomposition, any desired height of pile can be maintained by reducing or expanding the width of the windrow at the time it is turned.
>
> The initial width of a windrow probably will not exceed 8 or 10 feet at the base for convenience in turning. In dry weather, the cross-section is usually made trapezoidal, with the top width governed by the width of the base and the angle of repose of the material, which is something like 30 degrees from the vertical. In rainy climates or in wet weather, the cross section of the windrow should be approximately semi-circular like a haycock in order to shed water. In that case, the maximum permissible height of pile will govern its maximum width.

Sheet Composting

Another form of composting that is generally more closely associated with agriculture than with home gardening is sheet composting. In one sense, sheet composting is an open method, for it begins with layering various materials in a sheet on top of a garden or field, out in the open. Sheet composting, and the associated use of green manure crops, is in another sense, an alternative method of adding structure and nutrients to the soil. This is not an open method at all, for it involves tilling under plant refuse and manure and other wastes to a depth of up to a foot, and leaving them to decay, not in the controlled environment of a compost pile but in the earth itself.

Sheet composting is most useful for improving sizable plots of presently unused land. If you want to make spot applications of organic matter, finished compost made in a pile is a better idea for you than sheet composting.

Suppose, however, that both you and your old garden plot are tired and need renewal. If you have a year, or even better two years, to devote to rest and rehabilitation, and if you have good power mowing and tilling equipment, preferably tractor-drawn, sheet composting may be just for you.

When the gardening season is over, cut down all surface vegetation with a mower. Next, spread other organic waste materials over the entire surface of the garden, shredding them either before or after application. Add shredded manure and spread evenly, or add cottonseed meal, blood meal, or tankage, and then a sprinkling of rock powder. Then till the plot thoroughly to a depth of at least 5 inches.

The danger of sheet composting as a compost-making method is that the carbon-containing residues you use will call upon the nitrogen reserves of the soil for their decomposition. The high-nitrogen materials, on the other hand, may release their nitrogen too quickly or in the wrong form. What can be accomplished in a pile in a matter of weeks, given confined and thermophilic conditions, may take a full season in the soil.

Green manuring—the growing of cover crops to be turned under—is the most practical way to add substantial amounts of organic matter to a large garden or homestead field. A green manure crop, usually legumes like clovers, indigo, winter peas, cowpea, soybeans, lespedeza, fenugreek, or vetch, is planted after a food crop is harvested. Even weeds may be used; as you know, they plant themselves. The cover crop is then tilled or plowed under at least six weeks before the next crop is to be planted. Again, caution is needed about the possible short-term nitrogen depletion. Although it seems almost unfair, the worse shape your soil is in, the less quickly it can be returned to health by this method. Indeed, the first crop you grow after green manuring may startle you not by its excellence, but by its mediocrity. The second season, however, will almost certainly live up to your very greenest dreams.

Green manuring may be combined with sheet composting. In fact, it is a good idea to add natural rock powders when you till under, because the decay of the organic matter will facilitate the release of the nutrients locked up in these relatively insoluble fertilizers. Some farmers spread finished compost when turning under green manure, claiming this accelerates its decomposition.

In the sort of ideal circumstances few of us enjoy, green manuring and sheet composting go on in one garden plot while food crops are rotated onto another plot. Rotation is also an expensive but effective way of foiling pests and diseases.

Pit Composting

Ever since some primitive outdoorsman dug a hole to bury his orange skins or fish bones, garbage pits, in one form or another, have been with us. In most compost literature the word "pit" is used interchangeably with "bin" to refer to a masonry-enclosed, box-like structure sitting either on ground level or slightly under it. We will use "pit" only for compost-holding containers which actually go down into the ground at least a foot or so. Bins, pits, and the special methods they require are discussed in Chapter 10.

Commercial Composting Units

There are a number of manufactured composters on the market. Most of them use a cabinet or drum form, mounted on a stand to make turning easy. Some are even motorized for turning. Two types will be discussed in Chapter 10. Cabinets and drums, while they can function in

In composting with this type of commercial unit, the ventilated drum is turned each day, and compost is ready for use in 14 days.

large scale operations, are best suited to small gardens where space is at a premium. Some cabinets can be kept indoors. With proper materials, tools, and skills a composter can build his own drum or cabinet system.

Trench Composting

Trench composting is a less popular form of compost-making, for it shares some of the disadvantages of both pit composting and sheet composting. Some gardeners, however, swear by it for rapid improvement of unusually poor soils. Trench compost is like an underground mulch.

Nedra Guinn, a gardener in the southeast Tennessee chirt belt, dug trenches 12 inches deep and 18 inches wide, the length of a garden row. These were filled with compost materials including hay, leaves, weeds, tree trimmings, and grass. The material was then packed down and covered with manure, watered, and mulched. Nedra Guinn planted directly into the mulch and experienced no nitrogen deficiency in crops, but other gardeners who wish to try this method are cautioned either to top the trench with topsoil or to risk nitrogen depletion. The drawbacks of trench composting are the tendency to the formation of pockets of anaerobic activity, the slowness of decomposition, and the possibility of nitrogen-borrowing from plants.

Com-POSTHOLE-ing

Some gardeners have discovered that the traditional posthole digger is a quick and convenient tool for spot-composting. The following account describes the method used by organic gardener Michael Timchula:

Making compost in postholes can be done from early spring to the latest fall day. If you plan ahead, you can make enough holes in areas where the snow does not pile up too deeply or in sheltered places so that you can continue composting throughout the winter.

When cleaning up the garden and yard in early spring, keep the posthole digger handy. As soon as you get a small pile of debris, twigs, leaves, etc., dig a posthole about 12 to 18 inches deep and bury the debris, topping it off with a handful or two of manure. Cover the hole with the best of the topsoil which was removed and scatter the rest. Watering is usually not necessary as the hole tends to collect enough moisture to assure proper composting.

Keep the posthole digger with you at planting time. After planting and laying out your rows and hills, dig holes near a hill or in the center of a row or between plants and fill them as suggested above. In this way, feeder roots will seek out the fresh compost as the plants grow and a lush growth will result. The compost holes serve to hold the moisture and a weak compost-tea leaches out to feed the plants.

Cultivating time is when the postholer can be put to good use. In a row that will not need to be disturbed or cultivated for the rest of the summer (next to the carrots or chard or another vegetable that lasts all summer), start digging a row of holes very close together. Pack young weeds, clippings, trimmings, etc., a handful or two of manure and the day's garbage and cover lightly with topsoil. Keep one or two holes dug ahead so that you always have a place for making compost. In a large garden, you may need more than one row for the entire season.

Anaerobic Composting

It is possible to make compost without air. In 1968, J. I. Rodale

Covering the heap with heavy black plastic allows composting to proceed under anaerobic or semianaerobic conditions.

presented this thoughtful and succinct review of the method in the pages of *Organic Gardening and Farming:*

About 19 years ago, I first discussed a process of making compost by the Selby enclosed method which is for the most part anaerobic. Most readers who wrote in about their reactions were in favor of the new idea. But a few were highly critical. They considered it almost irreligious to abolish the aerobic concept of making compost, and said that anaerobic conditions lead to putrefaction.

Those who have criticized the enclosed method of making compost should realize that only in a portion of the period of composting in the Sir Albert Howard (Indore) process are the conditions aerobic. Let me quote from his *Agricultural Testament:* "After the preliminary fungus stage is completed and the vegetable wastes have broken down sufficiently to be dealt with by bacteria, the synthesis of humus proceeds under anaerobic conditions when no special measures for the aeration of the dense mass are either possible or necessary." About half the period is aerobic and the last half anaerobic.

In addition, two distinct drawbacks exist in the usual form of making compost which permits air to come freely into the heap. First, it causes oxidation which destroys much of the organic nitrogen and carbon dioxide, and releases them into the atmosphere. Second, valuable liquids leach downward and out of the mass into the ground underneath where they are wasted.

The purpose for making compost anaerobically is to prevent or reduce oxidation. Oxidation of nitrogenous substances is always accompanied by the production of a great quantity of free nitrogen compounds. Manure kept in efficient conditions in an open pit loses 40 percent of the nitrogen originally contained. Although this loss is relatively small in comparison with the 80 or 90 percent loss as a result of improper storage, it is also relatively large in contrast to the 10 percent or less obtainable by using closed pits. In them, fermentation takes place out of contact with air. Only a small nitrogen loss occurs.

One difficulty has been finding an efficient and simple way to practice anaerobic composting. One technique is to enclose the compost in a polyethylene wrapping, and gardeners and farmers in all parts of the country have reported highly successful results in covering heaps with heavy black plastic.

ANAEROBIC COMPOSTING IN THE GARDEN

Composting without air is not the most popular method used by gardeners, but it does claim some adherents and it is a useful method in certain situations.

The small-lot city gardener, for instance, might find that composting in a garbage can or plastic leaf bag is the only way he can produce compost without offending neighbors' sensitivities. Ethel Morton of New Bern, North Carolina, makes anaerobic compost in plastic bags because, in part, it solves the turning problem for her. Says Mrs. Morton, "I fill one of these 'compost cases' with damp garbage, grass clippings, a litle stable manure and dirt, dried-up flower arrangements, cut-up melon and grapefruit rinds, crushed eggshells—anything I happen to have—and when it is full I tie it around the neck with cord and place it in the sunshine anywhere convenient. I can roll it over every day if I like, for it is not too heavy for a woman to manage. Then I start on the next slip and repeat the process. By the time the fourth one is filled, the first one is ready for use, and so on. It is amazing how much compost can be made this way and how easily and quickly it is done."

Evaluating Your Compost

Following are several checkpoints with which you can gauge the success of your compost. These points will serve as a standard from which you can determine the effcency of your composting methods.

1. Structure: The material should be medium loose, not too tight, not packed, and not lumpy. The more crumbly the structure, the better it is.
2. Color: A black-brown color is best; pure black, if soggy and smelly, denotes an unfavorable fermentation with too much moisture and lack of air. A greyish, yellowish color indicates an excess of dead earth.
3. Odor: The odor should be earthlike, or like good woods soil or humus. Any bad smell is a sign that the fermentation has not reached its final goal and that bacteriological breakdown processes are still going on. A musty, cellarlike odor indicates the presence of molds, sometimes also a hot fermentation, which has led to losses of nitrogen.
4. Acidity: A neutral or slightly acid reaction is best. Slight alkalinity can be tolerated. Remember that too acid a condition is the result of lack of air and too much moisture. Nitrogen-fixing bacteria and earthworms prefer the neutral to slightly acid reaction. The pH

range for a good compost is, therefore, 6.0 to 7.4. Below 6.0 the reaction is too acid for the development of nitrogen-fixing bacteria. Under certain circumstances, a reaction of 5.5 is required; for instance, for potatoes, azaleas, rhododendrons, alpine flowers. In this case, add no lime to the compost and increase the amount of woods soil, leaves and conifer needles.

5. Mixture of raw materials: The proper mixture and proportion of raw materials is most important! Indeed, it determines the final outcome of a compost fermentation and the fertilizer value of the compost. On the average, we feel that an organic matter content of from 25 to 50 percent should be present in the final product. This means that one- to two-thirds of the original material ought to be organic matter: leaves, garbage, weeds, manure. The balance should be made up of good topsoil, old rotted compost and lime. If dead or mineralized soil and subsoil is to be used, soil which has frozen over winter secures better results. Ditch scrapings, or soil from the bottom of a pond, should be frozen and exposed to air for a season before being incorporated into a compost.

6. Moisture: Most of the composting failures we have seen have resulted from a failure to maintain the proper moisture conditions. Moisture content should be like that of a wrung-out sponge. That is, no water should drip from a sample squeezed in the hand. Never let the compost get dry.

9

Composting with Earthworms

If you let them, earthworms will do most of your composting work for you, in the garden, on the farm—or even in your basement.

Earthworms are amazing creatures, capable of consuming their own weight in soil and organic matter each day, and leaving behind the richest and most productive compost known. The castings of earth-

Earthworms are a necessary factor in maintaining good soil quality, and they can actually do most of your composting work for you if you provide for their simple needs.

worms contain from 5 to 11 times the amount of available N-P-K as the soil the worms ate to produce those castings. How do earthworms perform this magic? The secretions of their intestinal tracts act chemically to liberate plant nutrients with the aid of soil microorganisms. And what earthworms do for the three major plant nutrients, they do for the lesser nutrients, too. Earthworms literally tunnel through your soil, day and night, liberating plant nutrients wherever they go. Let loose in a compost heap, they will quickly reduce it to the finest of humus. Mulch your garden with organic matter of nearly any kind, and earthworms will never stop working on it until they have reduced the mulch to dark, rich humus. If you encourage earthworms to stay in your soil, or work with them in producing compost, they will virtually insure that you produce successful compost.

The secret in producing compost with earthworms is in learning a little about earthworms and their needs. If you buy a thousand Georgia red wigglers and thrust them into the middle of your compost pile, you will likely have a thousand dead red wigglers the next day. Most earthworms, you see, cannot tolerate the heat of an actively working

The ideal environment for earthworms can be provided in a shallow pit, like those used on this commercial worm farm.

compost heap. You will also want to learn to distinguish among the various major earthworm species, since their needs are quite different, and so are their capabilities in helping you make compost.

Most of the information in this chapter comes from *The Earthworm Book* by Jerry Minnich. This chapter will suggest ways to use earthworms in composting, but the gardener or farmer who wants to learn more about the topic should consult *The Earthworm Book* for greater detail.

Most people see earthworms as a welcome natural addition to their composting efforts and also as affirmation that they are doing things right. But gardeners could make better compost if they saw the earthworm as a necessary component of the whole process, just as important as air, water, or organic matter. The earthworms can do much of the work, and make composting faster—but in return, the gardener must learn to make compost with the earthworm's needs in mind, and discover which species of worms are suitable for various composting situations.

The Right Worm

It is important to be aware of the different species of earthworms and what they can, and cannot, do:

1. Red worms *(Lumbricus rubellus)* and brandling worms *(Eisenia foetida)*, are the species usually sold by earthworm breeders. They are commonly sold for fish bait under such names as red wigglers, hybrid reds, Georgia reds, etc. Any name which suggests a red-and-gold or banded worm is likely to be a brandling worm. The others are probably red worms. These cannot survive in ordinary garden and farm soils for very long, but they will thrive in compost heaps and manure piles. They can be used to good advantage in the Indore heap, and can greatly reduce the time required to produce finished compost and eliminate turning the heap. However, many will be killed off or driven away when the organic matter begins to heat up from bacterial action.
2. Field worms *(Allolobophora caliginosa)* and night crawlers *(Lumbricus terrestris)* will attack compost heaps and manure piles from the bottom, but prefer to retreat into the soil after having done so. They will not thrive in active compost and are killed by the heating process more easily than red worms and brandling

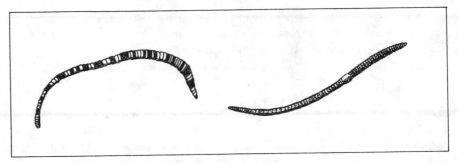

Red worms (above, right) and brandling worms (above, left) are most often raised and sold by commercial breeders, but the larger night crawlers (below, top) and field worms (below, bottom) are more familiar sights to gardeners.

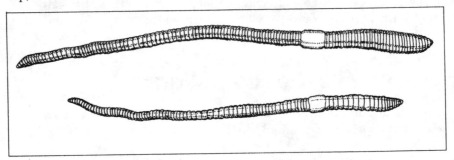

worms. Night crawlers demand cool soil temperatures and will not inhabit compost and manure piles. If they are thrust into active compost, they will simply die and melt.

3. The data on the *Pheretimas* are still incomplete, but they seem to have requirements similar to those of the field worm and the night crawler. They are soil-living species.

Earthworms in the Indore Method

Earthworms will naturally be attracted to an Indore compost heap, attacking it from the bottom. The base layer of brush will soon become reduced in bulk and filled in with finer debris. Field worms and night crawlers will quickly infiltrate this layer, to turn and mix the earth with the organic matter. They will also reproduce quickly, increasing their population many times over. If the heap is maintained for a year or more in one location, the earth below it will become rich, friable, and loaded

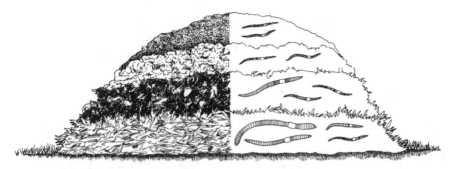

When earthworms are released into an Indore heap, night crawlers will penetrate only the bottom layer of brush, field worms will work in the bottom two layers of material, and red worms and brandling worms will be found throughout the heap.

with earthworms. With each rain, some of the nutrients from the compost will leach deep into the soil spreading out from the actual edges of the heap. Earthworms will mix these nutrients into the soil and stabilize them for growing plants. This enrichment of the soil beneath the heap is also a good reason for changing its location every year or so. Any prized plants grown where an old compost heap was built will flourish beyond reasonable expectations.

As the materials in the heap decompose and turn to humus, field worms will advance further up into the heap. Still, they will not flood the entire heap as will the manure-living species. The limiting factor is the high temperature; even an inactive, above-ground heap will not be attractive to field-living species. Night crawlers like even cooler temperatures, but will feed at the bottom of the heap. If in autumn and early spring they penetrate a well-advanced heap, you know you can use it for soil improvement.

Although manure-type worms can work at higher temperatures than field-living species, even they will be killed in the intense heat of a working compost heap, where temperatures can reach 150°F. (66°C.). Do not introduce them until the interior of the pile has cooled down to the outside temperature. Normally this will be in about three weeks after the last materials have been added to a well-constructed heap. At this point, dig holes at various points in the heap and drop 50 to 100 worms in each. About a thousand worms (a convenient number to order) will serve to inoculate a 4- by 6-foot pile. If manure-type worms and their castings were well supplied in manure that went into the heap and have survived the heat, there will be no need to introduce worms from an outside source.

In a matter of days, the worms will be consuming the organic matter, leaving rich castings wherever they go, and reproducing at a high rate. In a well-tended compost heap, a thousand reds or brandlers can increase to a million in one or two years.

Manure-type worms will do much better in the Indore heap if larger quantities of manure are included in the mixture. Instead of the 2-inch layer usually recommended, add 4 or 6 inches. If no manure at all is used, the worms will still have a good chance to thrive, although their progress will be slower.

NO-HEAT INDORE COMPOSTING

A variation of the Indore method makes it possible to produce compost quickly with very little heating, using earthworms. Construct the heap so that it is longer and wider than a normal heap, but only 12 to 18 inches high. Shred all materials as finely as possible and introduce manure-type worms immediately. They will go to work right away, and the heap will never heat up greatly because of the large surface area; the center of the heap is too close to the cooling effects of the outside air. The major disadvantages are that it takes up more ground surface area, and the shredding of materials takes time and requires fossil energy to operate a gasoline-powered shredder or rotary mower.

MAINTAINING THE EARTHWORM POPULATION

When removing finished compost for use on garden plots or farm fields, be certain to save a good number of earthworms for future composting operations. There are several ways to do this. The easiest is to remove only half the heap at a time, spreading out the remainder to serve as the base for the new heap. If your manure worm population is not as great as you wish it to be, you can save even more by "scalping" the heap in several steps. Earthworms are repelled by light; if exposed, they will quickly drive down beneath the surface. Remove finished compost from the outer parts of the heap, to a depth where worms are exposed. Wait for about 30 minutes, then take another scalping. Continue in this manner until you have removed as much compost as you want. The earthworms will have been driven into a compact area at the bottom of the heap. At this point, center spread out the remaining compost containing the earthworms, and cover it immediately with new manure and green matter. If, as so often is the case, the outer scalp of the heap has not composted fully (since it is the newest material), then set aside this first scalp and put it back after you have finished the operation. It will be the first material to be attacked in the new heap.

Earthworms in Bins and Pits

Red worms and brandling worms cannot survive northern winters without some kind of protection. Further, earthworms are the favorite food of moles, which can easily penetrate an Indore heap and decimate your earthworm population in an amazingly short time. The answer to both dangers is a compost pit dug beneath the frostline and outfitted with a heavy, coarse screen on the bottom to keep out moles but allow the free passage of soil-dwelling earthworms. Manure-type worms will not migrate deep into the soil.

Often, bins and pits are combined. The earth is dug out to a depth of 16 to 24 inches (deeper in areas such as Minnesota and Maine) and boards are used to extend the pit into an above-ground bin.

For the gardener who seeks to build a compost/earthworm pit for the first time, here are some basic instructions:

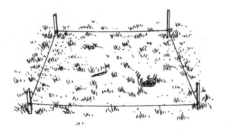

1. Stake off an area 3 to 4 feet wide and as long as you wish the pit to be.

2. Excavate the earth from this area to a depth of 16 to 24 inches. (If you live where winter temperatures get to −10°F (−23°C.) or

colder, make it 24 inches.) Pile the excavated soil to one side, in as compact a heap as possible, for later addition to the pit.

3. Drive two-by-four stakes into the four corners of the pit, if you will be using boards. (Scrap lumber from old buildings is fine.) A layer of quarter-inch, rustproof wire mesh will protect your earthworms from moles.

4. Nail boards all around the pit. Keep one end open so you can work with the material. Use stakes to hold loose boards in this area. Add boards on top of each other, leaving about a quarter-inch between each for aeration. Add boards only as the pile of materials requires them for support. The boards above ground need never be higher than 16 inches above the ground surface; if the pit is 16 inches deep, this will mean a total of 32 inches of vertical board area. (Remember that these earthworms will not work more than 6 to 8 inches below the surface of the heap, no matter how high it is built.)

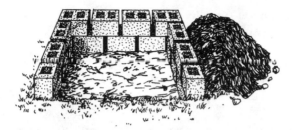

5. If you elect to use concrete blocks instead of wood, excavate the soil to a depth of one or two blocks, and add no more than two layers of blocks above the ground. At this low height, the blocks can be set in loosely, without mortar. Allow a little space between them for aeration.

Many gardeners find it helpful to divide the pit into two sections, one for new compost and the other for old. As finished compost is removed from one section, the earthworms are transferred into the newer heap on the other side, and a new heap is begun in the just-emptied side. In this way, there is always a ready supply of compost for garden use, and the earthworms are constantly maintained. An ideal setup would comprise two double pits.

Some gardeners outfit their bins with loose-fitting board lids, hinged on one side so that they swing up and open easily. This device

keeps out the sun and protects the surface of the heap from excessive heat during the summer, enabling the worms to work nearer to the surface where new material is deposited. It also keeps out predators during the night and conserves moisture during hot and dry periods. When a lid is used, keep a constant check on moisture. Add water as necessary, or—better—open the lid during rainfalls if moisture is needed.

WINTER PROTECTION IN THE NORTH

In the South, where winter temperatures rarely go below 20°F.

In northern areas, earthworm bins need to be protected for the winter. In areas where the winters are not too severe, covering the bin with a few layers of burlap will afford sufficient protection.

(−7°C.), red worms and brandling worms can be maintained easily in outdoor pits with a minimum of protection. A few layers of burlap bags and a mound of straw piles over the beds will offer all the insulation needed, even if they are occasionally covered with snow. In places like Minnesota, Montana, and Vermont, however, where winter temperatures routinely dip to −20°F. (−29°C.), special protection is a must.

The best winter-protection system we have seen is explained fully in a 46-page booklet, *Let an Earthworm Be Your Garbage Man* (available from Shields Publications, P.O. Box 669, Eagle River, WI 54521). It is essential reading for any northern gardener who decides to construct earthworm pits.

For winter protection, the booklet recommends digging a compost pit 16 inches deep, and lining it with two layers of concrete blocks below ground, with a third layer above ground. Pile the removed soil at the edge of the pit and cover thickly with straw. Line the bottom of the pit with garbage, cover with 2 to 3 inches of soil, then with burlap bags. Water if needed. The pit can be covered with wire mesh weighted down with bricks or concrete blocks.

In the winter, cans of garbage are added to the pit under the burlap and covered with a layer of soil.

Even in 20-below weather, the earthworms keep working and the composting process continues. By spring, the kitchen refuse added the previous autumn is ready for use in the garden.

Indoor Composting in the Winter

Earthworms can also be used indoors in the winter to produce a small amount of compost from kitchen garbage, dust from a vacuum cleaner bag, even newspapers. Generally, one pound of earthworms will eat one pound of garbage and produce one pound of compost each day, although this varies. There have even been a few family earthworm composting units placed on the market in recent years, including an effective "Ecology Box" by North American Bait Farms of California, but a simple homemade system is both easy and inexpensive and just as effective. It can be used anywhere, winter or summer, and it can be expanded into as large an operation as you wish.

It is best to begin on a modest scale. Construct a wooden box 2 feet wide, 2 feet long, and 1 foot deep. Or, get a vegetable lug box from your local supermarket and, if it has large spaces between the boards, tack in plastic screening to hold the earthworm bedding. If you construct your own box, provide for drainage and aeration by drilling a half-dozen

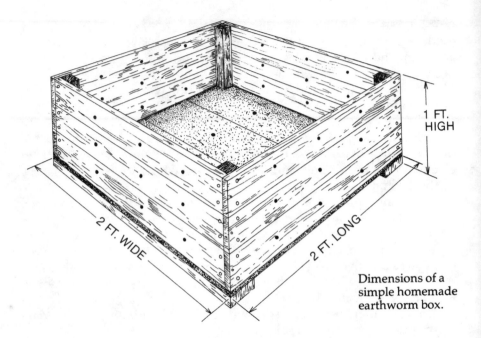

1 FT.
HIGH

2 FT. WIDE

2 FT. LONG

Dimensions of a
simple homemade
earthworm box.

⅛-inch holes in the bottom, and some more around the sides. A box 2 feet square, and 1 foot deep, will accommodate a thousand adult worms (or "breeders," as they are called in the trade) or you can order a pound of pit-run worms which will do as well.

You can prepare a bedding as follows: wet a third of a bucketful of peat moss thoroughly, and mix with an equal amount of good garden loam and manure; add some dried grass clippings, hay, or crumbled leaves, if you wish. (Don't use oak or other very acid leaves.) Soak this mixture overnight.

The next day, squeeze out the excess water and fluff up the material (which we will now call bedding). Line the bottom of the earthworm box with a single layer of pebbles or rocks. Then, place 4 inches of the bedding material rather loosely on top of the pebbles, and wait for a day to see if any heating takes place. If initial bacterial action forces the bedding temperature much above 100°F. (38°C.), all the worms will be killed. Any heating that does occur will subside within 48 hours.

When you are satisfied that the bedding will present no serious heating problems, push aside the bedding material, place the worms and the bedding in their shipping container in the center, and cover them loosely. Place a burlap bag, several layers of cheesecloth or wet newspapers over the top of the bedding and moisten it with a house-plant sprayer or sprinkling can.

Keep the bedding moist but never soggy. If the container begins to drip from the bottom, place some sort of container, such as a plastic dishpan, under the box to catch the drippings. Use the drippings to water your houseplants.

Start out by feeding the earthworms cautiously. If you give them more than they will eat in a 24-hour period, the garbage will sour, creating odors and attracting flies, or will heat up, killing the worms. Begin with soft foods, such as cooked vegetables, leftover cereal (including the milk), vegetable soup, lettuce, bread scraps, soft leaves of vegetables, even ice cream. A little cornmeal will be appreciated, and coffee grounds can be added at any time. Do not use onions, garlic or other strongly flavored foods.

Place the food on top of the bedding and tamp it gently into the bedding. After a week or two, your earthworms should have adjusted to their new home and should be on a regular feeding schedule. You can help them along, and build better compost, if you add a thin layer of partially decayed manure from time to time (being sure that it is past the heating stage, but not completely composted).

Every two weeks, the bedding in the box should be turned and aerated. Reduce the amount of food after such turnings, since the worms will not come to the surface as readily for a day or two after having been disturbed.

After a month, you can add another 2 inches of bedding material to handle the increased worm population, and after three months it will be time to start another box.

When you are ready to divide the box, prepare a second box as you did the first. Then arrange a good-sized table under a 100-watt hanging light, so that the light comes within 2 feet of the table surface. Lay a plastic sheet on the table. Dump the worms and bedding on the plastic, and heap them into a mound that peaks to within a foot of the light bulb. Pick off the pebbles and return them to the first box.

Any worms that have been exposed in turning the box will quickly react to the light by digging towards the center of the mound. This will allow you to scrape much of the bedding into a bucket. Wait another ten minutes, then scrape away another layer of compost. After several such scrapings, all the worms will have driven themselves into a compact ball at the bottom of the mound, where they can easily be divided and put back into fresh bedding in the two boxes.

Boxes can be stacked in tiers, by affixing half-inch-square wood strips, 14 inches high, into the four corners of each box. The strips will support the box on top of it. The boxes can be watered easily with a small houseplant hose or with a portable insecticide sprayer. The drippings from all but the bottom box will fall into the box beneath it.

Composting with Earthworms on the Farm

In the 1940s, U.S. Department of Agriculture scientists Henry Hopp and Clarence Slater found some very poor clay subsoil, containing no earthworms and virtually no organic matter and, by adding lime, fertilizers, and manure, grew a modest stand of barley, bluegrass, and lespedeza on two separate plots. On one, they left the growth untouched, while on the other they cut the top growth to form a mulch, and they added some earthworms to the soil.

By the following June, the plot containing earthworms was covered with a rich stand of all three crops, while the section without worms supported almost nothing but weeds. The total vegetation in the wormed plot was *five times* that of the wormless one. The plot with worms also had far better water-absorption and water-holding capacity, and twice as many soil aggregates—all the result of earthworm action.

The lesson learned here is one of which every organic farmer should be keenly aware. No soil should be left unprotected over winter. Large-scale mulching and sheet composting will protect earthworm populations, and the earthworms will improve the soil structure and crop-growing capacity.

RED WORMS IN SHEET COMPOSTING

Although manure-type worms (red worms and brandling worms) cannot exist permanently in agricultural soils, they can be used effectively in sheet composting, and their populations can be upheld each year through sound management practices. The following story will serve to illustrate the point:

The grandfather of earthworm pioneer George Sheffield Oliver employed earthworms as a key agent in his continual soil-building program. Oliver's grandfather, George Sheffield, operated an Ohio farm from 1830 to 1890, 60 years without a single crop failure. His 160-acre farm had a 2-acre barnyard directly in its center, with wide-swinging gates leading into each of the four 40-acre tracts. Thus, the stock could be led into any of the tracts simply by opening the appropriate gate. The barnyard featured an enormous compost pit, 50 feet by 150 feet, excavated to a depth of 2 feet. Each morning, the barns would be cleaned and the manure and litter deposited in the compost pit by an ingenious system of buckets, ropes, and pulleys. Because of the constant supply of material, literally millions of earthworms thrived in the pit at all times. In spring, the tons of rich compost, along with millions of manure-type worms and worm capsules, were distributed on the fields by horse and wagon. Immediately following the spreader was a horse-drawn plow, which turned the material under the soil within minutes, so that the vast majority of the worms would not be killed by the sun or eaten by the flocks of hungry crows that followed closely behind.

Sheffield was acutely aware of the value of the earthworm. In his spring compost distribution, he was certain not to clean out the compost pit completely, but left a few inches of material at the bottom so that the earthworm population would again build as the daily manure and litter were added. The pit, dug to a depth of 2 feet, afforded sufficient winter protection from ground frost, while the daily applications of hot manure created heat from above, enabling the manure worms to thrive through the snowy winter. The worms in the field probably survived until killed by winter freezing. In spring, they were replaced by the next generation of worms.

10

Compost Structures

Perhaps in no other area of gardening has the imagination of the gardener played so important a part as in the design and construction of structures for composting. Compost can be made in cages, in block or brick bins, in pits and holes, in revolving drums, even in garbage cans and plastic trash bags. A compost structure can be designed to be beautiful, to make compost in the shortest possible time, or to be moved from place to place with the least effort. It can be designed to make compost with no turning required, or to suit the needs of earthworms. Compost structures, in short, are designed to suit the user's needs and resources.

The choice of compost structure is, then, a very personal decision, one which should not be made without some prior research and, perhaps even more importantly, some experimentation. It is experimentation that leads to new structures.

The first decision to be made is whether a structure is needed at all. The gardener or farmer with plenty of room, ample materials and sufficient time may need no compost enclosure of any kind. He may find that the traditional Indore heap suits his purposes just fine.

If yours is a city or suburban lot, however, you might find that the open heap takes up too much room, or offends neighbors and family. If space is limited, an enclosure can produce more compost in a smaller land area. It can be more attractive and keep out animals and flies. If you cannot devote a permanent spot to compost making, you will want to investigate portable structures that can be broken down and moved in minutes. If your garden is located where winter temperatures are severe, a compost pit dug below the frost line can enable you to compost all winter long. If you want to work with earthworms in composting,

228

then you will need to consider some special outdoor structures, and perhaps others for basement composting. Perhaps a commercially built revolving drum suits your needs because age or infirmity prevents you from turning the heap, or simply because the drum produces quick compost and attracts no pests. Perhaps you even prefer to make compost in plastic bags because of its simplicity.

It is certainly true that one compost structure is not best for everyone. It may even be that everyone needs a structure designed especially for him or her. We hope that by describing different structures, you will gain some insight into matching construction with your individual needs. If you are like most gardeners, you will take one of these suggested forms, adapt it to your needs, use it for a year or two, and then make your own adjustments until you have evolved the perfect structure for you.

Pens and Bins

By far the most common compost forms are bins and pens. To simplify, let us call a "bin" any container with concrete, brick, wood or masonry sides that is fairly substantial and permanent, and "pen" any structure with wire, or hardware cloth sides, that is a less permanent installation. Not that they're that easy to classify—there are many kinds of structures called bins and pens.

In general, pens have the advantage of allowing for free circulation of air. Their disadvantage is that they also allow for free circulation of flies and four-footed pests. Bins are more stable and protecting structures, but they are often insufficiently ventilated. Neither the bin nor the pen has as great a tendency to go anaerobic as the pit, and both are easier to keep tidy than open composting forms.

A shady, sheltered spot not far from either garden or kitchen is an ideal location for either pen or bin. Often a space between house and garage or garage and shed allows the right amount of room. A three-compartment bin with tight floor and sides and with each compartment measuring a cubic yard in size makes for the neatest and easiest handling of turning. In such a structure there is at all times one batch working and one being used.

An advocate of bottom aeration claims to have made a free compost bin in one hour using available cement blocks and some leftover strong iron piping, plus surplus wire mesh with 1-by-2-inch apertures. The

4-by-8-by-16-inch cement blocks were laid horizontally with plenty of air between each block. Unlike other composters, this gardener preferred to have his compost bin in a sunny spot, feeling the compost would heat up faster in the sun.

The pipes were thrust across the bin from side to side over the third course of blocks to provide the pile with a strong bed. On top of the pipes, two lengths of wide wire mesh were laid to hold a bottom layer of coarse garden debris and twigs. This layer and the mesh and pipes held back finer material and allowed for bottom aeration. The gardener never turns his compost, but mixes materials together.

LEHIGH-TYPE BINS

The Lehigh-style bin is easy to erect and disassemble. It is adjustable in size, attractive, portable, long-lasting, and provides for proper ventilation and protection.

Construction is of alternating two-by-fours with the corners drilled out and held together with ⅜-inch rods. Five 36-inch two-by-fours to a side will make a bin capable of producing approximately 1 cubic yard of compost at a time.

The Lehigh bin.

A variation of the Lehigh bin, using poles instead of boards.

There have been several variations of the Lehigh bin, some using logs or poles instead of two-by-fours. However it is designed, the low cost, effectiveness, and portability of this structure has made it one of the most popular in use today.

CAGE-TYPE BINS

Cage-type bins are simple and inexpensive to build, allow good air circulation, are portable, and allow quick turning of the heap because of a removable front panel. The Lehigh bin lacks this last feature.

There are many variations of cage-type bins, all of which require relatively little lumber, since wire screening forms most of the panels.

Back in 1961, Lyman Wood, of Garden Way Research in Vermont, built the wire and wood bin shown here, using scrap 2-inch lumber which he covered with half-inch chicken wire mesh. Even allowing for inflation, it is a very inexpensive bin for general garden use.

Wood's bin was made of two L-shaped sections held together with

(continued on page 234)

BUILD A RODENTPROOF COMPOSTER

Once rodents discover your compost is a steady supply of kitchen leftovers, you may want to consider building this caged compost bin. Lap joint construction for the 2-by-4 framing was chosen for its simplicity and strength. A hardware cloth lining supported by 1-by-3-inch and 1-by-2¼-inch stock keeps the pile neatly contained and those orn'ry varmints out.

CONSTRUCTION

1. Assemble the base as shown in the illustration using 1½-inch #10 wood screws at the corners. The 2-by-4 pieces bearing the load of the compost are cut at 45-degree angles at both ends and nailed across the corners with four 16d common nails in each piece. The leg braces are also cut at 45-degree angles and fastened with 1½-inch #10 wood screws as shown.

2. To construct the bottom support frame, remove half the thickness of the wood on each end to a length that is commensurate to the width of the 2-by-4 (usually 3½ inches) on all five pieces. On two pieces, cut a dado half the thickness of the stock at the center to accommodate the middle support. Use 1½-inch #10 wood screws for assembly, two per joint.

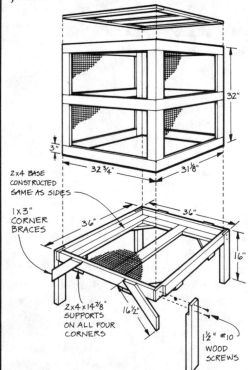

2x4 BASE CONSTRUCTED SAME AS SIDES

1x3" CORNER BRACES

32"

3"

32 ¾"

31⅛"

36"

16"

2x4 x 14⅞" SUPPORTS ON ALL FOUR CORNERS

16½"

1½" #10 WOOD SCREWS

3. The remaining side frames and top are cut and assembled the same way as the base with the exception of using 4d common nails instead of screws at each joint and clinching on reverse side.

4. For easy access to the compost, hasps are fastened to the top corners of the side frames and two 2½-by-1½-inch hinges are attached to the top. Paint the entire unit with a good grade of enamel or a nontoxic wood preserver. After the paint has dried, cut pieces of ½-by-½-inch hardware cloth to fit the interior of all frames and attach with ½-inch staples.

MATERIALS

2—36 x 2 x 4" (frame sides)
2—33 x 2 x 4" (frame sides)
4—16 x 2 x 4" (legs)
4—14⅞ x 2 x 4" (support braces)
5—32¾ x 2 x 4" (bottom frame)
4—16½ x 1 x 3" (corner braces) white pine
11—32¾ x 1 x 3" (top and horizontal white pine large frame sides)
6—31⅛ x 1 x 3" (horizontal small white pine frame sides)

4—32 x 1 x 3" (vertical large white pine frame sides)
4—32 x 1 x 2¼" (vertical small white pine frame sides)
In addition you will need four medium-sized hasps, one pair of 1½" x 2½" hinges, (36) 1½" #10 wood screws, (16) 16d common nails, approximately one pound of 4d common nails, 16'x36", ½" x ½" hardware cloth and ½" staples.

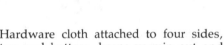

Hardware cloth attached to four sides, top and bottom, keeps vermin out and ensures good aeration of the compost.

The four side frames are joined at their tops with hasps and easily removed pegs.

The hinged top frame permits easy access to compost.

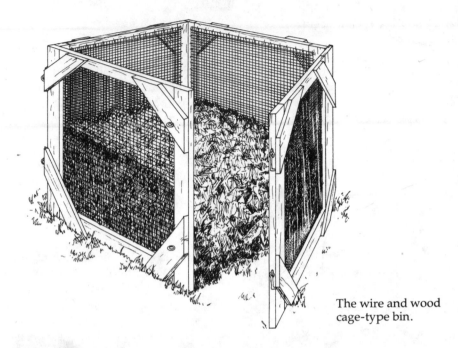

The wire and wood
cage-type bin.

screen-door hooks. The cage provided him with 18 to 24 cubic feet of finished compost in 14 days. The pile heated up to 140° to 160°F. (60° to 71°C.) in two days, and could be turned on the fourth day. He dampened each layer—leaves, grass, garbage, and manure—as he added it, and counted on the well-ventilated cage to encourage complete bacterial action.

Turning was extremely easy. He unhooked the sides, separated each of the L-shaped sections, and then reassembled them next to the square-sided heap. "You will be pleasantly surprised at how neatly and firmly the heap stands," he reported, adding, "It is now a simple and satisfying task, using a fork, to peel the layers off the pile and toss them in the now-empty cage." During the turning operation, he kept a hose handy to wet down the heap as the material was transferred.

THE NEW ZEALAND BIN

Perhaps the classic among compost bins is the wooden New Zealand box which was originally designed by the Auckland Humic Club to admit as much air as possible from all sides. It can be used to make several batches of compost in different stages of decomposition, insuring a continuous supply, and it can be a very attractive structure.

There are several variations of this box, but the simplest one is a wooden structure 4 feet square and 3 feet high or higher with neither top nor bottom. The frame is held together by two-by-fours. The wooden sides consist of pieces of wood 6 inches wide by 1 inch thick. A half-inch air space is allowed between every two boards so that air may penetrate into the heap from all sides. The boarding in front slides down between two posts so that the boards can be pulled upward and removed one by one when complete access to the contents is needed for turning or loading. The open side may also be built up gradually as the pen is filled. The top of the pen may be covered with hardware cloth, rolled canvas, burlap, or screen.

If you are using a single bin like the New Zealand box, be sure to allow for a working space in front of the box equal to two or three times the floor area of the box. This much space is needed for turning the pile. You pile up the material outside the bin and then replace it within the bin, mixing so the outside material is placed toward the inside of the new pile.

One variation on the New Zealand box, made by Treva Calder of Detroit, holds four separate bins for compost in different stages. The

The New Zealand box.

A variation on the standard New Zealand box, this bin is divided to allow production of several successive batches of compost at once.

dividers between the boxes are removable to permit quick and easy shifting of compost from one bin to another.

BLOCK AND BRICK BINS

Block and brick bins are permanent, if mortared, but cement block bins can be constructed without mortar and can then be moved at will.

The block or brick bin is easily constructed. Usually, blocks are laid to permit plenty of open spaces for air circulation. But the blocks or bricks can also be closely stacked, set into the ground, and mortared together, or formed into a cylindrical shape with an access gate at the bottom.

Gardeners who insist on a well-groomed compost area may prefer to have a large rectangular brick or block chimneylike structure with several compartments. Use wooden hinged lids to cover the structure. In a three-bin unit, the first two bins are used in turning while the third stores finished compost. The bottom of the bin, if made of concrete, should slant one way so drainage may be caught in a gutter leading to storage cans. A combination of bricks and boards may be used with

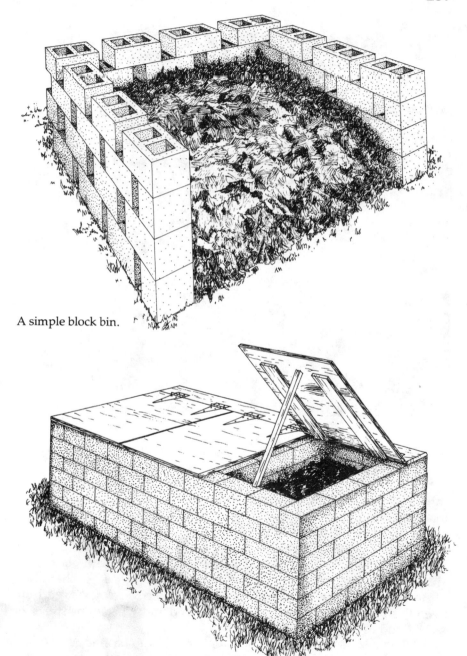

A simple block bin.

Block bins can be covered with hinged lids for a well-groomed appearance.

This variation on a standard block bin is mortared, with the inside blocks laid on their sides to permit aeration.

boards set into slots along the front opening. Boards can be removed for access to the compost.

Rough stones laid with or without mortar in an open-fronted, three-fourths circle (like a larger edition of a state park barbecue pit) make an attractive rustic bin.

Harold Burnworth of southwestern Pennsylvania spent a good deal of money—initially $70—for his 5-by-10 foot cement block bin. The Burnworth bin has a capacity of 2 to 3 tons, is covered with plastic and sits on a concrete slab. The liquid effluent—compost tea—is channeled off into an underground tub. In the spring, the cover is removed from over the tub, and the liquid is diluted and thrown around trees or shrubs and used in the kitchen garden.

"Heavy rains may require that our 5-gallon tub be emptied twice a day," reports Burnworth, "and practice will show you when the liquid is too diluted."

"Plan your construction carefully," Burnworth advises. "Insects and animals are difficult to defeat. Be certain your closures fit tightly. Prepainted or pressure-treated wood retards warping in the hot sun. Wood members should be heavy enough so rodents cannot chew holes and gain entrance. As your bin fills, pressure builds against the gate and may open it enough to admit rodents. Up to 3 tons of a soggy mass can exert great lateral pressure. Keep it wet but not soaked. After heavy rains, let it rest for a few days. The steady drip, drip, drip into your tub produces the priceless liquid that heals sick soils without wasting a drop."

Because his compost pile is also a garbage disposal, it has been placed "close enough to the kitchen for convenient use." Into it goes the familiar kitchen refuse, "bushels of cut corn shocks, apple pomace, vegetable tops, garden weeds and grass cuttings." For winter protection, it is recessed into a slope below the frost line and has a good southern exposure.

THE MOVABLE SLAT BIN

We have already discussed some movable bins. Here is another, designed by Bette Wahlfeldt. It is a sturdy wood slat design which needs no hardware for support—no hooks, nails, or screws.

To make it, she cut 10-foot-long 1 by 10 boards into 60-inch lengths,

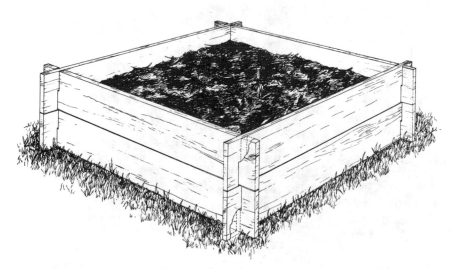

This simple bin is made from slotted boards and can be easily moved.

slotting each board 4 inches in from the end, and then 4⅝ inches across its width so that they can be nested. The finished bin is 50¼ inches square and 18½ inches high inside—perfect for even the tiniest city lot.

WINTER BIN

Winter composting does not have to be confined to a pit. Alden Stahr of Mt. Bethel, Pennsylvania, was frustrated for 15 years in his desire to compost during the winter. Finally, he rigged up a compost frame constructed very simply of four old blinds once used on his house and two storm windows which he placed to slant toward the south to pick up the long, low rays of the winter sun. Old bales of hay were stacked around the sides to serve as insulation. The glass lid kept out cats, dogs and wild animals, and prevented excessive rains or snow from over-soaking the heap, or high winds from drying it out. To help the heating process, Mr. Stahr mixed in manure with kitchen wastes.

The idea worked. The material had decomposed greatly by early spring, when it was transferred to the regular heap. One cold January morning, Mr. Stahr found a 50-degree difference between the inside and outside temperatures.

A hardware cloth cylinder
is the simplest type of pen.

PENS

The very simplest pen can hardly be called a structure at all. It is, however, quick to make, neat to use, and costs almost nothing. You just buy a length of woven wire fencing and, at the site of the compost heap, bring both ends of the fencing together to form a ring cylinder large enough to surround the heap. Fasten the ends of the cylinder together with three or four small chain snaps which you can find in a hardware

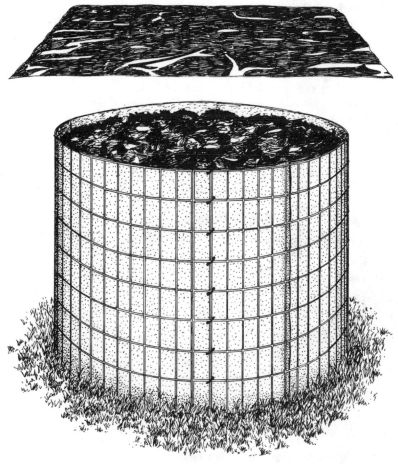

This partly anaerobic pen is lined with roll roofing and covered with a sheet of 6-mil black plastic.

store. Remove the cylinder to a free-standing position and start building the heap inside the cylinder. When it is half full, drive a stake into the pile. The stake should be as long as the total desired height. The cylinder can be removed for easy turning by removing the snaps. You set the cylinder up again and once more turn into it, shifting the ingredients from outside layers to inside, reversing the position of the material. The stake not only helps maintain the shape of the pile, but also aids in directing water into the heap.

A variation was made by Warren Tilsher of Rosemead, California, who describes his pen as "the most practical for gardeners with small plots." He advises having two for rotation.

A 30-inch-wide piece of 1-by-2-inch mesh woven-wire fencing is formed into a circle with a 30-inch diameter. Then, 30-inch lengths of roll roofing are cut, slipped inside the fencing, and wired to it. Vent holes are punched in the roofing. The roofing is durable and prevents small bits and pieces from falling out of the bin.

After the bin is full, it is covered with a layer of 6-mil plastic and the heap is left to rot. Because he doesn't take the time to turn the heap regularly, Tilsher gives the material sufficient time to compost and is very careful about the materials he uses.

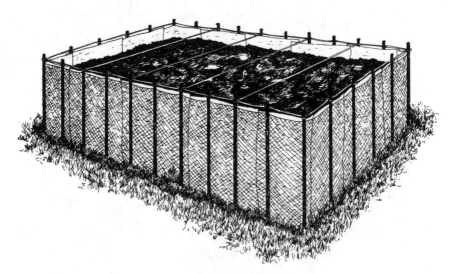

A pen made of wire mesh and tomato stakes.

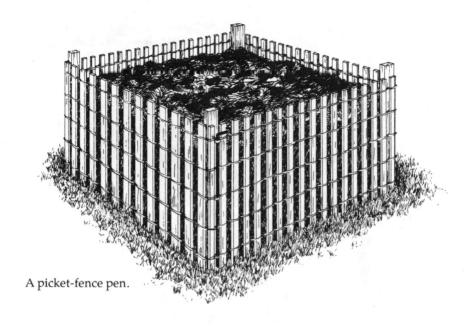

A picket-fence pen.

A refinement of the all-wire pen is the wire-and-tomato-stake pen in which one-half inch mesh poultry netting is placed inside an enclosure made by driving four-foot tomato stakes a foot apart in a 10-by-5-foot rectangle and looping baling wire around the top of each stake to weave all stakes together. Small pieces of wire hold the poultry netting to the stakes. Additional lengths of wire may also be used to reinforce the top. These pass from side to side and keep the stakes from spreading apart under the pressure of the compost. These wires are removed when the compost is turned. This type of structure is movable and reusable. However, neither it nor the simple wire pen will resist large dogs or tunneling rats.

Other materials that can be used to construct pens include snow fences, lattice fencing, steel posts and chicken wire, furring strips, prefabricated picket fence sections, woven reed or rattan fence sections, heavy window screens, storm windows with hardware cloth replacing glass, and louvered house blinds.

Pens and bins can be made to fit the contours of uneven land. One such structure consists of three bins in stair-step order going up a hill, partially cut into the bank. Compostmaking starts in the highest bin. Turning is done by dropping the partially decomposed compost down a

Stair-step bins.

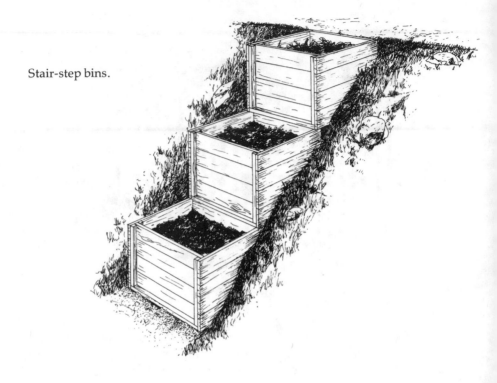

step, inverting it in the process. The third box receives the product of the second turning. From it the finished compost is used.

Pits

Pits for composting are dug into the ground and may be partially—or wholly—underground. The chief advantage of the pit form is its stable, secure, insulated structure. A masonry-lined, covered or coverable pit is secure from pouncing dogs, tunneling rats, clever racoons, most flies, and wind and rain storms. Pit composting is ideal for severe winter weather, for subsurface ground warmth and the heat-retaining properties of concrete enable bacteria to go on working longer. Some northern composters have a pen for summer and a pit for winter.

However, proper composting does not take place in a pit when compost becomes soggy and anaerobic. You must provide some drainage to lessen the possibility of anaerobic conditions. Improper aeration and the greater possibility of anaerobic conditions remain, however, the two greatest drawbacks to pit composting. We might, in fact, call them the pitfalls of this method. If you have the time to turn frequently and don't mind the extra strain on your back muscles in raising forkfuls of material from a lower than normal position, you may find ways to avoid these problems. Some pits are large and wide enough so that a person can stand down in them at pit-bottom level while turning, thus avoiding back strain.

A compost pit can be built of concrete or masonry. Other materials such as tile and pressure-treated wood are also occasionally used as pit liners. A pit must have subsurface walls to prevent drainage water from entering the compost from the soil or the ground surface. Such drainage water would leach nutrients from the compost.

Some experts suggest that a concrete pit bottom is a necessity to prevent leaching, while others prefer a natural dirt bottom which serves as a source for worms and microorganisms. Some concrete bottom proponents advise using a bottom layer of earth over the concrete, and others say that the masonry walls absorb bacteria from manure and help

This twin-bin pit has cisterns to collect run-off rainwater, which can be used as liquid fertilizer.

to "inoculate" new compost materials as they are added.

One kind of all-masonry pit has a drainage outlet and cisterns, so that leaching water or compost tea may be saved for special purposes. Elbert H. Coe, a composter who uses earthworms in his partially sunken, twin-bin pit (the two together measuring 4 feet by 10 feet, 8 inches) claims that after a heavy 1-inch rain early in the composting process, he recovered as much as 50 quarts of coffee-colored tea. His cisterns are 2-feet-square concrete containers centered behind each

A shallow, bottomless box, with or without a lid, can be combined with an earthworm pit for effective composting. If a lid is used, it is a good idea to leave some space between the boards to give the worms plenty of air.

section of his twin-bin pit. The cisterns taper down from 20 inches square at the top to 18 inches square at the bottom (inside dimensions).

In making the bins Mr. Coe set four rows of concrete blocks on a poured concrete base. The base was formed by digging a trench 8 inches wide and using cedar two-by-four lumber for the outside dimensions. After the concrete in the trench had set, he dug out the inside area, shoveling out the earth to form a slope to the rear, draining into the cisterns.

One ideal combination of a composting method and a compost-containing structure is the earthworm pit. A 10-foot square pit filled with a variety of material and watered well can support 10,000 earthworms. The more earthworms you put in the pit the faster the composting process works and the less need there is for turning the material. An earthworm pit can be of any width and length, and any shape—square, oblong, or round. It is usually masonry, tile, or poured concrete, but may be metal. Unlike ordinary piles or pits, earthworm pits should not be over 3 feet deep to prevent the high thermophilic temperatures that would kill the earthworms. Materials should be well mixed to prevent thermophilic pockets. Since earthworms dislike light but need air, a loose-fitting wooden top or boards set over the pit should be used as a cover.

One gardener combined the earthworm pit with the movable box method. He dug a rectangular hole about 18 inches deep in a flower bed. Over this he set a rectangular, bottomless and topless wooden box of slightly larger dimensions than the hole. The box frame sat at earth level above the pit. The hole was filled in layer style with kitchen garbage, manure, and green matter. When the frame was filled, too, the composter placed a board over the top and watered well. In three weeks when the heat of the pile had decreased, earthworms were added. Several pits can be made at the same time by this method, and the resulting humus can either be used where it is or distributed elsewhere.

Another successful pit is the one used by a New York State gardener. It is 4 feet wide, 4 feet deep, and 6 feet long with concrete sides and bottom. The bottom has an inset drainage grid similar to those used in basements and showers. Walls are 8 inches thick and project 18 inches above the ground. The top or roof is made of tongue-and-groove boards nailed to two-by-fours. A hinged lid provides the opening access. Earthworms do the work of aeration in this pit and garbage and leaves are the chief materials used.

An inexpensive pit may be made by digging a section of a masonry flue liner into the soil leaving about 3 inches of it projecting above ground level. A thin layer of concrete poured into the pipe serves as the bottom or floor. A small flue liner 2 feet square may not require bottom drainage if earthworms are used, but check frequently for anaerobic conditions.

Terra cotta tiles are also useful for lining pits. These can be used for the sides in combination with a hardware cloth bottom to prevent rats from getting in from underneath. If you build twin pits, you can make the turning job easier by forking from one tile-lined compartment to the other.

Drums

California gardener John Meeker solved the twin problems of running a compost pile in a congested suburban area without offending his neighbors, while getting enough compost to run his garden. He uses a steel drum raised 6 inches off the ground by a circular metal frame with legs. Other composters use 8-inch cement blocks, bricks, or even wooden bases.

There is always a bushel or two of compost ready, Meeker claims, even with so small a composter, "once the cycle has begun." This includes such seasonal bonuses as summer grass clippings, autumn leaves and crop residues which are "ready to enrich the garden by the time one gets ready for spring planting."

Meeker solves his odor problem easily enough. "When I have a large amount of lettuce leaves, beet tops, grass cuttings or kitchen refuse, I whiten the top of the dampened pile with a sprinkling of ground limestone, and over that I add a thick layer of dried steer manure. The limestone helps to decrease the smell and lessen the acidity of the green refuse and garbage."

A more complicated application of the steel-drum composter calls for nesting one drum on the bottom third of a slightly larger container, and installing a metal lattice grate between them to hold the pile up so air can get at it. Built by Ralph Poe of Canton, Illinois, the drum composter also featured a hollow, vertical, 3-inch wide pipe with quarter-inch perforations that was thrust down into the heap's center and left there for additional ventilation, as shown in the accompanying diagram.

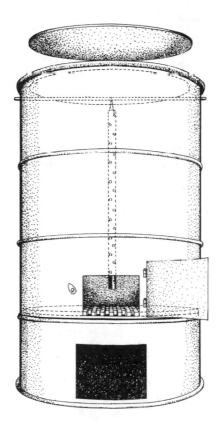

Structures for City Composting

Is there any perfect form of compost making for a city gardener? Helga and Bill Olkowski in *The City People's Book of Raising Food* suggest a well-built two- or three-bin brick structure set between two houses. Runoff is caught in sawdust at the bottom of the bin and the sawdust is turned with the pile. The Olkowskis' layer garbage as it accumulates on its way to the bin with sawdust in 5-gallon cans with tight-fitting lids. Sawdust is added every time fresh garbage is put into the can. The sawdust controls odor and putrefaction. In loading the bins, however, you should remember to compensate for the high-carbon content of the sawdust by using more high-nitrogen wastes.

(continued on page 253)

A BARREL COMPOSTER

If your composting operation is small and you neither relish nor have the time for turning garbage, then you'll find this composter suited to your needs. It is constructed with a minimum of hand-powered tools, and is not difficult or time-consuming to build.

CONSTRUCTION

1. Start by obtaining a good 55-gallon drum preferably one that has not had any toxic chemicals in it. Paint barrels are a good choice, as they already have a protective coating of paint inside. If not already painted, adding a protective coating is a good idea.

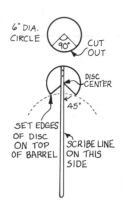

2. Drill a ½-inch hole in the exact center of both ends of the barrel to accommodate the ½-inch steel rod. (Refer to the illustration for making a simple tool to locate centers.) Hold the rounded end of the gauge anywhere along the circumference and scribe a line on the approximate center. Move the gauge 90 degrees and scribe another line. The intersection of these lines will be the exact center.

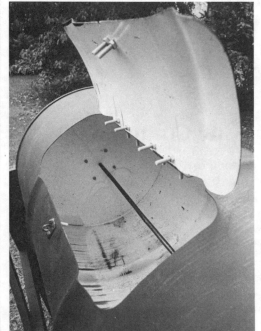

Barrel is notched at the ribs to facilitate opening the hatch.

Hinges and hasp are secured with 1-inch stove bolts.

3. Next scribe the lines for the opening in the barrel making sure to round the corners slightly. Drill a ¼-inch hole somewhere along one of the lines to start the saber saw. If your barrel has ribs, as most do, you will have to cut a 1-inch vee notch on each rib to facilitate opening the door. Attach the hinges and the hasp to the barrel and lid using 1-by-¼-inch stove bolts.

4. From ¾-inch white pine, cut two circles 7½ inches in diameter and two circles 2¾ inches in diameter. Drill a ½-inch hole in the center of each and apply glue to the 2¾-inch circles. Glue the 2¾-inch circles to the 7½-inch circles. This can be done easily if the circles are temporarily slipped over the ½-inch steel rod and clamped. After the glue has dried, remove the disks, insert the rod through the barrel, and assemble as shown in the illustration, using four 1¼-by-¼-inch stove bolts in each.

5. To build the support frame, cut the 2-by-4's to length and, using a corner lap joint, assemble with two 1½-inch #10 wood screws in each joint. The uprights will also have to be dadoed 23 inches from the bottom to accept a 1-by-3-inch board. To make a corner lap joint, simply remove one-half the thickness of the stock to a length comparable to the width of the stock on both ends of all pieces.

6. Half-inch holes to accommodate the rod will have to be drilled in the exact center of the top horizontal pieces before assembling the top portion of the support frame. Slip the ½-inch steel rod, with barrel attached, through these holes

The steel axle rod fits into ½-inch holes in the horizontal two-by-fours. Wooden bearing disks bolt onto the drum with four 1¼-inch stove bolts.

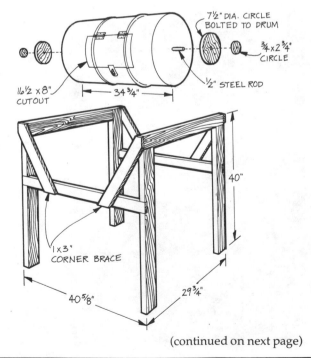

7½" DIA. CIRCLE BOLTED TO DRUM

¾ x 2¾" CIRCLE

½" STEEL ROD

16½ x 8" CUTOUT

34¾"

1 x 3" CORNER BRACE

40"

40⅝"

29¾"

(continued on next page)

and insert the cross members into the dadoed uprights. Fasten with 1½-inch #10 wood screws. Next cut the 1-by-3-by-23¼-inch piece at 45-degree angles at both ends, and attach with 1½-inch #10 wood screws across corners as shown in the illustration.

7. Drill several rows of ¼-inch holes along the bottom of the barrel exactly underneath the door opening to eliminate excess moisture. Paint the unit a flat black color.

MATERIALS

1—55-gallon drum (composter)
4—40 x 2 x 4″ (frame uprights)
4—29¾ x 2 x 4″ (frame horizontals)
2—40⅝ x 1 x 3″ (cross braces) white pine
4—23¾ x 1 x 3″ (corner braces) white pine
2—7½″ dia. x ¾″ (bearings) white pine
2—2¾″ dia. x ¾″ (bearings) white pine
2—1½ x 2″ hinges
1—small hasp
1—½ x 40½″ steel rod
8—¼ x 1¼″ stove bolts
12—¼ x 1″ stove bolts
28—1½″ #10 wood screws
Also approximately 1 pint of flat black paint.

For uniform compost, the barrel is rotated several times whenever new material is added. Air holes are drilled opposite the opening.

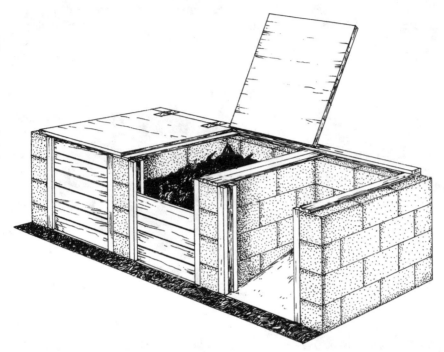

A covered, multi-bin structure is recommended for composting in urban areas.

Other city gardeners who lack even a small space between houses have composted successfully in garbage pails and metal drums. The danger with these methods is that they may quite easily go anaerobic and ferment. If you think it is hard enough dealing with garbage in a city, you should try to take care of a huge drum of fermented garbage. If, however, you really need to try these methods, provide aeration and drainage with holes in the bottom and sides of the drum or can. Set it in the basement or another protected area, preferably outdoors or on a flat roof. Elevate the can or drum on bricks or concrete blocks and set a pan larger in diameter than the drum underneath it to catch drainage. Layer garbage with high-carbon content materials just as you would in a regular pile. Composting is not really an indoor activity, and turning is especially hard to do in a limited space. We can only report that some people have succeeded in making compost in this manner.

Another much more sensible method is the indoor earthworm box which we discussed in Chapter 9. Worms are easily raised in basements

Special Project:

THREE-STORY TELESCOPING COMPOST BOX

To provide access to mature compost at any time, rather than having to wait for a pile to finish decomposing, Mr. C. A. Hensley of Victoria, British Columbia, designed a triple-decker telescoping compost box. Convenient to fill and mix, this arrangement allows even ventilation to all layers.

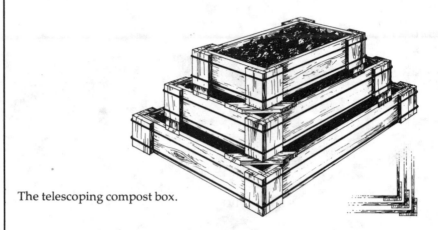

The telescoping compost box.

To begin a pile, the bottom box is filled, mixed and dampened, until overflowing. Second and third boxes are added as volume increases. As the heap settles, the two upper boxes are supported by 1-by-3-inch pieces at each corner. On further settling, the upper boxes are propped higher on bricks, flower pots or cans to increase capacity.

When the bottom layer is finished (usually by midsummer) the Hensleys telescope off the bottom box and use part of it to start the next season's heap. This leaves mature compost on the sides and ends of the bottom layer accessible for summer use.

The frames are made of oil-treated 1-by-10-inch boards, with 1-by-6-inch crosspieces at the ends for strong joints. Nails are 2¼ inch, well clinched across the grain. Each box is bound with two galvanized wires, drawn tight and stapled at the corners.

The size of the boxes is easily adapted to meet the gardener's needs. The Hensley's bottom box is 4 by 5 feet, with the other two boxes 6 inches and 12 inches smaller each way.

An alternative to the 1-by-6 crosspieces at the corners would be angles of heavy-gauge galvanized iron. This would permit the boxes to differ in size by only 2 to 3 inches, increasing total capacity.

where fairly stable temperature conditions can be maintained. Worms do the turning in worm boxes and the results of their labors are rich worm castings for compost and perhaps a little extra income for you during fishing season. If you live in an apartment, it would be just as well to discuss composting or worm-raising plans with your landlord before launching your career. Some city dwellers have strange prejudices.

Novel Ideas and Clever Adaptations

Every now and then, a composting idea comes along that staggers us with its simplicity and good sense. Samuel N. Fisher of Citrus Heights, California, persuaded his children that their above-ground portable swimming pool had seen its last season, and then he proceeded to appropriate it for parts of a compost bin. With a section 16 feet long from the sheet of aluminium that formed the outside of the pool he fashioned a 4-foot square bin braced with upright pipes and the connecting bars that came with the pool. The enclosure holds 56 cubic feet of compost. It is reinforced with long boards which serve as a brace and are sawed off flush with the connecting rods.

Improvisation on a smaller scale went into one Missouri gardener's use of bales of spoiled hay to build a temporary winter bin.

Commercial Composters

There are now several very good commercially built composting units on the market. In general, these are built on the principle of the revolving drum or the upright cylinder. They are designed to make compost in a short time, since they provide good aeration, and the manufacturers have gone to great lengths to ensure that their operation requires little physical exertion on the part of the user.

A list of known manufacturers of these units is included in the Appendix of this book. In general, the units are designed for the small-lot city gardener who wants to make compost quickly, without offending the neighbors by releasing unpleasant odors or attracting animals. Although we cannot recommend one unit over another, we do think that any city gardener who wants to have an efficient and attractive composting unit, and is willing to pay $25 or more for it, will do well to include one of these among his options.

11

Shredders and Other Special Equipment

Compost can easily be made without mechanical equipment. However, *more* compost can be made—in a shorter time—when the materials are first shredded or ground. For this reason, the compost shredder has become a standard fixture in many gardens and small farms, often second in importance only to the rotary tiller. In response to gardeners' demands, manufacturers have continued to improve the design and construction of shredders, so that today's models bear little resemblance to those primitive, bulky, and often dangerous models of 25 years ago.

The advantages conferred by the compost shredder upon its owner are many and impressive. Here are some of them:

1. Speed—your compost piles really will heat up and break down within two weeks because the shredder chews the compostable materials into small bits, making the job of the bacteria much easier.
2. Quantity—you'll have plenty of compost when you need it, providing you keep working at the shredder.
3. Quality—you'll have better, more uniform compost because the shredder breaks up the materials more thoroughly.
4. Mixtures—you can "mix your own" right at the machine, to insure a balance of nutrients or to make a compost specially designed to meet the needs of your soil.
5. Variety—you can set up a program using different kinds of mulches and composts which you want in various parts of the garden, easily and readily.

There is another factor about the compost shredder which will appeal to the hard-working gardener—it's a tool that you can bring to

256

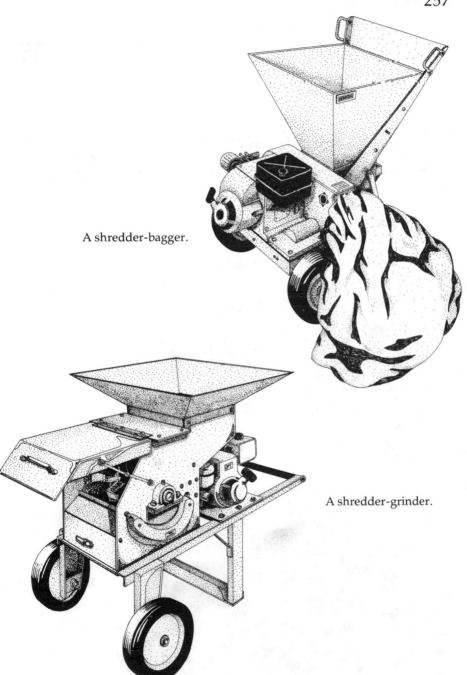

A shredder-bagger.

A shredder-grinder.

the work. This is a real boon to the compost maker who wants to have several heaps piled up in his garden where he will need them. The movable shredder makes this easy because it can go to work wherever the ground is reasonably level.

Compost shredders are designed to do big garden jobs for you. First they can speed and ease your task of preparing mulches. Today it is widely known that cut up and macerated leaves, weeds and other similar material make much better mulch than the rough raw product because they hold moisture better and form a thicker blanket which chokes off the weeds.

The shredder is a real friend in need when you are getting ready to build your compost heap. Again, it will take the raw stock and chew it

A small, electric-powered shredding machine can be used to shred kitchen wastes and for other small jobs.

A close-up view of the rotating knife of a wood chipper.

Soil Conservation Service photo

into the kind of shape that eases the job of the bacteria in your pile.

A third use which contributes to the shredder popularity today is the grinding and pulverizing job it can do with finished compost. The fine compost that can be achieved is ideal for potting soil and for use on lawns, flowerbeds, in greenhouses and in other "high-quality" jobs.

There are two main kinds of shredders: the low center of gravity shredder/bagger with its big-mouth hopper, and the classic stand-up shredder/grinder designed to handle a greater volume and variety of materials. *Organic Gardening* researchers have worked extensively with both kinds and have achieved the results they sought. (For a listing of shredder manufacturers, see the Appendix.)

Many combinations of accessories and functions are now available

Large-scale wood chippers are used by nursery owners and municipal crews to shred discarded Christmas trees, tree prunings, and large quantities of other tree wastes.

in one machine. The once-reluctant gas engine has been made a lot more dependable and easier to start. You can also find electric-powered shredders which are much quieter, simple to start, and also free of fumes. But they have to stay closer to the house and there is always the danger of playing around with electricity outdoors on the damp ground.

Many shredders—both low-profile baggers and the bigger grinders—are equipped with a chipping fixture that is usually a rotating knife which operates through a side slot and can handle branches up to 2 or even 3 inches thick.

Then, there are the shredder accessories or attachments that fit onto a small riding tractor or a walking power unit that also functions as a rotary tiller, a mower, a chipper, a snow blower, or even a dozer blade.

Jamming and Clogging

Overloading the machine—any machine—will result in jamming and stalling it. This especially holds for the shredder whose job it is to chop up fibrous, damp, or wet materials and then eject them through a screen or grid. The best idea is to work with as large a screen as

If possible, leaves should be shredded when they are dry. If you must shred wet, soggy leaves, remove the screen from your shredder to prevent jamming and clogging the machine.

possible—1¾ inches is ideal. Some manufacturers offer a grating of rods or square roller bars that seem to be nearly jam-proof. Another solution to the problem is a rack which encloses only half the shredding chamber, available on some models.

If you are shredding very wet, soggy, and rubbery leaves, here's a sure way to eliminate frustration and loss of time: remove the screen. Without it, the action of the cutters chops the leaves into a satisfactory aggregate which can be used either for compost or mulch. If you are working with a shredder/bagger, you might find that it speeds up the process to remove the bag. You will also find that it's a good idea to deposit the aggregate immediately into the compost pile or the planting row.

A clutch—either centrifugal, which depends upon the speed of the motor to activate it, or one that is manually operated—helps to avoid jams. This calls for alert operation of the machine, but it can save a lot of time spent in clearing out the innards of your shredder. Some models also offer a king-sized, spring-held stone-ejection plate that is a real timesaver. A quick tug on its handle opens up the mixing chamber and spills the damp mass out to save you still another jam. By all means, ask about these plates when shopping around for a shredder.

Bringing the Machine to the Work

Wheels are important. In the spring and autumn, you will want to wheel your shredder right down the garden rows, shredding leaves and crop residues right where the next crop will be planted. Check the wheels on the shredders you are considering. They should have at least a pair, rugged and rubber-tired, and placed so that they will support the machine with ease, comfort, and safety when you move it. Some of the larger models come with three wheels, and some have four. Make sure that the machine you are thinking of buying handles easily over rough ground.

The Cutting Mechanisms

There are three or four basic systems for reducing and mixing your organic wastes. Hammermill tempered steel flails revolve freely on a rotating shaft, and so have the ability to absorb shocks from hitting stones. There also seems to be a minimum of blockage in the mixing chamber caused by wet materials.

Sets of hardened steel teeth or knives, fixed rigidly on a revolving shaft, work in combination with interior baffle plates and the bottom screen which, together, tend to keep the material in contact with the knives.

The smaller shredder/bagger machines work with a series of two or three rotary blades similar to those of a lawn mower. In some models, these whirling knives pass between stationary cutters that are part of the frame or chassis to achieve more complete cutting. The turbulence created by the rotary blades also whirls the aggregate out through the vent which, as noted, permits you to deposit it right where it is needed—either in the compost pile or in the planting row.

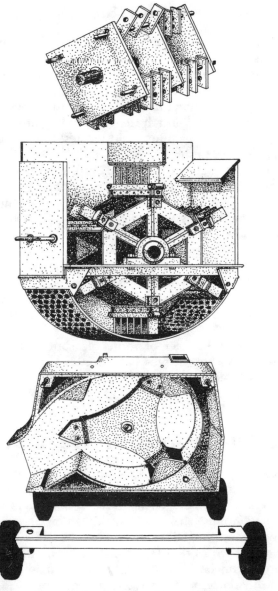

The three types of cutting mechanisms used in most shredders are:
(top) steel flails which revolve freely on a rotating shaft;
(middle) fixed steel knives on a revolving shaft, that work in combination with
    baffle plates and the bottom screen;
(bottom) rotary blades similar to those on a lawn mower.

Materials

Anything that is organic and compostable, and can be reduced to a workable aggregate or mass in your shredder, is grist to your grinding mill. Large-scale gardeners find that there is plenty of material on the home grounds to keep the shredder busy for a series of weekends, particularly in the late summer and fall. There are the weeds, the grass clippings, the crop residues, and the leaves. Add to these the contents of your garbage pail and other household wastes, and you will have no trouble finding material to shred.

Next, you might be able to get wood chips from the municipal road department, sawdust from a local lumberyard, and corncobs from the nearest feedmill. All of these varieties of cellulose are fine for mixing with the garbage (so long as the cobs are ground up). If the cobs have not been ground, then you should go slowly. Experimentation is called for here, since tough cobs have a habit of flying back up out of the hopper, right at your head. Some *Organic Gardening* readers have reported that a thorough soaking—up to a week under water—of the cobs softens them and makes shredding easier and less dangerous. In addition, some of the larger machines can handle cobs with no difficulty at all.

No garden chore is easier or more pleasant than shredding dry autumn leaves. But if your leaves have wintered over and are tough, wet, and rubbery, feed them into the shredder in very small handfuls which are followed by dry sawdust, and again, be prepared to do this kind of shredding without a screen.

Shredder Design and Wet Materials

Al Wonch, a gardener from La Port, Indiana, believes that the design of the machine has much to do with its efficiency in shredding wet or dry materials. In general terms, he says, shredders can be divided into two groups. Group 1 shredders work well on dry or damp refuse, but perform poorly on wet, sticky compost, soils and manures. Group 2 shredders handle both dry and wet materials, though some designs within this group work better on wet materials than others.

Why this difference between these two groups? The main reason lies in the design of the rotor assembly and its relationship to the feed hopper throat. Figure 1 shows the generalized construction and refuse flow of Group 1 shredders. The feed hopper is mounted on the side of

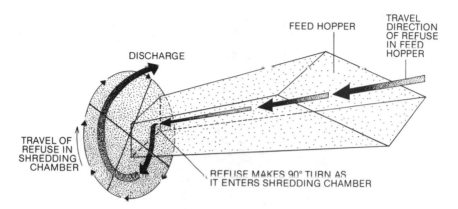

Figure 1: Group 1 shredder.

the shredding chamber, and the rotor assembly (the rotating hardware that does the shredding) passes in front of the hopper throat at 90 degrees to the movement of refuse in the hopper. When the refuse enters the shredding chamber, the rotor assembly blades smash into it. Because the rotor assembly spins rapidly, the time interval between blades striking the refuse is very short. Therefore, the rotor blades smash the material into very small pieces. The spinning rotor assembly sucks the fragments around the circular shredding chamber before they're blown from the discharge chute.

Figure 2 shows a typical shredder with rigid tines on the periphery of the rotor assembly. The tines are short, narrow pieces of steel which tear refuse apart. For fragment size control, most rigid-tine shredders use some combination of (1) adjustable discharge door; (2) semipermanent screen or bar grate; or (3) baffle plate.

The baffle plate forces the refuse in the shredding chamber against the tines. A powerful spring holds the baffle closed while the rotor assembly tries to push refuse past the baffle. The greater the spring tension, the more the baffle will slow the travel of refuse through the shredder. Once shredded refuse moves past the baffle, the tines carry the fragments over a curved piece of perforated metal.

If the piece of metal has round holes, it's called perforated metal. If it has slots, it's called a bar grate. The screens and bar grates in this style shredder are securely bolted to the lower front of the shredding chamber. Fragments smaller than the holes or slots are driven through, while larger pieces are swept around the shredding chamber and further

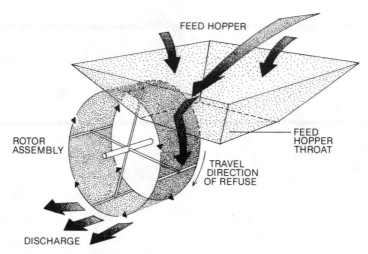

Figure 2: Group 2 shredder design.

reduced in size. Screens and bar grates perform well for sizing dry leaves, stems and vines. The fragments pass easily through the screen and pile up near the front of the shredder.

But if you try shredding wet, sticky material, the screens and bar grates will soon plug. Therefore, most rigid-tine shredders have an adjustable discharge door located at the top front of the shredding chamber. The rotor assembly twirls any soggy refuse around the shredding chamber, across the plugged screen, and to the open discharge door where it is kicked from the shredder. Since this refuse is only partly shredded, when your pile is drier, you'll probably want to reshred it with the discharge door partly closed. This second shredding will give you smaller fragments, which will decompose quicker in your compost pile.

However, if you want to aerate wet, half-finished compost, you may run into problems. Since wet refuse tends to plug screens, you may have to remove the screen before feeding the refuse. Shredding without a screen won't give you much size reduction, but will aerate your compost, thus speeding it toward complete decomposition.

Using the Shredder

It took Ellie Van Wicklin, a composter who now depends on her shredder, a day or so to get up the courage to use it for the first time. She

Stalks and other plant materials that would take a long time to decompose if left whole are easily shredded for quicker composting.

says that shredding pea vines and bean plants was the trickiest operation she had to perform because the tendrils and stems of the plants have a tendency to wrap around the ends of the drive shaft or roller. She now feeds them through by pushing the central stem of one plant down through the branches of the next, making a compact clump of several plants at one time and then feeding the clump to the machine. Ellie finds that corn stalks, tomato vines and asparagus stalks, even tall goldenrod plants—materials that would have taken a long time to decompose unchopped—are quickly shredded.

Peter Tonge, another gardener who considers a shredder indispensable, suggests using wood chips to unclog a shredder and keep it operating efficiently when working with soft, green vegetation. The brittle chips break up quickly and fly out, taking the softer, clinging material with them. Like most experienced compost makers, Peter shreds all the materials he uses—from leaves to manure—at the same time. He finds it easy to mix materials this way. He also reshreds the compost after it has started to decompose. By this method, he is able to obtain a rich, crumbly compost and also a small quantity of fibrous residues which he uses for mulching.

Reshredding compost material after it has begun to decompose will yield a finer, richer product.

Some composters have found that partially rotted hay goes through the shredder much more quickly than dry hay or straw. Wet corncobs shred more easily than dry ones, but wet leaves often clog a small machine.

Safety First

It is a good idea to get into the habit of wearing both safety shoes and safety glasses when operating the shredder. If yours is an electric model, be certain that it is properly grounded, and do not operate it under wet or damp conditions. To avoid danger in feeding materials into the hopper, make use of a flexible stick as a pusher. A large sunflower stalk works well and later can be fed to the machine as "dessert." A rigid stick may jam the machine, or even bounce back to injure the operator. It is also well to stand clear of the exhaust chute while the machine is in operation. Flying shreds and pellets of cellulose can feel like buckshot. Some shredder or mulcher models come with pivoting metal rods with which the operator maneuvers the material into place and directs it downward. The temptation is to use your hands instead. Resist this temptation. Shredders have no way of discriminating between sticks and fingers, and will shred either quite easily.

Rent or Buy?

Gardeners on a small scale might find that the most economical way to gain the advantages of a shredder without making the investment is to rent a machine in the spring and in the fall, and to prepare enough material for several compost piles at one time. Material to be shredded can be stored in heaps located strategically around the garden, until the shredder is rented. Materials, once shredded, can again be stored until garbage or partially rotted manure becomes available to use with it. It is less important to grind soft garbage than to reduce the size of fibrous material; and, since garbage is often the slowest material to accumulate and the hardest to store, stockpiles of fibrous material already shredded are handy to have around.

Rental fees for shredder use are high, but then so are the costs of purchasing shredders. Part of the high rental rates reflects the fact that shredders are in high demand during certain weeks of the year, while they stand idle for most of the rest of the year. Nevertheless, if you can manage your operations so that you can get by with shredding facilities for only a few days of the year, then you will save money by renting one.

A shredder also lends itself well to group ownership. A garden club, a group of friends, or a neighborhood might well consider making a joint investment, sharing the responsibilities for its care and fueling.

One Gardener's Experience

Lois Patterson of Houston, Texas, likes to do her shredding on Sunday. She reports that she uses her shredder to combine family garbage with other compostable material. She shreds enough material to fill three bins, and now finds that the shredder has become an integral part of her gardening operations. "It all began," she says, "when, tired of turning one heap into another for the third time in as many weeks, I decided that there must be an easier way to make compost.

"I sat down in the shade to rest, somewhat consoled by the fact that each time I turned the compost the leaves and hunks of earth and manure were smaller, and would eventually turn into fertile, fluffy soil. If they were in small pieces to begin with, I reasoned, wouldn't they break down sooner and eliminate a lot of shoveling?

"Eureka! A shredder would take care of that.

"I bought one, and if I were to insure it I'd place its value at many times what I paid for it. I don't turn compost any more. I use the time-honored practice of layering garden, yard and kitchen wastes with soil and manure. At some time before the wire bin is full, I run the contents through the shredder into an adjoining bin and water it, then let it alone. It heats up and decomposes rapidly with no further effort from me.

"Meanwhile, in the first bin I start accumulating another heap to await the shredder. This goes on the year around, and I'm seldom without a few wheelbarrow loads of finished compost when I need it.

"As vegetables such as corn, tomatoes, okra and eggplant complete their life cycles, I roll the shredder into the garden and shred the plants as I pull them up, letting the pieces fall right back into the garden where they belong. I don't have to move them to the compost heap, turn it several times, then haul it back and spread it."

Substitutes for the Shredder
THE ROTARY MOWER

If you have no access to a shredder or grinder, you can use a rotary mower to grind up straw, weeds, and leaves. Sometimes a mower works even better than a shredder on dry leaves.

For mowers with side exit ports, use a carton or fence, or the side of your compost bin as a backstop. If your mower can be adjusted, set it for cutting high. Pile up the material in low piles. Then depress the handle of your mower and push the machine forward until the blades are positioned directly above the pile. Lower the machine gradually into the pile, lifting it and dropping it again several times. If the mower seems to be on the point of stalling, depress the handle again to lift up the cutting blades. For really fine grinding, repeat the process. The mowers advertised as "self-mulching" are ideal for this use, since they cut the materials more than once on a single pass.

A CONVERTED AND MOUNTED REEL MOWER

A reel lawn mower can be converted into a shredder by making a suitable frame for it. Remove the handle and braces of the mower and

An old reel mower can be converted to use as a tabletop shredder.

mount it in such a position that the cutting bar is flush with the bottom of the feeding trough of a wooden table. A simple wooden table can be constructed of scrap lumber. It should be of a convenient height and braced with stout boards. The feeding trough on the table top should have sides 3 or 4 inches high and a bottom which will permit easy feeding of material. It is desirable to line the trough with a smooth, hard-surfaced material such as masonite or galvanized metal.

The machine may be operated by hand, or with a motor mounted on a platform attached to the leg or frame of the table. For hand operation, drill a small hole halfway between the center and edge of one wheel and, with a bolt and nut, attach a handle. For machine operation, a small pulley is attached to the motor, while a relatively larger pulley is attached to the lawn mower wheel.

A rectangular piece of board with a handle makes a handy pusher for material being fed to the machine. The operator uses the pusher with his left hand while operating the machine with his right hand—or vice-versa for southpaws.

One gardener made a power-run shredder from a reel mower by using a secondhand ¼ h.p. washing machine motor with a 2-inch pulley. The mower was set into a support frame 19 inches wide and 28 inches long. The cutting edge of the reel mower was set up so that leaves could be fed to the machine in a way similar to the way the machine cuts grass, except that after it had been converted, the machine was stationary and the material moved toward it. The Oregon gardener who constructed this model said it could cut up dry leaves at the rate of a bushel every few minutes.

Building your own shredder can save you quite a bit of money, but always remember that even more care should be exercised when working with homemade machines than when using purchased ones which have been designed with safety features.

THE MEAT CLEAVER

Helga and Bill Olkowski in *The City People's Book of Raising Food* report that they discovered that coarse materials like melon rinds, dry weed stalks, or straw decompose more rapidly when cut into short lengths of from 3 to 8 inches. Convinced of the need to reduce the size of their materials, the Olkowskis bought a shredder. The noise, the danger, the tendency to jam, and the fuel consumption of their machine soon persuaded them that they had made an unwise investment. Finally, they went back to their old method of using a cleaver to shred and chop material.

We mention the Olkowskis' experience because we want to point out once more that the choice of grinding or chopping method, like the many other choices in composting, is up to you. No one will tell you that you must have a shredder to make good compost. Composters agree that shredders and grinders save time, especially in large gardens. Shredded material composts more rapidly, and machine shredding is quicker than hand shredding. Time saving, then, is on one side of the ledger. Fuel consumption, machine cost, and noise are on the other side. Only you can place a value on your time in relationship to these other factors.

THE MEAT GRINDER

Some composters use meat grinders, electric blenders, or food processors to reduce household garbage to particles. Meat grinders are painfully slow. Blenders are quicker, but rapidly reduce garbage to a pulp which tends to cake when dried out. Food processors are perfect—highly efficient, miniature shredders that will quickly and easily shred materials to your specifications.

Kitchen garbage, of course, doesn't have to be shredded or ground in order to break down sufficiently, since it is the first thing to be attacked by bacteria in the compost heap. Nevertheless, shredding does speed up the process.

THE DISPOSAL WITH A DIFFERENCE

Another means of grinding garbage is a sink disposal unit made with a special trap for saving the garbage after grinding, instead of adding it to our already overtaxed sewers where it is lost to the garden. One model spin-dries shredded garbage so that it is in perfect condition for adding to the compost heap.

Tillers and Tractors

Rotary tillers and garden tractors with tiller attachments are valuable tools in the composting process—particularly in sheet composting and green manuring.

Green manure plants, which can add tremendous amounts of organic matter to the soil, are easily handled with the proper garden power equipment. Fertility-building crops such as rye, clover, and buckwheat can be fitted into the garden rotation schedule. The practice is especially worthwhile in large gardens, where at little cost, time, or effort, a great amount of organic matter is returned to the soil.

Green manuring is an idea and a method that has long been used by farmers to build soil, but has largely been overlooked by gardeners. By taking full advantage of tillers and garden tractors, however, you can do as good a green manuring job as any farmer. You can work into the soil a green manure crop that soon will decay into fertile humus.

Sheet composting is accomplished by spreading extra organic material on the bare ground, or over a green manure crop. Then, both the crop and the extra material are tilled into the soil, where they will quickly decompose.

Green manuring and sheet composting are often more efficient methods than heap composting, since the decay occurs right in the soil and there is no turning and far less hauling of materials.

The secret behind fast sheet composting is rotary tilling. For example, suppose that, at the end of the summer, you have several good stands of flowers or other plant debris, which you ordinarily gather up and take to the compost heap. Unless shredded, they can take anywhere from three to six months to decompose. But with a rotary tiller, you can

Green manuring adds large amounts of organic matter to the soil. The crop (in this case, rye) is sown in fall, and turned under early the following spring.

till them in to a depth of 3 or 4 inches, and—at the end of only a few weeks—you will find scarcely a trace of the plants left. Instead there will be only a more fertile soil.

The tiller and the shredder, in fact, go hand in hand in any large gardening operation. Using both to maximum advantage, the gardener can gain farmlike efficiency on even a half-acre plot.

12

Using Compost

Your compost is finished. After carefully following the recommended steps for turning the year's bounty of organic materials into rich, mellow humus, you want to be certain that it's used to your best advantage—that it benefits your soil most and helps to insure a natural abundance and health in your coming crops.

It is not possible to stress too heavily the "soil bank account" theory of fertilizing. The real purpose of the organic method is to build permanent fertility into the soil by adding to its natural rock mineral reserves and to its humus content. Practically all the natural fertilizers are carriers of insoluble plant food. They start working quickly, but they don't drop their load of food all at once, as does a soluble fertilizer. An insoluble fertilizer will work for you for months and years.

So you can see that, as an organic gardener or farmer, you are adding fertilizer not only to supply immediate plant food needs, but also to build up the reserves that future crops will draw upon.

When to Apply Compost

The principal factor in determining when to apply compost is its condition. If it is half finished, or noticeably fibrous, it could well be applied in October or November. By spring it will have completed its decomposition in the soil itself and will be ready to supply growth nutrients to the earliest plantings made. Otherwise, for general soil enrichment, the ideal time for applying compost is a month or so before planting. The closer to planting time it is incorporated, the more it should be ground up or worked over thoroughly with a hoe to finely shred it. The special tools and equipment we discussed in Chapter 11 will come in handy when you wish to add compost to your soil close to planting time.

If your compost is ready in the fall and is not intended to be used until the spring, keep it in a protected place. If it is kept for a long period during the summer, water the finished compost from time to time.

For organic farmers and gardeners, it's not a bad idea to make applications of compost either in the fall or winter or in the early spring. The big advantage here is that application at such a time helps to equalize the workload. Usually this time of year is the least crowded with busy schedules, and the farmer or gardener can devote more time to doing a good job without interfering with the rest of the crop program. Also, there is less chance of damaging the soil or of injuring crops.

It is a good idea to give the garden a dressing of compost in the midst of the growing season, when plants are mining the soil for nutrients and the soil microorganisms that make the nutrients in compost available to plants are at their most active.

Photo by Jerry Gentry

Just before the spring plowing is a particularly good time to apply fertilizer. Then when the plowing is done, the fresh organic matter can be worked down into the soil to supply food for the spring soil organisms. These organisms are what give life to the spring soil. They become active and start to grow at about freezing temperatures. However, soil temperatures must rise to 50°F. (10°C.) before they really take on the dynamic action that so characterizes a living organic soil. In early spring, the temperature is just about to rise to the level where the vital soil organisms can make use of it.

In summer, plants take more nutrients from the soil than they do in any other season. Everyone knows that. But perhaps you didn't realize that in summer the soil has more nutrients available to give to plants than at any other time of the year. During the summer the increased activity of bacteria and other soil microorganisms is primarily responsible for the abundance of plant food. These same microorganisms are one of the primary forces that act on organic and natural rock fertilizers to make them available to plants. It is a good idea, then, to apply these natural fertilizers when the activity of microorganisms is greatest.

Summer can be a fine time to apply compost and the natural rock fertilizers—rock and colloidal phosphate, greensand, granite dust and diabase dust. Organic fertilizers of all types are needed even more in the summer, because they hold moisture in the soil and stimulate the bacterial activity that takes place during the warm months. You will get a fast return on your money, and the added fertility will quickly transform itself into strong roots and tops. The nutrients you add in the summer will continue to benefit your plants next year and the year after.

General Rules for Applying Compost

Apply at least ½ inch to 3 inches of compost over your garden each year. There is little if any danger of burning due to overuse, as is the case with chemical fertilizers. You can apply compost either once or twice a year. The amount would depend, of course, on the fertility of your soil and on what and how much has been grown in it.

When applying either half-finished or finished compost to your soil, turn over the soil thoroughly and mix the compost in with the top 4 inches of soil. If you have a rotary tiller, you can simply spread the compost on the soil surface and go over it a few times to work it in.

To improve the structure and fertility of poor soil quickly, give it a thorough compost treatment in the fall. Spade it 12 to 18 inches deep

Half-finished compost can be tilled into the garden in the fall. Leaving the garden rough-surfaced will allow winter's freezes and thaws to mellow the compost by spring planting time.

and mix in all the half-rotted compost you have. Then leave the surface rough and cloddy so that the freezing and thawing of winter will mellow it (or plant a green manure crop that will add more fertility when it is dug or tilled under in the spring).

Putting compost down deep in the soil will also give your plants built-in protection against drought. Having humus down in the lower levels of your soil means that moisture will be held there where plant roots can get all they need in dry weather.

Too, this moisture will prevent the plants from starving during drought, since their roots can pick up food only when it is in liquid form.

The Vegetable Garden

Your vegetable garden will thrive if you give it liberal amounts of compost. Dig it in during the fall, bury it in trenches, put it in the

COMPOST APPLICATION GUIDE FOR VEGETABLES

Nutrient Requirements
EH = Extra Heavy   M = Moderate
H = Heavy   L = Light

Vegetable	Nitrogen	Phosphorus	Potassium	pH factor
Asparagus	EH	H	EH	6.0–7.0
Beans, bush	L	M	M	6.0–7.5
lima	L	M	M	5.5–6.5
Beets, early	EH	EH	EH	5.8–7.0
late	H	EH	H	same
Broccoli	H	H	H	6.0–7.0
Cabbage, early	EH	EH	EH	6.0–7.0
late	H	H	H	same
Carrots, early	H	H	H	5.5–6.5
late	M	M	M	same
Cauliflower, early	EH	EH	EH	6.0–7.0
late	H	H	EH	same
Corn, early	H	H	H	6.0–7.0
late	M	M	M	same
Cucumbers	H	H	H	6.0–8.0
Eggplant	H	H	H	6.0–7.0
Lettuce, head	EH	EH	EH	6.0–7.0
leaf	H	EH	EH	same
Muskmelons	H	H	H	6.0–7.0
Onions	H	H	H	6.0–7.0
Parsley	H	H	H	5.0–7.0
Parsnips	M	M	M	6.0–8.0
Peas	M	H	H	6.0–8.0
Potatoes, white	EH	EH	EH	4.8–6.5
sweet	L	M	H	5.0–6.0 or 6.0–7.0
Radishes	H	EH	EH	6.0–8.0
Rutabaga	M	H	M	6.0–8.0
Soybeans	L	M	M	6.0–7.0
Spinach	EH	EH	EH	6.5–7.0
Squash, summer	H	H	H	6.0–8.0
winter	M	M	M	6.0–8.0
Tomatoes	M	H	H	6.0–7.0
Turnips	L	H	M	6.0–8.0

furrows when you plant and in the holes when transplanting seedlings. When the plants begin to grow rapidly, mix compost with equal amounts of soil and use it as a top-dressing; or mulch the plants heavily with partially rotted compost or with such raw compost materials as hay, straw, sawdust, grass clippings, or shredded leaves.

One rule to remember when mulching is: the finer the material, the thinner the layer you will need.

This kind of treatment will give you a rich, loamy, friable soil that will reward you with big yields of all kinds of vegetables, without fear of drought, disease, or insect troubles.

For sowing seeds indoors or in a cold frame, put your compost through a ½-inch sieve, then shred it with a hoe or even roll it with a rolling pin to make it very fine. Then mix it with equal amounts of sand and soil. The ideal seeding mixture is fine-textured and crumbly, and tends to fall apart after being squeezed in your hand.

Applying a layer of compost to flower beds in autumn affords extra winter protection for perennials and builds better soil for the annuals to be planted in spring.

The Flower Garden

Finely screened compost is excellent to put around all growing flowers. Apply it alone as an inch-thick mulch to control weeds and conserve moisture, or top-dress it mixed with soil. In the spring, you can loosen the top few inches of soil in your annual and perennial beds and work into it an equal quantity of compost. And use compost generously when sowing flower seeds.

Compost watering is an excellent way to give your flowers supplementary feeding during their growing season. Fill a watering can half-full of compost, add water and sprinkle liberally around the plants. The can may be refilled with water several times before the compost loses its potency.

Plenty of compost has been found to keep the moisture level of the flower bed too high for ants, an extra plus for flower gardeners.

Your Lawn

To build a lawn that stays green all summer, has no crabgrass, and rarely needs watering, use compost liberally when making and maintaining it. Your goal is to produce a thick sod with roots that go down 6 inches, not a thin, weed-infested mat laying on a layer of infertile subsoil.

In building a new lawn, work in copious amounts of compost to a depth of at least 6 inches. If your soil is either sandy or clayey (rather than a good loam), you'll need at least a two-inch depth of compost, mixed in thoroughly, to build it up. The best time to make a new lawn is in the fall. But if you want to get started in the spring, dig in your compost and plant Italian ryegrass, vetch or soybeans, which will look quite neat all summer. Then dig this green manure in at the end of summer and make your permanent lawn when cool weather comes.

To renovate an old, patchy lawn, dig up the bare spots about 2 inches deep, work in plenty of finished compost, tamp and rake well, and sow your seed after soaking the patches well.

Feed your lawn regularly every spring. An excellent practice is to use a spike tooth aerator, then spread a mixture of fine finished compost and bone meal. Rake this into the holes made by the aerator. You can use a fairly thick covering of compost—just not so thick it covers the grass. This will feed your lawn efficiently and keep it sending down a dense mass of roots that laugh at drought.

When planting a tree, make the planting hole twice the size of the root ball, and fill in around the tree with a compost-rich planting mixture.

Trees and Shrubs

"A 5-dollar hole for a 50-cent plant"—that's the rule the experts follow in planting new trees and shrubs. A good job of planting will pay off in faster-growing, sturdier specimens every time.

Always make the planting hole at least twice the size of the root ball in all directions. The best planting mixture we have found is made up of equal parts of compost, topsoil, and peat moss or leaf mold. Fill this in carefully around the plant, tamping it down as you put in each spadeful.

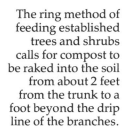
The ring method of feeding established trees and shrubs calls for compost to be raked into the soil from about 2 feet from the trunk to a foot beyond the drip line of the branches.

Soak the ground well, then spread an inch or two of compost on top. A mulch of leaves, hay and the like will help keep the soil moist and control weeds.

Established shrubs should be fed yearly by having a half bushel of compost worked into the surface soil, then mulched.

The "ring" method is best for feeding trees: start about two feet from the trunk and cultivate the soil shallowly to a foot beyond the drip line of the branches. Rake an inch or two of compost into the top two inches.

Another way to feed established trees is to apply liquid compost, beginning around the base of the trunk and working out toward the drip line.

When hilling up the soil around your rose bushes for winter protection, mix plenty of compost with it—they'll get a better start next spring.

Fruit Trees

The ring method is ideal for fruit trees, too. You can work in as much as 3 or 4 inches of compost, then apply a heavy mulch, which will continue to feed the trees as it rots. Some gardeners merely pile organic materials as deep as 2 feet around their fruit trees, adding more material as the covering decomposes. You can even add earthworms to speed the transformation to humus. Berry plants may be treated the same way, with lower mulches, of course, for low-growing varieties.

Another good trick for pepping up old fruit trees is to auger holes a foot apart all around the tree, and pack these with compost.

House Plants

Lots of humus means extra-good moisture retention and air circulation in house plant soil. A good potting mixture is composed of equal parts of loam, sand, and compost, the last put through a ¼-inch mesh. Leaf mold compost makes a fine, loose soil, while for acid-loving plants like azaleas, compost made from pine needles or oak leaves is best. Feed your house plants every two weeks during their growing season with compost tea, made by suspending a cheesecloth bag of compost in water and using the liquid when it is a weak tea color. In general, compost can be added to potting mixtures as one-fourth of the total.

To rejuvenate the soil in window boxes, tubs and indoor plant boxes, scratch an inch or so of compost into the surface twice a year. Occasional light top-dressings of compost are also excellent for the soil in greenhouse benches. All of these will benefit from regular feeding with compost tea.

Soil-Compost Mixture for Starting Seedlings

You can help to insure good germination by adding compost to seed starting flats and beds. Make a mixture of two parts good garden loam, one part fine, sharp sand, and one part compost. Mix well and put 8 inches of the mixture into the hotbed, cold frame or flat. It's a good idea to let this growing medium age for several months before seeding. Sift the soil mixture through a ¼-inch mesh screen to provide a fine-textured bed for planting. When screening the mixture, place coarse screenings in the bottom of the flats to provide better drainage.

This mixture provides adequate nourishment for young plants; you don't need to add manure or other organic fertilizers high in nitrogen. Used too soon, these fertilizers can cause the young plants to grow too rapidly, unbalancing their natural growth.

When starting plants in flats, some gardeners prefer to place a layer of sphagnum moss in the bottom quarter to half of the flat. Then after the seed has been placed in the rows, finely screened compost is sifted on top of them. When the seedlings are ready for transplanting to another flat, fill the flat with one part compost, one part sand, and two parts leaf mold.

Starter Solution for Plants

Starter solutions made from compost or manure can be a big help in the growing of vegetable plants. The home gardener as well as the commercial grower can benefit from the rapid and unchecked growth of his plants, if the plants have reached a sufficiently advanced stage of growth, and if the solution is used before they are moved to the field from the greenhouse, hotbed, or cold frame. Greenhouse operators have long made use of this method to bring their crops to a rapid and profitable production. Earlier yields have also been reported in the field.

The main benefit received from these solutions is that of providing the plant with immediately available plant food. This stimulates leaf and root growth, giving the plant a quick pickup after transplanting. These solutions are used especially on young lettuce, tomatoes, celery, peppers, melons, eggplant, cabbage, cauliflower, and all kinds of transplanted plants.

Here is a recommended starter solution you can make from compost:

Fill a barrel or other container one-quarter full of compost. Continue to fill the container with water, stirring several times during the next 24 to 48 hours. To use the liquid, dilute it with water to a light amber color. Pour one pint around each plant when setting out or later as necessary to speed growth. Liquid compost can be used at 10-day to 2-week intervals especially when soils are not high in fertility.

Tests have shown that seeds sprout more than twice as well when soaked in a solution of this kind. In the wild, practically all seeds depend upon the moisture which seeps to them through a layer of nature's compost. In soaking the seed flat, place it in a large container holding an inch or two of starter solution. Allow the flat to soak until its sandy surface shows signs of dampness.

As an additional bonus, seed flats containing mature compost and handled in this way seldom suffer loss from the "damping-off" of the seedlings.

How to Use Compost Tea

The juices of compost can be the best part. Often, some of the valuable nutrients in compost are dissolved in water quite readily, and in solution these nutrients can be quickly distributed to needy plant roots.

Since plants drink their food rather than eat it, the use of compost tea makes quite a bit of sense, particularly during dry periods when plants are starved both for food and water.

Many problem plants and trees can be nursed back to health by treating them with compost tea. You can use it on bare spots on your lawn, on trees that have just been transplanted and on indoor plants that need perking up. You can even use it on vegetables in the spring to try to make them mature earlier. Compost tea is especially effective in greenhouses, where finest soil conditions are needed for best results.

It is really no trouble to make compost tea on a small scale. For treating house plants or small outdoor areas, all you have to do is fill a sprinkling can half with finished compost and half with water, stir gently 10 or 12 times, and pour. Nothing could be easier than that. The

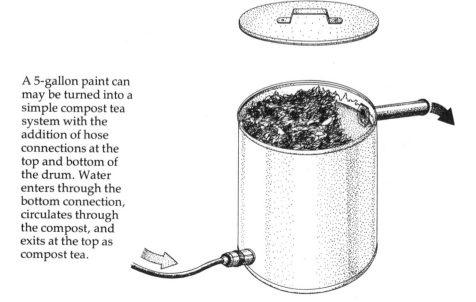

A 5-gallon paint can may be turned into a simple compost tea system with the addition of hose connections at the top and bottom of the drum. Water enters through the bottom connection, circulates through the compost, and exits at the top as compost tea.

compost can be used several times, as one watering will not wash out all its soluble nutrients. The remaining compost is actually almost as good as new, and should be dug into the soil or used as mulch. It takes the action of soil bacteria and plant roots to extract the major value from compost.

Developing a continuous system for making compost tea for the home grounds requires a little more ingenuity and mechanical skill.

One method is to weld hose connections onto a metal can with a lid that will stand up under normal water pressure. One setup we have seen uses an ordinary 5-gallon paint drum. The water intake is located at the bottom of the can, and the exit at the top. Therefore, the water has to circulate up and through the compost before it can get out of the can. Although the large lid on the paint drum allows compost to be placed in it easily, it does not provide a perfectly tight water seal. A can with a screw-type lid would be better, even though loading and unloading of the compost would be more difficult.

The operation of this compost watering can is simple. You attach the water supply to the intake connection, and the hose or sprinkling device to the exit connection. The can may be carried to different parts of your garden, and one charging of compost lasts for about 15 minutes of watering. A screen placed over the exit hole on the inside of the can prevents solids from escaping and clogging the sprinkling heads.

Making Compost to Sell

Bob Doroska once introduced himself to a garden club audience as "the little guy with a manure fork who makes 3,500 buckets of compost a year and sells 3,500 buckets a year."

When he moved into his suburban home in Brockton, Massachusetts, he started making compost simply to improve his own soil. When it began to accumulate, he decided to sell some of it. A $50 income the first year became $250 the next, and $1,000 the year after. Soon, sales climbed to nearly $3,000 a year, giving Bob a good and steady source of extra income.

Each week, Bob makes the rounds gathering up raw materials: hardwood shavings from a furniture factory, leather dust from a shoe factory, treated sludge from the sanitation department. His sources are many, and mostly free. The compost is sold mainly to gardeners at the community plots in Boston's Fenway Gardens, and in the Brockton area.

IS COMMERCIAL COMPOSTING FOR YOU?

The commercial production of compost is not for everyone. Most gardeners, in fact, have enough trouble getting sufficient organic waste materials for their own composting use. However, some farmers and homesteaders might find that the sale of compost brings in good auxiliary income, much as earthworm raising and rabbit breeding do. In fact, producing compost, earthworms, and rabbits can form a combined operation with good profit potential. The rabbit hutches are placed over the earthworm pits, since the manure is good earthworm food; and the spent earthworm castings form the best imaginable compost material. Nothing is wasted, and everything produces a profit.

Commercial compost production requires good, steady, and low-cost (or free) sources of materials. It also requires a steady and sizable market for the finished product. Perhaps the ideal location for commercial production would be a 10- to 20-acre homestead not far from an urban area, where materials can be collected quickly and with little transportation cost. The urban area would supply the purchasers of the finished product. Commercial production also requires some experience and composting know-how, so that composting time can be shortened to a point of profitability.

Anyone considering such a move should check all the local and state regulations which apply to the production and sale of soil conditioners and plant foods. Begin with the county agricultural agent's office and with the city or county attorney, and go on from those points.

Most small commercial compost producers did not set out to get into the business, but rather fell into it by accident or were talked into it by friends. Here is one good example, drawn from the pages of *Organic Gardening and Farming* magazine.

COMPOST FROM SCRATCH

Long-time organic grower Malcolm Beck of San Antonio, Texas, says his 15-acre truck farm was so bountiful, he decided to market the rich compost he knew to be the source of his success.

The unique thing about Malcolm's compost-making is its simplicity. Horse manure from local stables, rotted hay, earthworm castings and wood shavings are the basic ingredients. Before he bags it for sale, he adds rock phosphate, granite meal, marine humus, kelp and more earthworm castings.

Listening to Malcolm talk about making compost is like hearing an experienced cook explain how to bake a cake from scratch: a little of this, a dash of that, watch it close, add a splash of water now and then, stir it, and let it heat up properly.

Malcolm makes tons of compost. He started the business in June, 1975, on a part-time basis and has composted enough raw materials since then to make over 800 cubic yards of his special fertilizing mixture. When he is not at work at his regular railroad job, people come to him for the compost. He sells it loose or in 4-cubic-yard recycled bags.

Using old bags to market his compost is only one of Malcolm's practical business ideas. The composting business is a family business and 90 percent of the work is done by family members. Beck's two sons got involved when they were 15 and 17 years old. Hauling stable manure at three dollars a load taught them that hard work has its rewards. They are also learning the ins and outs of operating a business—a business that may be theirs to manage some day.

Collecting and hauling raw materials is the greatest expense for the Becks, since a request is all that's usually necessary to get barnyard manure for the hauling. Malcolm does collect some material free but usually pays a nominal fee just to remind the seller that the "waste" is really valuable.

"The highest cost of compost is transportation," Malcolm says. "Get the raw materials that are closest to you and save. Don't be overly concerned about the type of manure or leaves (or other ingredients) you use. Get what you've got. If you locate organic wastes that are readily available close by, you fulfill the goal of every organic grower. The philosophy of recycling is the basis for composting. Down here, wood shavings, rock phosphate, marine humus, kelp and worm castings are all available in the neighborhood.

"People think there's some kind of magic when it comes to making compost, but there isn't," says Beck. A nitrogen-producing manure; some deteriorating organic matter such as hay, grass clippings or leaves; a little moisture, all in a proper ratio, and you've got a pile started.

How do you know if the materials are mixed in the right amounts? Malcolm says that if the proportions are wrong, the pile just won't heat up. If it isn't "cooking," add more nitrogen in the form of cottonseed meal or blood meal, he advises. A properly-made compost pile can reach a self-generated temperature of 160°F. (71°C.) at the right time of year. After two weeks at that temperature, the compost is ready to use.

How can you tell when it's ready? "It will cool off when it's ready for the garden. If you don't turn it often enough or it gets too wet, a smell will remain, and that's a signal it's not ready," Malcolm says.

13

Composting on the Farm

The efficient utilization of organic farm wastes could save American farmers hundreds of millions of dollars annually in fertilizer costs, and at the same time significantly reduce energy consumption and the further depletion of the nation's mineral supplies. Today, farm composting is a sound idea. Tomorrow, it might well be a national necessity.

The post-World War II agricultural trend toward mechanization, specialization, and consolidation of farmland into the hands of fewer and larger owners has resulted in a curious situation: Today, many large farms produce no manure at all. The tendency to specialize, to produce large quantities of one crop for market in what is called monoculture, plus the substitution of machines for horses and mules, has led to this imbalance and removed the primary ingredient for compost—manure—from the farm.

By the same token, livestock and dairy production, through the same process of mechanization and specialization, has become concentrated on large farms and feedlots. There, manure accumulates in enormous quantities where there is insufficient green matter with which to compost it, and not enough land on which to distribute it in a balanced fashion. This accumulation of manures actually harms the soil rather than helping it.

In a paper entitled, "Animal Agriculture and Waste Recycling," Gordon A. MacEachern of the Canadian Economics Research Council commented on the growing awareness that "the major output by weight or volume from the present agriculture-food system is not the food and fiber consumed but waste by-products." He gave these statistics: About 64 pounds of manure are produced per steer per day in feedlots; 3 pounds of manure are produced for each pound of milk; 8 pounds of

The concentration of livestock on commercial farms leads to huge accumulations of manure where there is insufficient cropland on which to distribute it, and not enough available plant matter with which to compost it. Serious disposal problems are the inevitable result.

manure per pound of broiler meat; 6 pounds of manure per dozen eggs; 6 pounds of waste per pound of vegetable product consumed. At present, the vast bulk of this manure constitutes not a valuable asset, as it should, but a liability to the feedlot, dairy farm, or poultry farm operator—an unwanted substance to be disposed of at the least cost possible, while still staying within guidelines established by the EPA. How different it would be if we saw manure for what it is—a rich and renewable national resource that can pay cash dividends when it is managed intelligently with today's technological resources.

Economic experts have long accepted the logic of borrowing money to boost crop yields. Thus, with the blessings of financial wizards, farmers have been advised to go to their local bankers for loans to buy fertilizer, tractors, pesticides, and just about anything else that can be bagged or put on four wheels.

In fact, skyrocketing costs have made some farm chemicals almost as valuable as precious metals, and much easier to steal. One newspaper reporter who interviewed southern farmers was convinced that "the nation's newest crime wave is not in the streets but down on the farm." According to a North Carolina sheriff, stolen pesticides sell for nearly as much as whisky.

Meanwhile, machinery costs have doubled for many farmers; farm machines have become so large, complex and costly that only the most prosperous can even qualify for loans at the banks to purchase them. Worse, expensive machinery means expensive repair bills. Where formerly a 60- to 80-h.p. tractor was enough, you'll see the same farmer today on a 125-h.p. unit. As the heavier machines pack the soil, hardpans are created—requiring bigger and still more expensive tractors to till deeper. The Great American Dream for many farmers these days is to get off the treadmill that leads to bigger debts.

About the only commodity farmers have not gone into hock for is humus. Yet, according to research findings, soil organic matter content may be the most worthwhile "product" for which to borrow money.

At the University of Minnesota experiment station, when organic matter levels were raised 125 percent and nitrogen 180 percent after application of 10 tons per acre of natural fertilizer, corn yields jumped from 105 to 160 bushels per acre.

In trials at Bushland, Texas, the dollar value of natural fertilizers that build organic matter was again confirmed. A. C. Mathers, soil scientist with the U.S. Department of Agriculture, found that 10 tons per acre resulted in more grain sorghum per acre over a five-year period than did chemical fertilizer applied for maximum yields. The reason stems from the added organic matter in the manure, which results in the cumulative buildup of soil fertility.

The Food and Agriculture Organization in Rome dwells upon the fact that world shortages and price increases in raw materials have created a fertilizer crisis in many areas. "It is now of the utmost importance and urgency to increase utilization of agricultural, municipal and certain industrial organic wastes as sources of plant nutrients, particularly of nitrogen. Consequently, it is imperative that developing countries should immediately organize and adopt adequate and safe methods for the collection, processing and utilization of their organic waste materials."

The work of soil scientists, like T. M. McCalla, Department of Agriculture microbiologist at the University of Nebraska, has helped us to understand the interrelationship between organic wastes applied to the soil, and microorganisms which decompose them. "If it were not for the soil microorganisms breaking down the plant and animal residues, these materials would soon accumulate in such quantities that man would be unable to move around," Dr. McCalla explains. "All the nutrients would soon be tied up in a form unavailable to higher plants. So it is absolutely essential that we have this microbial transformation in order for man to survive."

An example of the research that will get farmers "borrowing humus from a bank of organic wastes" instead of money from a bank to buy chemical fertilizers was started at the University of Nebraska. The research was unveiled to Nebraska farmers at a 1975 workshop entitled, "The Use of Agriculture Residues and Organic By-Products in the Agricultural Economy of the Seventies."

Project leader Warren W. Sahs, assistant director of the Nebraska experiment station, credits the stimulus for the research to the needs of dryland farmers "searching for cost-benefit answers other than the copious use of agricultural chemicals." The long-term research will compare the use of legumes, rotations and manure with a conventional program of continuous corn using chemical fertilizers and insecticides.

The rotation of one of the plots will be oats-clover, corn, soybeans, corn with nutrients supplied by feedlot manure. The nitrogen equivalent for all treatments is 100 pounds of actual nitrogen per acre, with the assumption that the sweet clover will contribute 40 to 60 pounds of nitrogen per year. Dr. Sahs estimates that the study will continue for 10 to 15 years. At the end of each 4-year cycle, the soil will be sampled for organic matter content, phosphorus availability, zinc and potassium levels, and soil compaction.

Unfortunately, it will take drastically revised policies throughout the U.S. Department of Agriculture, land grant college and extension network to alter the patterns which have reduced soil organic matter levels in United States farmland. Borrowing humus from the "bank of organic wastes"—those produced on the farm and in the city—makes good economic sense for farmers if:

1. Wastes are consistently available at the right time and place.
2. Wastes are uniformly free of toxic amounts of heavy metals.
3. Wastes are viewed by government officials as an agricultural resource.
4. Wastes are considered an integral part of an agricultural program in a closed system.

Composting will go a long way toward satisfying those criteria for using organic wastes on the farm. But little composting research is being done by agricultural researchers at experiment stations although improved methods would help all farmers.

Most of the innovative work in large-scale composting techniques is being done by organic farmers themselves. Richard Thompson of Boone, Iowa, found he was losing too many nutrients by stockpiling his feedlot manure during the winter and applying it in spring. He decided he would compost it, but had nowhere to go for help. His local extension agent had no suggestions. Finally he found another farmer who had composted chicken manure many years ago and got some ideas. Beyond that he had to simply experiment as he went along.

When he first began his organic program, Thompson's yields were 70 to 80 bushels per acre of oats, and 35 to 45 bushels of soybeans. These yields were good and also competitive with his neighbors'. The hay fields seemed to improve each year. After about seven years of organic farming, the field of corn following soybeans in rotation, dropped to the 80- to 90-bushel range. The cornfield following hay remained in its previous 120-bushel range. Thompson was able to make some profit on the lower yield because his expenses per acre were $40 to $50 lower than those of his neighbors using chemical methods. However he felt with all the manure he used, something must be wrong to produce only 80 to 90 bushels. This was where composting came into the picture.

In the spring of 1975, he decided not to spread the manure on frozen ground during the winter. Instead, the manure was pushed up into large piles in the yards during the winter. On June 5, he started to clean out these piles and haul the manure to his chosen compost site on the edge of the hay field. This manure was cold and had large chunks of ice in it.

A bacteria starter was spread on the manure piles in the yard, loaded in the spreader and taken to the compost site located centrally between Thompson's farmstead and his neighbor's. The manure was pushed into long piles about 8 feet wide at the bottom and 4 feet high. In two days time he saw what he thought was a miracle. The cold, frozen manure heated up to 140°F. (60°C.) and steam rose from the tops of the windrows.

As we have seen, one of the keys to good composting is keeping moisture content in the 40 to 60 percent range. If the manure is wetter than 60 percent, it will have to be turned more often with the spreader to get it dry enough. If the manure is too dry, water needs to be added.

Thompson solved this problem by mixing some wet manure with dry manure to obtain the proper moisture level. Much has been written about C/N ratios in composting (they should be 20 to 30 parts carbon to one part nitrogen). For the farmer, Thompson believes that a good rule by which to judge C/N ratios is simply that what creates a good environment for livestock will make good compost. If cattle or hogs are kept clean and dry with bedding, the ratio will be excellent.

Thompson's windrows were turned by reloading the spreader and unloading to make a parallel windrow. The windrows need to be turned until their interior temperature stays below 100°F. (38°C.). However, if time is a problem, incomplete compost that is still steaming can be applied to fields and disked in the same day.

If composting has a drawback for farmers, it is the amount of time it takes to turn the windrows. But the recently developed compost-turning attachments for tractors provide a solution to the time problem. Thompson found that an Easy Over attachment on his tractor allows him to turn the more than 500 tons of compost he's making in an hour, as opposed to the two days it took using a stationary manure spreader and loader. Although the turner was expensive, he feels it was a good investment. On a family farm time is often the critical commodity, and the turner frees up a lot of time. It is not necessary for every farmer to own a turner; if there is one in your area, you may be able to hire it for custom work. Turners are generally easy to transport on the highway, and moving them seldom presents a problem.

Another farmer who successfully composted manure for some time is Robert Steffen, former farm manager at Boys' Town in Omaha, Nebraska. While at Boys' Town, Steffen got manure from local horse stables, and made over 2,000 tons of compost a year. He converted a manure spreader so that it not only aerated the manure, but applied a biological starter at the same time. The spreader was run with a power take-off from a tractor and built the windrows about 6 feet high.

Near Sheridan, Oregon, a research and educational group called the Delphian Foundation needed to apply compost to over 200 acres of moderately heavy clay soil. Director Jay Nunley encountered considerable problems in setting up composting on a farm scale. (Every step required in composting a small plot would be magnified many times over unless shortcuts could be found.) The solution was found by composting mixtures of cattle manure and sawdust anaerobically under plastic.

"Seven piles of compost were constructed at strategic locations in the fields to minimize distances the material would have to be transported for application," Dr. Nunley writes. "Each pile built was 15 to 20 feet wide, 7 to 9 feet deep, and the lengths of the piles varied from 35 to 150 feet. Manure spreaders were loaded with equal volumes of manure and sawdust and, as spreaders advanced, long windrows were built up. Two men were able to make the windrows at the rate of 18 tons per hour."

Upon completion, each pile was wet down and covered with sheets of black polyethylene plastic. Hundreds of discarded tires obtained free held the plastic sheeting in place. With this technique, the farmer-researchers at the Delphian Foundation successfully "borrowed" more than 2,100 tons of compost over a 2½-month period.

Statistics compiled in a Foundation report show: the original 200:1 C/N ratio of uncomposted material went to 18:1 after composting, thereby ensuring availability of nitrogen of plants; 227 acres were composted at a rate of 4 to 21 tons per acre.

Despite the brisk activity in improving farm composting methods, there are still relatively few farmers who carry out any kind of composting practice. Indeed, there are few who even use manure with any degree of efficiency. The reasons are two: First, farmers have not been educated adequately concerning the value of organic wastes and the proper methods of utilizing it. Second, the machinery has not yet been developed to make farm composting economically viable on large acreages. Both situations are changing, however, and the very recent development of new compost machinery gives bright promise to the future in this area.

Farmers who do carry out a systematic composting program report significant improvement in their soil structure, crop quality, and animal health. In addition, there are other practices closely related to composting and sharing its principles, which a larger number of farmers have found feasible. We will look first at some more agricultural composting methods and then, briefly, at some related practices.

How Some Farmers Make Compost

In 1950, Friend Sykes, an English organic farmer and agriculturist, explained in his book *Food, Farming and the Future* how a thousand tons of compost were made and applied on his farm, Chantry:

> A number of our livestock are collected in yards during the winter. . . . Our barley and oat straw are of excellent feeding

quality, and form part of our winter fodder. The wheat straw is used for bedding the cattle. Fresh supplies are put into the yards every week, and sometimes more frequently if the weather is wet. This material, with dung and urine, provides muck in the good old-fashioned way. . . . When the cattle go into the fields, this material is dug out with a Rapier Muck-shifter. . . . To make muck-shifting socially attractive, we try to get nearly the whole of the farm staff on the job; and in about a week or fortnight the whole of the muck is dug out of the yards, so speedy is the method of handling. It is taken to the fields where it is to be used, and here we build a very long pile, about 12 feet wide, and of indefinite length. The material is already damp, and as it is out in the open receives no further watering.

In a few weeks' time the muck is turned by the mechanical grab, by being lifted from its first position, swung round, and dumped in a new pile on the other side of the crane. This is the only turning in the field it usually receives, and in the space of about three months it breaks down into a very satisfactory compost, which is subsequently spread out on the field. Chalk and soil are added when the heap is being assembled.

Friend Sykes goes on to explain that the cost of the operation is extremely low. To spread the compost he uses a machine which, he claims, will spread the compost as quickly as his grab will dig it. He acknowledges that both the method and the product are rougher than those of a small-scale gardener, and he advises horticulturists or greenhouse operators to use two turnings.

The ingredients of the Chantry compost, in addition to manure and bedding straw, are "straw, bracken, roadside cuttings and weeds." Sykes emphasizes not only the importance of urine as an activator, but also that of vegetable matter as a source of cellulose and fiber, which he calls "the base of the compost." These vegetable wastes, he says, "are to be found not only on the farmland, but in all the lanes, the woodlands, the ditches, and the wastelands. . . . It should be cut and collected. Millions of tons of this material go to waste every year and, if the collection were properly organized, the cost of it would not be serious."

Clarence Golueke considers manures, "because of their highly putrescible nature," especially amenable to composting. He cites a system developed at the University of California at Los Angeles School of Public Health for the treatment of dairy manures containing bedding materials.

Careful management of livestock wastes is essential—improperly stored or disposed animal manures are harmful to the environment. Animal bedding and barnyard manure should be collected to be composted and returned to farm-lands.

Manure is air dried until the moisture content drops to 60 percent or less. In an ongoing process the drying step needs to be done only once at the beginning of the operation, since dried manure or drying manure continues to serve as an absorbent for fresh manure. The dried material is mixed with fresh manure to keep it from caking. The mixture, then, is put in a bin equipped for forced-bottom aeration.

A variation of this method is to spread the composted manure and straw in the animals' stalls for bedding and to absorb urine. Bacteria in the material help control the odor of the fresh waste.

In *Biological Reclamation of Solid Wastes,* Golueke stresses the importance of careful management of dairy and feedlot wastes. These manures can have a disastrous effect on the environment if not properly stored. Not only do they attract flies, but runoff from them, or even volatile ammonia air-blown from them, can cause nitrogen pollution in ground and surface waters. In large-scale dairy farming, he says, grazing is at a minimum and most wastes are concentrated in one site.

The most serious problem in composting manures is that they must be either dried or liquefied to slurry before they can be handled efficiently. If liquefied, they can be digested anaerobically for methane

Machinery for loading and turning compost is available in sizes suitable for the family farm . . .

. . . as well as for larger commercial operations.   Compost Science *photos*

production or used in spray irrigation. Composting, however, demands that manure be dried. This can be accomplished either by mixing wet and dry manures, or by mixing wet manure with larger quantities of dry material, usually straw, dried leaves, sawdust, or woodchips. Once the drying and mixing have been done, the material can be composted in windrows. The trick is to get the manure wet enough so that the composting process goes on, yet dry enough that it will not pack or form balls.

Most farmers find windrow systems more economical than the mechanical digesters that are used in municipal compost operations. Fairly recent technological advances have produced machines, such as the one used by Richard Thompson, to turn windrows and reduce the time it takes a farmer to make windrow compost. In fact, compost can now be made in windrows as quickly as in mechanical digesters. Because the material is used in a few weeks, farmers who use windrows no longer have to sacrifice land to the storing of compost and they have fewer problems with flies and pests. If manure or green vegetable matter is used, windrow compost can be stabilized within 12 days. The higher the C/N ratio, the longer the compost takes.

Windrows are several feet wide, and often hundreds of feet long.

R. G. Bell of the Department of Microbiology at the Medical School, Dunedin, New Zealand, writing in *Compost Science*, gives this description of the windrow composting process:

> The material to be composted is placed into windrows: heaps about 6 feet to 8 feet high, 10 feet wide and often hundreds of feet long. Aerobic conditions are maintained by turning the windrows. Turning is most frequent at the early stages of decomposition when the microbial activity is the most intense. Windrow turning can be effected by means of a front end loader, a grab crane or, with a specially designed self-propelled windrow composter. Windrow composting takes from between 4 and 12 months to complete depending upon climatic conditions, the nature and texture of the wastes and on the degree of maturity required. This composting system has been widely adopted by commercial mushroom growing establishments.

Bell, like Golueke, particularly favors composting as a means of disposing of manures. The stabilized product resulting from composting

Turning windrow compost with a front-end loader.   Compost Science *photo*

manures with high-carbon materials contains most of the nutrients found in fresh manure, but can be stored and applied to the land at the farmer's convenience. The high cost of composting equipment, especially high-rate digesters, however, leads Bell to recommend that composting ventures be carried out cooperatively in areas of concentrated livestock production. A compost cooperative could provide both processing and storage facilities and exchange finished compost for raw manure. Eventually such cooperatives could form alignments or "symbiotic relationships" with municipalities to obtain garbage as an ingredient of their compost. City garbage lacks the nitrogen of manure, but contributes balancing carbon materials.

A small farm or homestead seldom accumulates in a week or less enough manure and litter to permit the building of a compost stack or windrow that is large enough to heat up properly. Instead, small-scale farmers must use stacks which permit the addition of material as it becomes available. On homesteads and small diversified farms, manure and litter are usually stacked and handled by hand with a pitchfork. Machinery can, however, be used to convey material to the stack and to load the final humus into carts, trucks, or spreaders. Assess your needs carefully; if the time you spend forking litter every week could be more wisely spent, a loading machine can be a good investment.

On a small farm, compost pits may be preferable to windrows if flies are a problem and if there is a central farmyard from which litter and manure can be taken directly to the pit. A pit may be entirely or partly sunken with material also stacked above ground level. The walls of the pit prevent leaching, but they also cut off air and make turning a difficult task. Sump pumps can be used both in bringing diluted urine from the stable or barn, and in recirculating the compost liquid over the stack or pit. Cellulose material on the bottom of a concrete pit can also absorb moisture.

H. B. Gotaas suggested that in manure pits the manure should be kept toward the center of the pit and all droppings should be cleaned up promptly to minimize fly breeding.

There is some current research being directed toward composting on an agricultural scale. Among continuing research projects is the one at the Research Institute of Biological Husbandry in Oberwil, Switzerland, where new ways are being designed for farmers to make best use of solid and liquid manure and plant residues. The project includes work on making and spreading compost, techniques for saving energy in composting, and the prevention of odor problems and nutrient leaching.

Windrow Compost Technology

According to Michael Allaby and Floyd Allen in *Robots Behind the Plow*, the building of a windrow is simple with the equipment found on most farms. They report on a method employed by Douglas Campbell, a former farm director of the Soil Association in England.

> In early spring, when the cattle left covered yards for the fields, the yards were "mucked out" using a tractor with a front-loader attachment, onto a conventional muck-[manure] spreader, which is no more than a farm tractor with a flailing device at the rear, and which throws out the contents of the trailer as they are pushed toward it. The muck-spreader made the heap, the flailing action ensuring adequate aeration. The heap was shaped by a three-sided "mold" made of corrugated iron, which looks like a small hut open at both ends. This was towed on skids behind the muck-spreader, so that the material was thrown into it. As soon as it was filled, the whole unit of tractor, trailer-spreader, and "hut" moved on a few feet. As it worked, a second man (the first was driving the tractor) forked green matter into the trailer to be mixed with the manure, and added lime. The entire operation took three men (the third drove the front-loader) about a day. The compost can be turned, again using the front-loader, but the Soil Association heaps were left to mature without turning. . . . The compost made by this method is rougher than garden compost, but perfectly satisfactory for farm use.

Though the Soil Association method of composting may be unique in some ways, this description and earlier descriptions of windrow-making methods give you some idea what kind of equipment a farmer needs for composting.

In some respects, equipment for composting on the farm differs from that used in the garden only in size. Shredding equipment, for example, is available in large tractor-driven models equipped with conveyer belts. Mowing equipment, though much larger, is basically similar in design to what a gardener uses.

The farmer needs special spreading equipment for applying compost. Manure loaders and spreaders can be used to mechanize the handling not only of manures, but also sawdust, corncobs, and other organic materials. A 30-inch-wide loader scoop on a hydraulic or

Farm-scale shredding equipment operates along much the same principles as the smaller shredders used by gardeners.
Compost Science *photo*

mechanical lift can pick up several hundred pounds of manure or other material at one time.

A farmer with an extensive woodlot or with access to thinnings or slash from a logging operation may find a wood chipper an excellent buy for making fine wood chips for bedding, composting, and mulching.

Automatic turning machines are most often used in municipal composting operations, but they can be beneficial for agricultural windrows and they have been widely used with manures for making mushroom compost. One type of machine consists of a tractor equipped with a rotary scoop in the front. The scoop collects the material and drops it onto an endless belt that passes over the cab of the tractor. The belt drops the material into a mobile form (something like the English "hut") attached to or towed by the tractor. The machine works head-on into the pile, reforming it as it progresses the pile's length. Automatic turning machines have an advantage over front-end loaders for turning windrows because they can turn more material in a day and are less apt to compact the material.

A manure spreader can serve double duty as a compost turner.

An English firm has developed a compost mixer, a machine approximately 15 feet long, 7 feet 10 inches high, and 4 feet wide, mounted on wheels and driven by a three h.p. electric motor. Dry material used for composting is forked onto a feeder conveyer which throws the material into a revolving drum where water is sprayed on it as needed. Other materials such as limestone, rock phosphate, or organic fertilizer can be added from a hopper as the wetted material passes from the drum onto another conveyer. These ingredients, too, are damped down by a fine spray of water. A third conveyer takes the mixture to a spinner mechanism which breaks up the material and aerates it. It is then thrown on the pile or windrow until the pile reaches 6 feet in height. For turning or further digestion, the process is repeated.

Small aerobic and anaerobic digesters can be used on the farm, but their cost is usually prohibitive. A possible exception is the small methane gas collector which produces both humus and fuel.

Agricultural Methods of Composting
SHEET COMPOSTING

In sheet composting, as we saw in Chapter 8, the raw organic material instead of being decomposed in the compost heap is left on top of the planting area, or incorporated into the surface layer of soil. The obvious advantage of this method is that it saves time and effort. Most gardeners find sheet composting unsatisfactory because, if the organic matter is spread on top of the soil, nutrients are added to the soil very slowly, and if the material is put into the soil, garden plots must be taken out of use for several months while the organic material decays within the soil. Because the farmer's holdings are more extensive and his land is less intensively used, he can often spare a field temporarily while its productiveness is being built up.

Russell Wolter, an organic farmer from Carmel Valley, California, describes his method of sheet composting:

> We till our land with a 60-inch Rotavator behind our Case tractor, about 30 h.p. We have a disk, and we use it, but we are fond of rotavation because it does a thorough job. Ordinarily it will rotavate our crop residue under, along with any fertilizer we are going to add to the ground, such as chicken manure. We have added chicken manure about 1 ton per crop. We use chicken manure as our main nitrogen source.
>
> We also add, at various times, and in various amounts, rock phosphate, fish oil, dry seaweed, gypsum, oyster shell, sawdust, and, of course, the crop residue, inferior heads of lettuce or whatever, and cover crops. I include in that the legume crops, the beans, peas, fava beans that you can grow. These all add nicely to your soil.

Sir Albert Howard considered sheet composting a supplement to the practice of composting in heaps, and a device to keep the land actively producing humus at all times to prevent the loss of nitrogen through the leaching which occurs on bare land. He particularly advised using vegetable residues in the form of stubble and the roots of corn, and deep-rooted weeds.

Gene Logsdon, a homesteader who uses his sheet compost as a surface mulch and then tills it in later, says that ideally the ground during every growing season should be mantled with either 4 inches of manure, 6 inches of grass clippings, or 8 inches of hay, straw, or leaves. He makes an effort to gather and use all these materials on his large vegetable fields. He acknowledges, however, that there simply isn't enough time for him to gather or spread enough material to do the job, so he has worked out alternative means of enriching his soil and has integrated them into a total management plan for his 22 acres. His program involves a combination of sheet composting, crop rotation, intercropping, and green manuring.

GREEN MANURING

The green manure crop is the backbone around which a good sheet composting program is built. Green manuring is the growing of cover crops to be turned under the soil surface. It is the most practical way for the farmer to add substantial amounts of organic matter to land areas. The green manure crop, usually a legume, is most often planted after a food crop has been harvested or as a nurse crop with it, and is turned under about six weeks before the next crop is to be planted.

In selecting your green manure crop, pick one which will produce the greatest amount of organic matter in the time allowed. This may mean growing several stands in one season, or it may mean planting a green manure crop interspersed with a maturing food crop and left to mature after the food crop is harvested. Alfalfa, for example, can be planted in with wheat in the spring, or it can replace wheat after wheat is harvested in July. Wheat straw and alfalfa are plowed under together and provide balanced soil additions. Rye grass can be planted alone in the fall and plowed under the next spring.

Another system is to follow bean crops with wheat because the beans can be harvested or plowed under in the fall before wheat planting time, and the beans fix enough nitrogen for the wheat crop. This system combines green manuring with crop rotation.

The crops most widely used for green manuring are alfalfa, buckwheat, common sesbania, brome grass, rye, cowpeas, hairy indigo, red clover, soybeans, sudan grass, kudzu beans, sweet clover, and vetch. Even weeds are better than bare soil and they can add nutrients to the soil as well, especially if they are deep-rooted.

Green manure crops decay in the soil fairly quickly, particularly if the plants are young and succulent. To derive the greatest benefit from their soil-enriching qualities, plant them soon after the decay is partly stabilized, or in as little as six weeks. You can check the degree of decomposition simply by digging into the soil.

Green manure crops can either be plowed or tilled under by themselves, or more organic materials and rock powders can be sheet-composted with them and the whole accumulation tilled under. Experiments have shown that the plowing in of a green manure crop every year will prevent the depletion of organic matter, but not really increase the organic matter content. If the soil is rich in humus but needs minerals or nitrogen, cover crops can be plowed under when they are at a young stage. If the main objective is to increase humus content, however, they should be allowed to reach maximum growth.

In *Humus*, Selman Waksman points out:

> A plant changes in chemical composition during growth; hence during decomposition of plant materials representing different stages of development there will be differences in the nature of the processes, in the rapidity of decomposition, and in the transformation of the nutrient elements into available forms. . . . When plants are young, they decompose rapidly; . . . a large part of the nitrogen found in the plants is liberated as ammonia. When the plants are mature, they decompose much more slowly; their low nitrogen and high carbohydrate contents are responsible for the fact that not only is there no nitrogen liberated, but some of the nitrogen is actually removed from the surrounding medium by the microorganisms active in the decomposition processes.

With some crops like Indian corn, the seeds may be planted before the sheet composting or green manuring process is entirely complete because the corn kernel contains sufficient food to feed the corn seedlings for about two weeks. Humus in the soil should, however, be stabilized by the time the fibrous roots develop on the base of the young corn plants. Otherwise, root-feeding bacteria in the soil will be diverted into breaking down the green manure matter and will not provide enough nitrogen for the corn.

Some of the other means to greater fertility and better soil structure employed by organic farmers include crop rotation; spray irrigation using watered cow manure, seaweed sprays, chicken manure slurry, or sewage sludge; applications of municipal compost or commercially produced organic fertilizers; compost irrigation; shallow plowing and the use of disks and diggers or chisel plows in place of moldboard plows; the use of slag, a by-product of steel-making which is particularly rich in nitrogen and potassium; subsoiling, a means of using a special machine to place organic matter under the soil in the root zone of plants; the placing of manures or sludges in deep covered furrows; and the production of compost through methane digesters. Of these, methane digesters alone are directly related to the making of compost. Some of the other practices will be discussed in connection with subsequent chapters on the use of sludge, and on municipal compost and the use of industrial waste.

Methane Digesters

The methane digester is a chamber or unit (often a mechanized drum) in which anaerobic digestion is carried on within a controlled environment. Anaerobic digestion differs drastically from composting in its oxygen requirements. The presence of oxygen or any highly oxidized material can inhibit methane-producing anaerobic bacteria.

In his *Biological Reclamation of Solid Wastes*, Clarence Golueke defines anaerobic digestion as a process in which "wastes are 'stabilized' through biological activity in the absence of atmospheric oxygen with the concomitant production of methane (CH_4) and carbon dioxide (CO_2)."

According to Golueke, the anaerobic digestion of farm wastes was practiced on a small scale on a few farms in France and Germany during World Wars I and II. The gas produced was used for cooking. Methane production on farms has been practiced in rural India, where both

A methane digester of this size is adequate for use on a small farm.

human and animal wastes were being used in more than 1,500 digester installations by the late 1960s, and in mainland China, where low technology digestion has been advanced to a high level. Interest in methane production in the United States is increasing as natural gas prices rise.

A project planned a few years ago for a Washington State prison dairy farm was to establish figures for cost, upkeep, and production of a 100,000-gallon methane gas plant.

A methane digester operates in two stages. In the first stage organic matter—manure, crop residues, bedding, sawdust, and other dry and wet material—is liquefied into volatile solids of an acid nature by anaerobic bacteria and chemical processes. In the second phase, methane-forming bacteria consume the volatile acid to produce the bio-gas that is captured in the digester. Bio-gas contains about 55 to 70 percent methane. Methane is the major ingredient of natural gas, and it burns virtually pollution-free.

The Washington State Department of Ecology planned to finance the prison farm project. The project would have sought to improve the fertilizing qualities of dairy manure as well as to produce enough gas to run the prison creamery.

Plans called for the use of two 50,000-gallon glass-lined steel manure storage tanks and a high-rate digester similar to those used at sewage treatment plants. The digester would have employed a gas recirculating system to achieve a continuous hydraulic flow which mixes the material and keeps fiber scum from forming. Although the concept was a good one, funding problems kept the prison project from being put into operation.

In the dairy barns of the prison, cow manure falls on individual sawdust-bedded stalls and is scraped up by tractor. One part water is added to two parts manure; the watered manure is added to the digester daily and finished humus is removed. Average retention time is 17 days.

In the methane-forming process, nitrogen from the raw manure is transformed into organic ammonia and bacterial protoplasm. The digested slurry, therefore, has a higher available nitrogen content than raw manure.

Several different materials can be used in anaerobic digesters. Manure sludges or slurries generally have a higher nitrogen content than sludges or slurries made with nitrogen-poor wastes. Digested hog manure, for example, contains from 6.1 to 9.1 percent nitrogen, while digested municipal refuse is only 0.6 to 2.5 percent nitrogen. Sludges from refuse, however, tend to have larger particles and may do more for soil structure.

Methane production alone will not make a small-scale digester pay for itself. Energy is spent collecting and hauling materials for the digester, and this energy must be balanced against the energy produced. If compost for soil improvement is sought, however, the added bonus of fuel production may give the edge to a methane digester when you compare it to a medium- to large-scale windrow composting system for dealing with dairy and feedlot wastes. As the price of natural gas continues to rise, we will be hearing more about methane digesters.

The Economic Efficiency of Composting

A combination of economic factors is throwing a more favorable light on agricultural use of organic wastes instead of energy-intensive and costly chemical fertilizers. It's beginning to make sound financial as well as agronomic sense for farmers to build up soil humus.

A study by The Center for the Biology of Natural Systems at Washington University in St. Louis, conducted by Dr. Barry Commoner and six associates, concluded that farmers who have built up soil humus, fertilized with green and animal manures, and practiced crop rotations achieved a net profit about equal to that of conventional farmers, and had comparable yields, but used one-third less energy in production. According to the study:

> The dollar value of the crops produced per acre on the organic farms was slightly lower because organic farms must rotate high-value crops like corn with lower-value crops like hay. However, because they do not use pesticides or fertilizer, their operating costs also were lower, so that in the end their income was about the same as the conventional group's income.

The farms examined in the study ranged in size from 175 to 785 acres. They included 16 organic farms in the Midwest matched to similar-sized farms with conventional crop production practices. The main crops of both groups were corn, soybeans, wheat, oats, and hay. Unlike over half the conventional farms in the same midwestern states, the farms in this study, both organic and conventional, raised cattle or hogs and had manure available. The report pointed out that "on the conventional farms, expenditures for fertilizers, other soil amendments and pesticides constituted about one-half of variable operating costs, amounting to an average of $23 per acre of cropland. This compares to an average of $7 per acre on the organic farms."

Yields per acre on both sets of farms were about equal. Conventional farmers averaged five bushels per acre more corn, while organic farmers produced three bushels per acre more wheat.

In discussing the implications of the findings, the report said that the results indicate that organic farmers will be much less influenced by the disruptive effects of growing energy shortages and price increases.

Another important implication, the researchers concluded, is that the profit-making ability of organic farms is much less vulnerable to the impact of declining crop prices (operating costs averaged only 19 percent of the total value of production for organic farms, compared to 27 percent for conventional units).

If the current trend continues and farmers are forced to turn to organic methods to make their land pay, just as old fashioned organic farmers were once forced off the land or into chemicals, then the whole pattern of agriculture in America may change. Organic farming, as we've said earlier, demands economy of value rather than economy of scale. Small-acreage labor-intensive management works best with organic systems.

It will also become imperative to develop networks of quasi-cooperative, quasi-political alignments between cities and the agricultural communities that serve them and need their recycled wastes. Proposals for humus management systems are being worked out by several groups who are concerned about the urban-rural waste connection. The advantages of structuring such a connection include: (1) cities would have a solution to their waste problem—more economical and environmentally sound than any other available; (2) rural development would benefit from the potential jobs in waste treatment and composting plants (including transportation and resource recovery efforts for materials not used in agriculture); (3) farmers would benefit from lower fertilizer costs and higher profit potential; (4) energy would be saved.

The Example of China

The most widely studied example of a labor-intensive system of agriculture involving connections between cities and farms is found today in China. The land in China has been farmed far, far longer than ours, and yet it remains fertile despite the large human population it must feed.

China's agricultural system depends on the recycling of a tremendous quantity of human, animal, and plant waste. Nightsoil, animal manure, and city garbage are collected, composted, and applied to fields and gardens. During the winter silt and other material are scraped from the bottom of canals, fish ponds, and rivers. In the scraped mud are materials from algae and other water plants, wastes from ducks and fish, and soil eroded by monsoon rains. The mud is transported to sandy fields and poor land to build up fertility.

More than 109 agricultural communes use garbage from Shanghai and in turn raise enough vegetables to supply the city's needs. City garbage is brought to the communes on concrete boats that ply China's vast network of canals. Silt from the canals is spread over the garbage after it has been spread on the land, and before it begins to ferment.

Animals, chiefly pigs and chickens, are raised in small numbers both on communes and in the cities themselves. Their manure is carefully collected and composted. When pigs are found in larger feedlots, the feedlots are located where food processing wastes are available to use as food suppliers. At the Red Star Commune, for example, pigs consume the by-products of a dairy plant and a grain processing operation.

Straw, fodder, and thatch are worked into the fields for fertilizer. Heavy metals are removed from waste water and waste from industrial plants in cities so these materials can be used in the fields without fear of pollution or toxicity. Highly sophisticated technology is used in this process, but as one Chinese spokesman pointed out, by starting from scratch his country had the advantage of being able to avoid mistakes made by other industrialized nations. Farmers in China stress crop rotation, the composting of agricultural wastes, and green manure crops—all essential organic processes.

14

Composting and the Law

Making compost on a garden or farm scale violates, of itself, no law that we know of. While individual states vary somewhat in regulations *related* to composting, no state legally prohibits the practice as such.

It would, of course, be an indefensible contradiction of the basic principle of soil conservation for any government to restrain or prevent the return of needed organic matter to the land. At the same time, where actual danger to health results from *malpractice*—or, in other words, from improperly made compost—the responsibility of government is clear. Here, then, is where some of the regulations relative to compost-making appear. A number of others are primarily concerned with the commercial production and sale of compost.

Virtually all composting limitations or restrictions fall into one or the other of the two categories just mentioned: commercial manufacture and distribution, and public health danger.

Nearly every state has what is generally termed a "Commercial Fertilizer Law." In part, these stipulate requirements for registering, grading, labeling and selling all products intended "to supply food for plants or to increase crops produced by land." In order for such products to meet the law and be sold in most states, they must be registered with the agriculture department, show that they maintain various minimums of plant nutrients (N-P-K), and be labeled in accord with the particular state's code, usually to include a guaranteed analysis of these major fertilizer values. Other provisions in most states limit the percentage of inert matter permitted, instruct that any toxic or "injurious" ingredients included be identified, their quantities listed, and adequate directions for use and warnings against misuse be given.

Regulations such as these apply, of course, only where a product is manufactured or processed *to be sold*. If you plan to distribute a compost

316

product commercially, your wisest first step is to check with the agriculture department in your own state to determine its requirements. Some states do not consider compost—along with various other materials such as limestone, gypsum and manure—as a "commercial fertilizer" at all. A number of them direct that these be called "soil amendments," "soil-improvement mixtures," "manipulated manures" or some similar designation, and insist that they be tagged as "not a plant food product." Again, it is important to emphasize that any state's fertilizer-law provisions control only products actually marketed. None of them affects preparation and use of compost or other fertilizer material for yourself.

Protecting Public Health

The other half of the legal aspect to composting concerns itself with avoiding any "health hazards" which may be involved. This segment is

The decision to start making compost in the backyard carries with it a responsibility to use proper methods, and to build containers that are securely constructed and located where they will be inoffensive to neighbors.

of far more significant and frequent consequence to the usual home gardener or farmer making compost than the legislation regarding fertilizer trade. Yet, there need never be any difficulty or conflict at all regarding the health-protective statutes anywhere. The one important thing to keep in mind is that properly made compost breaks no rules, endangers no one's health, and legally offends nobody. Quite the contrary, as shown clearly throughout this book, it is of irrefutable value to all plants and soils—and therefore *beneficial* to everyone who derives life from the land.

Almost all states have sections within their Sanitation or Health Codes dealing with waste disposal and public welfare as it may be affected by waste disposal. Most often, the latter is called a "nuisance" regulation. It is essential to understand that by a "nuisance" these laws do *not* mean something which is simply "annoying" or an arbitrary "bother" to anyone. In this instance, the legal terminology specifically designates a "nuisance" to mean a condition dangerous to health or a likely hazard to personal or public well-being.

A look at one state's wording may help make this clear. The Texas General Sanitation Law of 1945 defines a nuisance as: "Any object, place or condition which constitutes a possible and probable medium of transmission of diseases to or between human beings."

Under the provisions of most of these statutes, the state may restrict a composting project or prosecute a violator (to the extent of the particular state's edict) if unhealthy conditions exist. A typical law might stipulate the following conditions as unacceptable:

1. Storing, discharging or depositing sewage, human wastes, wash water, garbage, or other wastes in such a way as to make them a potential agent in the transmission of disease.
2. Storing or disposing of any kind of wastes in a manner that pollutes a water supply or contaminates surrounding land to the extent that public health is endangered.
3. Depositing, storing or disposing of garbage, manure or any other wastes in a manner that attracts vermin, insects or other pests, or allows the wastes to become a breeding place for mosquitoes, flies, or other disease-carrying insects.
4. Keeping or leaving human wastes, refuse, bodies of dead animals, etc., within specified distances (usually about 300 to 500 feet) of any street or highway so as to create a nuisance (that is, endanger the public health).

Your home garden or farm composting will not create any of these conditions if it is handled with even a moderate amount of care and attention. Correctly following any of the methods recommended in Chapter 8 will make certain that these conditions will not occur.

First of all, your compost will not transmit disease. When any heap or pit method is correctly used, the heat promptly generated raises temperatures more than high enough to kill any pathogenic organisms which may—or may not—be present in the raw materials being composted.

Second, the compost will not pollute water supplies or nearby land. If properly made, no part of a compost heap will ever enter a pond, lake, river, or other water supply. It cannot contaminate any type of soil because any harmful bacteria that may have been present were destroyed by the heat of the process.

Third, properly made compost draws no flies, other insects, rodents, or animals. The conditions favorable to attracting or breeding such pests are contrary to those established in the compost heap. The heat, layering, and rapid decomposition of the organic matter being composted are biologically unfavorable to insect life. These same factors, along with a proper cover or enclosure, very effectively prevent any animal attraction.

Finally, regardless of where compost is made, it cannot become a "nuisance" of any sort, especially in the legal sense of creating a threat to health, when the practice is correctly followed. Naturally, it is only sensible for a gardener or farmer to use good judgment and courtesy in the placement of his heap. Almost invariably, it is to his or her own advantage to keep it a reasonable distance from any thoroughfare. In heavily populated areas he or she should, of course, be considerate of a neighbor's landscape or home as well as of any business establishments and public buildings. A well-kept compost heap does not produce objectionable odors of any kind, and there is no need for it to be an eyesore. Most laws stipulate that decomposing animal bodies present a threat to health if left within a certain distance of public thoroughfares. Few gardeners include animal bodies in their compost, but those who do must be careful to see that they are incorporated properly and do not lead to any potential complaint or danger.

Practically every state leaves the general application of its health laws in the hands of local authorities. Each city or town has, usually, a board of health and a health inspector. Seeing that the regulations are upheld, attending to complaints and making inspections and rulings are their responsibilities. Ordinances and usage in different communities may vary slightly, but in general the legal pointers regarding composting adhere quite closely to what has been discussed here.

Recourse to Court

A gardener or farmer who has a complaint placed against him in connection with his compost is not compelled to accept the decision of a health board or inspector. His legal rights entitle him to take the matter to court. If his composting is done properly, if he believes it violates none of the specific legislation of his area (especially any of the infractions detailed here), he certainly may seek a court's opinion.

Frequently, a complaint is the result of a cantankerous neighbor or an over-zealous inspector. Where this is the case—and there actually is no breach of the law or of reasonable consideration for others—the gardener would best serve his own interests and those of other gardeners in his community by appealing to a court. A considerable number of gardeners in many sections of the country have successfully appealed complaints.

On September 29, 1971, Sybil Fabricant of Englewood, Colorado, was given a choice of paying a $100 fine plus $20 court costs, or spending 60 days in jail for having a compost pile in her backyard. A neighbor had insisted that Miss Fabricant's pile smelled, and she complained to the authorities. Even though the other neighbors testified at the trial that there were no offensive odors, Miss Fabricant was found guilty by Englewood Municipal Court Judge Haydn Swearingen of violating a city ordinance requiring residents to keep dwellings in "a clean and sanitary condition."

She appealed the case—and won. The district judge found in favor of composting for the entire county, and even made specific recommendations explicit on composting procedures. Miss Fabricant's fine was not reduced, and it cost her nearly a thousand dollars in legal fees to appeal her case, but the victory was nonetheless sweet to her. Gardeners throughout Arapahoe County, Colorado, can compost without fear because of Sybil Fabricant's courage and initiative.

In the summer of 1977, Bill Martin of Omaha, Nebraska, was similarly threatened, and attended a public hearing to determine if his compost pile was really an "illegal storage of brush, weeds, and branches" that constituted a health hazard. Health official E. C. Willoughby, after inspecting the heap that had been newly fenced, ended the dispute by deeming the pile "neat, nice, and beautiful." He also admitted that technically all compost piles violate an anti-litter ordinance which bans piles of grass, leaves, and "worthless vegetation," but said that he would support a revision of the law that would allow properly kept compost piles to be maintained. The Omaha Health Department even announced plans to hold seminars to teach interested people how to build proper compost heaps.

The sharply contrasting experiences of Sybil Fabricant, in 1971, and Bill Martin, in 1977, are symbolic of how far the law has come in the last decade or so in recognizing the nature and benefits of compost. Today, a compost heap is far less likely to be viewed as an illegal storage of potentially hazardous materials, and more as an ecologically sound method of restoring the land's fertility. Any compost heap can also be said to contribute to the public good, since it contributes to the reduction of waste collection expenses, and to the burden placed on sewage systems and landfill sites. If more city and suburban gardeners composted part of their organic wastes, the expense of these city services could be reduced significantly.

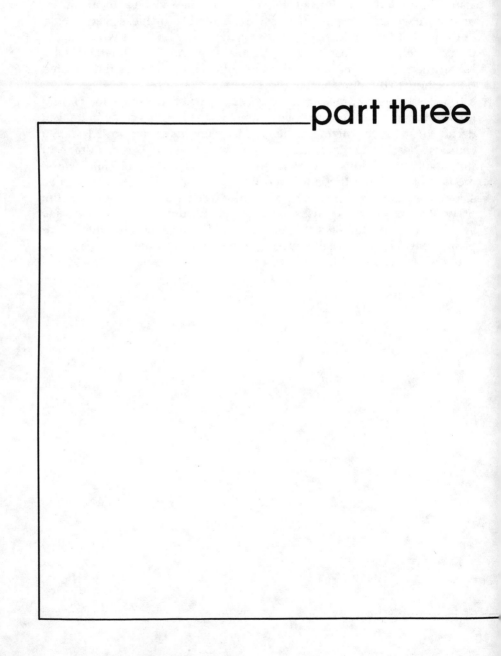

part three

Large-Scale Composting: Recycling Society's Wastes

15

Municipal Composting

The ever-growing population and the general migration of the populace from rural to urban and suburban areas continue to intensify the problems of municipal waste disposal in the United States. The best solution will be one that satisfies all sanitary requirements, does the job economically, and provides a useful end product.

Today, the three most widely used methods of garbage disposal, which account for more than 99 percent of the country's waste, are incineration, landfill, and dumping. All three have disadvantages. Drawbacks to the sanitary landfill include: the frequent necessity for long distance hauls to suitable sites; scarcity of suitable sites in heavily populated areas; winter conditions, like ice and snow, that make operating almost impossible; the limited future use of fill sites; and lack of available cover material which may prohibit the use of this method entirely. Dumping has the obvious disadvantages of health and fire hazards. Disadvantages of the incineration method include air pollution, difficulties in salvaging useful material, waste of potential organic matter, high capital cost, high operation and maintenance costs, and the high degree of skill required for successful operation.

Composting has clear advantages over all three and they can be summed up as follows:

1. Conversion to a highly usable end product.
2. Compared with the sanitary landfill method, a centrally located compost plant would reduce hauling costs which often approximate one to three dollars per ton. Getting rid of the non-compostable residue from the composting operation is less costly than relying on landfill.
3. Salvaging metals, rags, etc., is more economical in a composting operation because of the plant's design.

4. A well-designed compost plant can handle dewatered sewage solids, especially if mixed with ground refuse. (The cost of treating sewage solids by composting is about half the cost of conventional disposal methods in a modern sewage plant.)
5. Composting principles used for garbage and trash disposal also apply to any industrial wastes, so that a municipal plant could be used for the combined disposal of these wastes.

Of course, another basic advantage to composting is the fact that use of compost by gardeners and farmers would be increased tremendously, thereby aiding in the conservation of our nation's soil.

Despite composting's advantages and the increased level of technology which now makes municipal composting practical, America's cities have been reluctant to let go of their traditional disposal methods. According to the Salt Lake City Municipal Research Center of the U.S. Bureau of Mines:

The daily per capita discard of domestic, municipal, and commercial components of urban refuse amounts to 2.24, 1.2, and 2.3 pounds, respectively. This total quantity of 5.74 pounds per capita per day is equal to a national total of over 100 million tons per year. Most urban refuse is disposed of in landfills, and salvage of materials from these landfills is discouraged by health authorities. About 30 million tons is burned in municipal incinerators. An annual composite urban refuse could produce about 12 million tons of ferrous metals, over a million tons of nonferrous metals, and 15 million tons of glass.

Costs for incineration and landfill are soaring with energy and land shortages, while the price of fertilizer is increasing rapidly because of current or expected shortages of essential minerals, including the oil which is necessary to the fertilizer manufacturing process. Meanwhile, the demand for compost is at an all-time high and is rising annually at a significant rate. It would seem that the time is right for municipal composting in America.

Europe Leads

Nevertheless, it has been the European cities that have taken the lead in municipal composting, showing us the way if we will only follow.

In Europe many of the municipal compost operations which started in the 1950s or before are still in existence and some have grown and taken in more communities, though composting is still not a major means of refuse disposal in Europe. Other new plants, some using new technology and methods, have begun recently abroad. The relative success of European operations as contrasted with American ones says more about the social and political differences between our country and others than it does about comparative technologies.

In Holland, several years ago, the Dutch government set aside large sums for study of the problems of maintaining soil fertility and disposing of urban refuse. It created a "Compost" group charged with developing methods of composting urban wastes. The group's study led to the founding of The Refuse Disposal Company, Ltd., or VAM, a non-profit utility which was formed in 1932 and which still receives state subsidies through the Ministry of Agriculture.

In Hungary there is a national organization for the management of all organic wastes. All sales of commercial fertilizer are under government authority, partly to eliminate possible undesirable competition with government-directed composting, and partly to synchronize production requirements of the various areas of the country. Production and demand are controlled in a planned economy. The sale price of compost is subsidized by half its manufacturing cost.

Germany, however, has been perhaps most active in this area. In West Germany, there are 20 large-scale composting sites and also five companies engaged in the composting of wastes. (A list of them appears in the January-February, 1977, issue of *Compost Science.)*

Why, then, is the United States lagging? Perhaps it is because, when municipal composting first emerged as a serious waste disposal alternative in the 1950s, some manufacturers entered the field convinced that public wastes could be turned into a profit-making product. Some manufacturers of composting equipment thought that they could recoup some of their initial losses by selling patented inoculums to other entrepreneurs and managers. This hope was founded on bogus biology and proved illusive. The sale of salvage (newspapers, scrap metal, etc.) plus the income from the final composted product never was able to meet the costs of operating the early plants.

Clarence G. Golueke says it all in *Composting.* "The fallacy of judging the success of a compost operation in terms of its money-making record is a misconception that has always plagued composting, and is one that must be corrected. Thus, if the product cannot be sold, and a deficit results in terms of operational and capital costs, the entire enterprise is regarded as a failure—regardless of how well the plant may have operated. Yet, no one expects an incineration operation to earn money. Since composting also is a method for treating wastes, its success should be judged on the basis of performance and not the amount of profit."

Golueke goes on to comment that higher air quality standards and rising costs may in the future rule out incineration until "the only technology available for solid waste processing will be composting." He looks with hope at the current moves toward regional management of waste, and sees composting as becoming part of the public sector's responsibility, thus obviating the need for profit.

There are some additional causes for hopefulness, though not for the unrealistic idealism (or the economic rapaciousness) of the 1950s. First, the technology for satisfactory, relatively problem-free composting is now available. The only technical problems remaining are in the pretreatment or sorting phases of the operation, phases which composting shares with incineration in any case.

Compost, furthermore, is now beginning to compete with fertilizer on the market. This is especially true of sludge composts, and when sludge is composted with municipal wastes, two urban problems are solved.

Since the Solid Wastes Act of 1965, the federal government has been in the composting picture. In fact, the U.S. Department of Agriculture and the EPA are sponsoring large-scale experiments on urban composting which may eventually develop better ways of treating refuse.

What Is Refuse?

When speaking of these large-scale operations, it will be helpful to define the terms associated with them. Basically, *garbage* is composed of rapidly decomposable or putrescible organic matter, mainly wastes from the preparation, cooking, and consumption of food, and wastes from the storage and sale of produce.

Refuse is a mixture of garbage and trash. *Trash* is decay-resistant material including metals, paper, tin cans, glass containers, leaves, rags, sweepings, hedge trimmings, plastic bags and containers, cardboard, and all kinds of miscellaneous objects.

Garbage, of course, is an extremely useful ingredient of compost, a moderately efficient nitrogen source, and an excellent source of bacteria. Analysis, however, shows that only an optimistic 20 to 30 percent of municipal refuse by volume consists of garbage. Municipal refuse does not generally include food-processing wastes from canneries, slaughterhouses, and packing plants. In high-income residential communities, more food waste—particularly high-nitrogen meat waste—goes into refuse than in low-income communities. But in all communities, less home preparation of food is taking place now than went on ten years ago. As people rely increasingly on prepackaged foods and fast-food restaurants, city refuse will contain more packaging material and less garbage.

What is in refuse, then? Here's an analysis of waste from Madison, Wisconsin, compiled in connection with experiments involving particle size separation:

CHARACTERIZATION OF MADISON REFUSE SAMPLES

Material	Percent
Metals	
Ferrous	5.7
Nonferrous	0.3
Moisture (varied between 5 and 30)	12.4
Nonmetal	
Paper	41.0
Dirt and glass	15.9
Cardboard	15.3
Cloth and leather	4.4
Plastic	2.9
Wood and plants	1.5
Rubber	0.6

And here is comparative data on the wastes of two New England communities, tabulated in connection with a computerized analysis of wastes aimed at developing new sensor sorting devices:

BULK COMPOSITION OF REFUSE SAMPLES

Percent By Weight (Wet Basis)

Material	Cambridge, Mass.	Middlebury, Vt.
Paper	35.8	48.9
Newsprint	(7.8)	(3.0)
Metals	9.2	9.1
Ferrous	(8.3)	(8.8)
Nonferrous	(0.9)	(0.3)
Glass	18.6	16.6
Plastics	4.1	2.4
Cloth, rubber, leather	5.2	2.5
Wood	1.1	0.4
Food waste	5.9	4.7
Yard and garden	0.5	0.3
Misc. and uncategorized	19.6	15.1

As you may have gathered from examining these percentages, modern municipal wastes generally have too low a nitrogen content for the best, or even for practical, composting. The usual way of compensating for the lack of nitrogen is to add either sewage sludge or animal manure. Most ground refuse without nitrogen additions will form humus eventually, but the process is a long and costly one.

The Municipal Composting Process

The steps in municipal composting are sorting, grinding, composting or digestion, and windrowing or storage. Some systems call for a second grinding after the composting step, and others for screening as well. Some reduce the size of materials before the initial sorting. The sequence of steps is essential whether the composting is to be carried on in windrows or in a digester. We will examine various systems for the composting phase of the municipal refuse operation later, but first let's look at each of the steps necessary to the total process. We will skip the composting step and then return to it when we discuss individual systems.

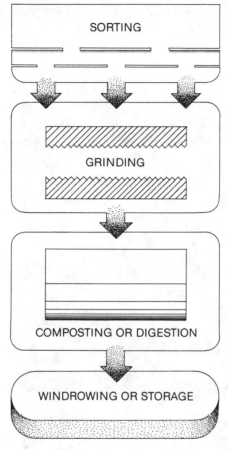

All municipal composting systems consist of these four basic steps.

SORTING

In discussing sorting, we'll move from the simplest to the most complex methods either now in use or proposed. First a word of caution: more complex is not necessarily of greater value any more than bigger is necessarily better. Both St. Louis and Baltimore have experienced dramatic failures of the complicated mechanical separation equipment at their incinerators. The result has been higher costs, delays, and the need for even more sophisticated technology to correct problems. In Nashville, a highly mechanized plant had to default on 16 million dollars in bonds.

The simplest way of separating compostable material from that which is uncompostable is to have those who accumulate garbage and trash do the separating as they discard material in their home, restaurant, or business. In this way, garbage never soils paper (a recyclable commodity), glass splinters never contaminate garbage, and metal never gets near damage-prone grinding machines. By general consensus, the

The simplest method of sorting municipal refuse is for each family to do it at home.

Compost Science *photo*

main problem with this method is that it won't work because people are unwilling to separate their wastes.

A mechanized system set up on the basis of supposed total home separation would be open to damage from the accidents and carelessness of a few people. Legislation would be necessary to mandate compulsory participation, and penalties would need to be imposed on offenders. This would not only burden our courts and investigatory agencies, but variations on the theme of the popular 1960s song "Alice's Restaurant" would bring forth cries that individual liberty had been threatened. Moreover, many cities have a large investment in compacting garbage trucks and prefer, because of transportation costs, to collect garbage and trash at the same time.

On the positive side, a pilot project in Nottingham, New Hampshire, a town of 1,200 residents, has shown that most people don't object to separating and hauling their own refuse to a central location. Financial savings for those who elect to separate materials for collection have attracted wide participation for a project in Oregon. Recycling centers for salable wastes have become, if less popular than fast-food chains, at least a recognized phenomenon of the 1970s, and these could feasibly be extended into composting operations. We have discussed some of these enterprises in Chapter 5.

Another simple way of dealing with separation, perhaps the easiest of all, is to do it after collection. In Holland, when VAM was first founded, refuse, excluding garbage, was collected and dumped into viaducts from railway cars. The refuse was mechanically levelled, sprinkled with bacteria-rich water, and left to decompose for four to eight months. Only then were metals and large objects taken out of it. Bacteria and natural processes had reduced much of the remaining waste. The problem with this method—VAM has since gone over to presorting and grinding—is that refuse today contains easily fractured glass and plastic. When compost containing glass splinters, plastic bits, or plastic film is applied to pastureland, the plastic and glass are eaten by grazing animals and stay in the rumen. Eventually enough accumulates to result in serious, even fatal, consequences.

There are four main reasons for sorting refuse: (1) Salable or recyclable scrap can be recovered. (2) Metal objects cause direct breakage or wear and tear on size reducing equipment. A hammermill hammer can be broken by a piece of steel. Grit, glass, and even dry paper can gradually wear down a hammer. (3) Metal and glass also pose a potential danger to farmers and gardeners working with compost. Also the more nonorganic material (glass, metal, plastic) or high-carbon material (paper, wood) is removed from refuse, the higher in nitrogen the finished compost product will be. (4) Finally, the potential danger to livestock of composting unsorted refuse must not be forgotten.

The simplest sorting method is hand sorting from a conveyer belt. This method is widely used in Mexico, where a development program cosponsored by that country and the United Nations is underway, and plants have begun operating in four cities.

About 60 percent of the refuse which comes to the Mexican plants is compostable. The figure is higher than it would be in the United States because Mexico is less industrially developed. Composting in Mexico is part of a total recycling activity, and authorities hope to recover part of the cost of operating the four 500-metric-ton-per-day plants by sale of scrap. Sorting can be quite important to the success of the project. All sorting is done manually by employees for whom the government provides housing and some meals. These employees have been chosen from among individuals who formerly eked out a living by scavenging the dumps.

The motivation, training, and supervision of workers is essential to any good manual sorting operation. In Mexico, each worker is responsible for removing all the materials in one or two categories. These can include metal cans, artificial fiber cloth, large wood objects, glass bottles, plastic containers, cardboard, newspapers and magazines, plastic bags and wrap, and several others. These the worker drops into separate chutes that lead to containers or carts on lower floors. In the United States, hand sorting usually has been accompanied by magnetic sorting for iron-containing cans and objects. A magnetized belt frequently follows the conveyer belt and attracts ferrous metal. In Mexico, however, magnets are only used after grinding to catch small pieces missed by the hand sorters.

The obvious problem with this method is that it is labor-intensive. In the United States where the minimum wage is relatively high, the cost of labor for a large plant might well be prohibitive.

As we go up the scale toward complexity, we come to a sharp break between manual and automatic sorting systems. We have seen that magnetic devices can pull "tin" cans and other iron-based metals from a conveyer belt. There are many other devices that attract, trap, or catch individual materials by taking advantage of some property inherent in them.

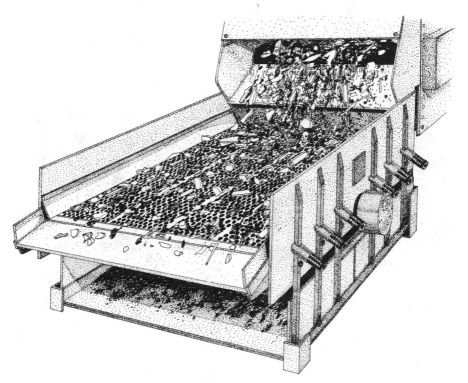

A separating screen for sorting particles of shredded refuse.

There are dry, wet, and combined sorting processes, but all of them subject materials to tests of one sort or another in order to identify them. In wet processes, the wastes are converted to a slurry. In combined processes, much dry sorting goes on first, and then a small portion of mixed wastes is slurried before further sorting. Centrifuges spin heavy materials out of slurries, filters screen them out, and settling takes advantage of the fact that some materials float and others sink. Wet processes are generally uneconomical unless a provision for wastewater treatment is included in the plant's design. But let's look more closely at some dry sorting processes.

Dry mechanical systems are based on the physical, electrical, and electromagnetic properties of wastes. We've already mentioned how magnets are used to draw metallic wastes from refuse. Another separa-

A ballistics separator in the Netherlands, used to remove glass, metal, stone, etc., from compostable refuse.

Compost Science *photo*

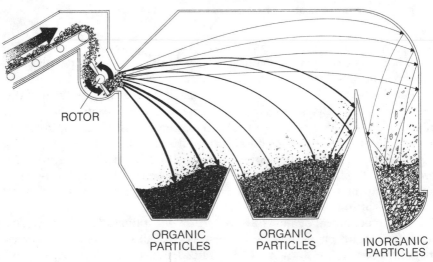

ROTOR

ORGANIC
PARTICLES

ORGANIC
PARTICLES

INORGANIC
PARTICLES

Diagram of a ballistics separator.

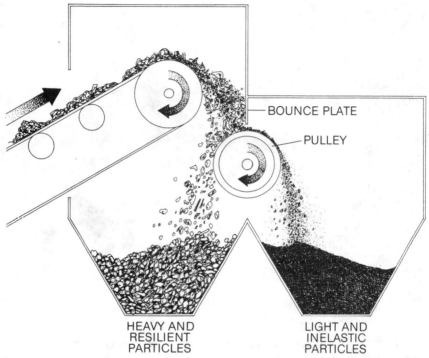

Secator separator.

tion device is a ballistics separator. In one model of the ballistics separator, material to be sorted is flung by an impeller horizontally at a slightly upward angle into a divided bin. The heavier and more resilient pieces leave the impeller at higher speeds and travel to the far end of the bin. Less dense objects with more drag go into the near end. Similarly, in a *Secator* system, a high-speed conveyer belt discharges particles against a metal plate. Particles bounce off the plate and drop onto the surface of a rotating drum from which they are propelled varying distances, depending on their elasticity and density. More resilient particles bounce further from the plate while denser ones fall off one side of the drum.

In inclined conveyer separation, material is dropped from a conveyer belt onto an upward-sloping, steel-plated conveyer. Heavier particles bounce downward and fall into a bin. Lighter ones are carried over the top to another bin.

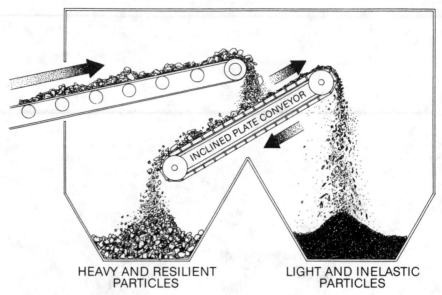

HEAVY AND RESILIENT
PARTICLES

LIGHT AND INELASTIC
PARTICLES

Inclined conveyer separator.

The air classification system is one of the most commonly used sorting procedures. In one variation, air is drawn upward through a tube of rectangular cross sections set in a vertical zigzag pattern. Dry, granulated, or shredded material is introduced to the tube about halfway up. Heavy particles fall down and lighter ones are blown upward to pass out the top of the tube. Metals and garbage tend to fall down, while plastic film and paper go up.

In another, more sophisticated, air classification system developed by the U.S. Bureau of Mines, material is discharged from a variable-speed belt feeder into an enclosed sloping chute which in turn enters the top of a device called an elutriator. There the refuse strikes a baffle which causes it to drop vertically into a horizontally moving air stream produced by a blower. The air stream blows the feed material into a 12-inch-wide, 6-foot-long compartmented chamber open at the upper front end. Metals, hard plastics, hard rubber, and other materials of high density fall into the front compartments, while paper, textiles, fibers, and other light materials are collected in compartments more distant from the blower. A baghouse at the opposite end from the blower collects the fine material and dust.

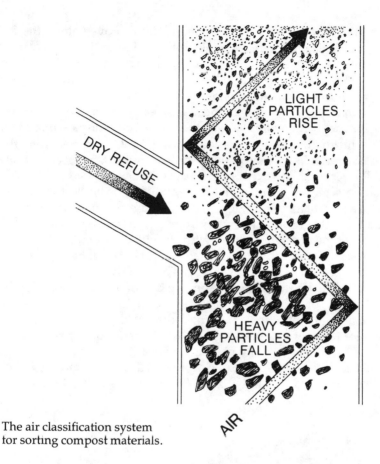

The air classification system
for sorting compost materials.

Another type of elutriator, vertical model, works on much the same principle, but depends on gravity for the initial drop with a variable-speed drum serving as the feeder. Heavier particles drop down, and lighter ones are carried upward. From either of these classifiers, the "heavies" can go on to magnetic separation of ferrous metals and further screening. The "lights" are also screened on a 4-inch mesh and then further classified.

Another air system, one developed in England, uses a perforated table with air blown through the holes. One-third of the table inclines upward at five to ten degrees. A dry granular substance flows over the table. The refuse is ground so that it is either slightly smaller or slightly larger in particle size than the flowing medium. It is then dropped on the table. Lighter material floats on the medium and is moved along the flat part of the table. Heavier material sinks into the medium and is carried up the incline and deposited with the medium, which is then screened and reused. By this system it is possible to capture aluminum foil for recycling or sale without using expensive electrostatic devices.

The trommel screen, a long cylindrical screen of wire mesh which is set on an incline and rotated, is another relatively simple separation device. The inclination can be varied from 5 to 20 degrees from the horizontal. Material is carried downward through the screen while tumbling. Proper tumbling occurs when the material, carried up the side of the rotating screen by centripetal force, falls onto the bottom where there is little accumulation of material. In this way the finer materials are not blocked by the other materials from going through the screen openings. This type of screen is used with shredded materials.

Through the use of a trommel screen, all or nearly all of the material of particle size less than one-half inch can be removed from shredded refuse. It is particularly important to remove fine material when refuse is to be incinerated, or when fiber is to be recovered from it. But even when the material is intended for composting, taking fine material out makes it easier to separate heavier materials. Material under two inches and over one-half inch is usually plastic or paper. The plastic film of bags or wraps frequently clogs or blocks conventional screens and traps fine material like dust and ground glass. Among the more conventional

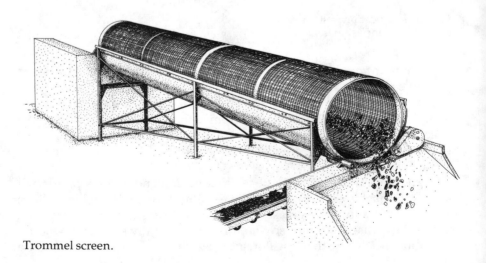

Trommel screen.

screens used in separating municipal refuse are flat screens and screens with several decks.

One of the most serious problems in sorting is presented by the need to separate film plastic from loose paper. Both are light and both respond to air separation or suction methods, but paper is compostable and plastic is not. One solution is to pulp or slurry the combined light mixture. In a slurry, plastic particles remain unchanged, while paper is macerated into fibers. In fiber form paper can be cyclone-centrifuged and cleaned. It can sometimes be recovered for use in fiberboard. The recovery of paper in this manner is part of a complex process developed at the University of California, Richmond Field Station.

All this may sound so highly technical that you'd be more than willing to go back to hand sorting. You'd be in good company, for many people who accept composting and recycling, but not gadgetry, fear that high-level technology may once more reduce composting's viability as an economical disposal method. We've dwelt on the problems of sorting at length because this is the principal area where development is going on right now.

GRINDING OR SIZE REDUCTION

Grinding, shredding, or other reductions in size go on either before or after sorting, and often depend on the way the refuse is to be sorted. Often some sorting is done before grinding and the final sorting is performed afterward. This is necessarily true if a combined wet and dry system is to be used, or if machines are equipped for using shredded material.

Refuse is reduced in size by pounding, tearing, or shearing. Size-reduction machines all employ one or more of these principles, usually with greatest emphasis on one of them.

The two principal types of grinders for municipal wastes are hammermills and ring grinders. A hammermill uses flailing hammers to strike material as it falls through a chamber or rests on a surface. Material is hurled at a surface, or batted between moving hammers and a fixed outlet or discharge grate. Small pieces leave the horizontal or vertical battering chamber first, and large ones remain until they too fit through the grate or the discharge opening. In a vertical mill, pinching and crushing also go on as the chamber narrows. Some models have grinding cylinders at the bottom of vertical hammermills between which material is forced like clothes through a wringer. Hammers continue to strike any material that resists the wringers.

Materials for municipal composting must be ground or shredded after noncompostable materials have been sorted out.

The ring grinder has a vertical shaft in a funnel-shaped housing. Ring-shaped grinders move outward as centrifugal force is applied. Pieces of material are ground away much as the edge of a knife grinder. One model, the *Eidal* grinder, uses an initial reduction through tearing action accomplished by rotating breaker bars. The liner that houses the grinders has fixed bars projecting from it. Particle size can be adjusted by decreasing or increasing the distance between the "choke" ring and the ring grinders.

Vertical mills or grinders are less apt to overload and jam than horizontal ones, but they are more difficult to repair.

A rasping machine to substitute for hammermills and ring grinders was developed by the Dutch organization VAM. It has a perforated horizontal bottom through which refuse is rasped or grated by means of

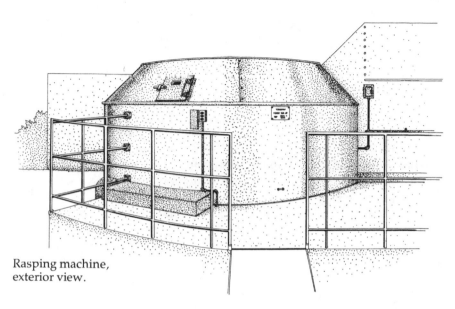

Rasping machine,
exterior view.

slowly rotating arms. The bottom is formed by alternating rasp plates
and sieve plates. The sieve plates have openings which allow particles of
one inch or less to pass. Rotating arms move the wastes over the plates.
The rasp plates are made of manganese steel bars welded onto the plates
in a staggered pattern and protruding above the plates.

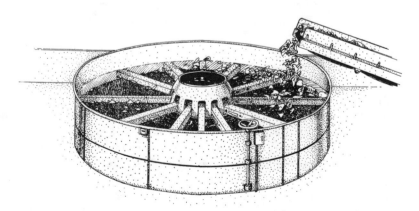

Rasping machine,
interior view.

The *Egseter* was developed by the Dano Corporation as an important feature of its Biostabilizer process. It is a drum-type cylinder which rotates at about 12 r.p.m. around an axis. Hardened steel bars are set approximately 30 inches inside the outer shell and a screen or sieve is located between the bars and the shell. The pieces of waste rub against one another and against the bars as the drum rotates. When they have been reduced to a size that can pass between the bars and through the screen, the particles drop out.

Both the VAM rasping machine and the Dano Egseter are relatively simple and require less power and less maintenance than hammermills. Neither machine can reduce refuse that has much paper, textile waste, or plastic film in it, but both are suitable for cities in developing nations.

In Heidelberg, Germany, the *Cascade* mill, a short ball-type mill with a large diameter is employed. This type of mill was originally developed for grinding ore. The chief advantage of the *Cascade* mill is that it can finely grind bulk refuse in one operation, while at the same time mixing it with dewatered sludge.

The Heidelberg plant also uses the *Eirich* shredder, which consists of an inclined dish with a rapidly rotating set of knives. As the dish rotates, the material moves toward the knives. The rotary motion also helps to sort out size particles. The pulverized material leaves the shredder through a calibrated gap in the center. This machine can be either continuously or batch-fed. Glass, and especially metals, must be carefully separated and screened out in order to protect the machine.

FINAL PROCESSING

The final processing of compost may come before or after storage, aging, and further decomposition toward a point of stability. Especially when municipal refuse is composted, however, the further the decomposition has progressed, the easier it is to do the final screening or grinding. Some compost plants both screen and grind for the last time, while others employ one process or the other. In Mexico two grades of compost are produced, a fine grade screened of glass shards and plastic particles, and a general grade which is left unscreened.

The texture of the windrowed or stored material and the use for which it is intended will usually determine the need for a second or final grinding. In a small plant the main grinding mill can be used at off-peak times for the faster and easier final grinding. In larger plants, a second and smaller mill is needed if final grinding is to be done. Composting will have reduced the particle size of the original material considerably, though, and a second or final grinding may not be necessary.

If there is plastic in the compost or the particles are large, a horizontal shaker screen may not work for the final screening, because screen perforations may become covered or clogged. An inclined trommel screen like the one used in sorting may offer a solution to this problem.

Modes of Municipal Composting
THE WINDROW

In windrow composting, material is placed in windrows immediately after sorting and milling. Windrows have been described earlier in this book, and windows of ground municipal compost make use of the same equipment, follow the same principles, and are the same general size and shape as the windrows used in agricultural or sludge operations: they are 4 to 6 feet high and round or conical in cross section

Municipal refuse may be composted in windrows after it is sorted and ground. Windrows must be turned regularly, or employ a forced-air system to ensure sufficient aeration for the composting process.

The Scarab Compost Turner, powered by a 250-h.p. engine, straddles the windrow and turns the compost as it moves along the pile.

to shed rain. Since municipal refuse is apt to be dry and resistant to decomposition, moisture control is particularly important.

The volume of finished compost will be only 20 to 60 percent of the volume of the original pile, depending upon the character of the materials and the degree of compaction. Compost with a lot of organic matter or garbage in it loses volume and weight faster than material with a higher cellulose or ash content.

To maintain aerobic conditions, windrows are turned every other day from the third day after they have been made. Turning is accomplished by breaking down the piles and reconstructing them, in the process tumbling the material to fluff it. If possible, inside material should go on the outside when the windrow is rebuilt. If it is impossible to reverse the position of material in the pile, then it should be turned once a day. As you can see, the procedure is very similar to the California method of garden composting which was described in Chapter 8.

This large machine picks up compost material, mixes it, and distributes it in windrow form.

Even plants where manual sorting is employed, like those in Mexico, use machinery to turn the piles efficiently and economically. The Eagle Crusher Company manufactures a machine, the Cobey Composter, designed especially for the purpose.

Satisfactory compost can be made in windrows without turning, if air is pushed or pulled through the windrows. Sludge, even when composted with other material, is more homogeneous than municipal compost and more moist. Although forced-air systems have been used with refuse composts, many experts advise against them because channels form in refuse material when air is forced through it, causing dryness in adjacent areas.

In less industrialized parts of the world, municipal refuse is still being composted by the Indore or modified Indore methods in pits, bins, and layered piles, formed and turned by hand labor.

Clarence Golueke whose excellent books, *Composting* and *Biological Reclamation of Solid Wastes*, discuss the principles and processes of composting in greater depth, has pointed out that the so-called high-rate composting methods are something of a misnomer perpetuated by the public relations and advertising people working for the manufacturers of mechanical compost equipment. All compost has to age in windrows or storage piles in order for the biological processes performed by the microorganisms in the piles to be carried out within their predetermined biological limits. What mechanical digesters are in effect doing is putting greater emphasis on grinding and on the initial "hot" phase of composting, and less on the sitting period during which bacteria do the grinding, and aeration is provided for them by turning.

Recent technological developments in windrow composting—specifically turning machines and pregrinding and sorting—have shortened the time of windrow composting to at least the equivalent of any existing mechanical system. Not only does this advance reduce the amount of land needed for windrow operations, but it also reduces odor problems.

MECHANICAL DIGESTER SYSTEMS

The first large-scale digester systems were largely anaerobic silos such as the Beccari process which was originally used with manures. The Beccari process silo was an insulated cell with air vents which were opened to make the second phase of the process aerobic. This process was used in Italy and France and has been modified in the Verdier process where drainage liquid or sometimes gases are recirculated through the mass in order to achieve more aerobic conditions. In the Bordas modification, material falls through the silo in stages, passing through grates or chambers as forced air dries and aerates the mass.

In general, mechanical systems are designed to speed up the decomposition process by providing a controlled environment. This is accomplished through aerating by tumbling if the system is horizontal, and by dropping if it is vertical. Moisture is supplied by spraying. Sometimes the compost is stirred for additional aeration and mixing. Some digesters use a combination of forced bottom aeration and stirring by means of an endless belt. All digesters are enclosed in one way or another.

One of the more successful digestion methods is the Dano process, which uses a large, slowly rotating drum with baffles inside it to move material along in a screw path during its average three-day digestion. Aeration is accomplished both by tumbling action and air injected into the drum through valves spaced along the cylinder. As dry wastes are delivered to the drum they are ground in an *Egseter* and sprayed with water or sewage sludge. Aerobic bacteria in the material respond to the

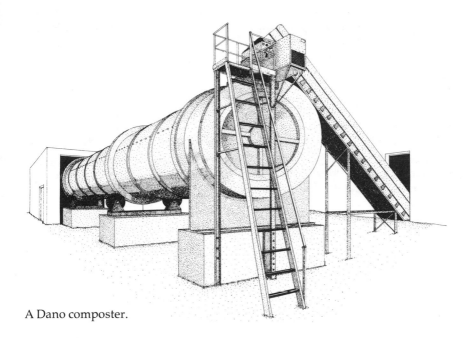

A Dano composter.

controlled environment and assist in rapid decomposition, raising temperatures up to 140°F. (60°C.). The compost is screened as soon as it leaves the "Biostabilizer" unit, and is then cured in windrows for one month if turned, and two months if not turned. The Dano system, developed in Denmark, evolved from a separating and grinding process. It is still used in a number of small and moderate-sized plants, most of them in Europe. The system is, however, expensive to operate.

One floor-to-floor tumbling design which is being used in Norman, Oklahoma, is the Naturizer system. It consists of two three-floor structures. A conveyer belt takes ground material to the top floor of one structure where it remains tumbling for 24 hours, then drops as V-shaped floor troughs pivot upside down like the shaker grates on an old wood stove. On leaving the bottom floor after a total of three days in the first building, the material is reground and transported to the top floor of the second structure where it repeats the process by the end of six days. One to two months' windrowing with occasional turning is sufficient for aging the Naturizer compost.

Another system currently in use is the Metro system, which makes use of continuous bottom aeration along with stirring and tumbling. The stirring and tumbling are accomplished by an endless belt which moves from one end of a long bin to the other. The belt is attached to a rail which moves over the bin. As the belt moves, it picks up composting material at its front, lifts it 3 feet, and drops it behind. The bins have perforated bottoms with an air stream moving through the perforations. The endless belt stirs the bin contents once a day during retention of up to six days.

The more complex Fairfield Hardy digester combines stirring with forced aeration by having large hollow augers rotate through the mass. Air comes out of nozzles in the augers. Ground refuse is placed in a cylindrical tank, and augers are supported by a bridge on a central

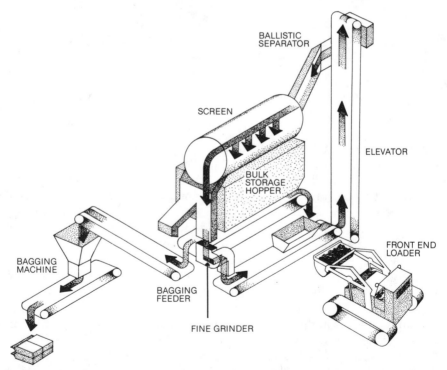

This type of efficient mechanical system can sometimes lead to the use of unfinished compost. In this system, the composting process begins when unsorted refuse is loaded into the elevator. After separation and screening, the refuse must be fully digested by a mechanical digester located inside the hopper in order for ripe compost to be produced.

pivoting structure that resembles a lawn sprinkler. Detention time can be varied, and windrowing usually follows digestion.

Mechanized digesters, obviously, cost more to buy and operate than windrows cost to build and turn. Capital investment usually reaches five-digit sums, and energy costs are also high. The Dano system, for example, uses 12 to 15 kilowatt hours to process a ton of refuse. These figures can be compared with the four kilowatt hours per ton for sludge compost windrows. In addition, mechanical digesters require more highly skilled manpower for their operation.

A temptation to the managers and owners of mechanical plants where economy can result from rapid turnover of material is to minimize space-requiring windrow time by selling or transporting unripe compost. If composting is done properly, however, land requirements for digester and windrow plants are the same. Both systems involve windrowing for comparable periods of time.

According to Dr. Neil Seldman, who is principally interested in resource recovery in his booklet, *Garbage in America,* large corporations are promoting high-technology resource recovery plants (and presumably high-technology composting plants as well), while small businesses and conservation-minded citizens push for low-technology projects such as neighborhood recycling centers. Dr. Seldman feels that a "major national battle [is] underway over who should control and profit from recycling the 150 million tons of municipal garbage processed each year."

Some proponents of composting as a means to soil building and enrichment feel that low-technology windrow composting, combined with some mechanization of sorting, grinding, and turning, is the most sensible way to use urban refuse. This sort of composting would build more satisfactorily upon neighborhood or city-wide recycling projects which remove much uncompostable but salable inorganic wastes, than upon massive mechanized refuse disposal plants.

Municipal refuse composting is only now getting underway again in this country. Gardeners who wish to use municipal refuse compost for their gardens or for further composting in their own piles, should keep informed of developments in the field and look out for products as they appear. Most municipal products now contain composted sewage sludge, but not composted refuse.

16

Sewage Sludge and Composting

Municipal garbage and refuse is one form of human waste that is generated in our urban and suburban areas. Another is sludge—the end product of our sewer systems. Fortunately, our sludge composting techniques have developed further than our methods of composting solid wastes. In many areas of the country, treated sludge is available for all gardeners who choose to pick it up and take it home. In some areas, sludge is being used on farm fields.

Sewage treatment plants like this one produce great quantities of sludge which are too often dumped, buried, or burned. Sludge is a valuable agricultural resource which we have too long overlooked.

USDA photo

Traditionally, America's sludge has been dumped, buried, or burned, resulting in pollution of our water, air, and land, and the waste of large amounts of energy and resources. The federal Water Pollution Control Act of 1972 required that all towns stop sending raw sludge into waterways. But near coastal cities, as rivers have become cleaner, the ocean has become more polluted, for the most common practice has been to dump the sludge produced by sewage treatment plants into the ocean. Although the 1972 law also gave the EPA the authority to end most kinds of ocean dumping, ocean dumping has remained a serious problem, especially along the New York and New Jersey coastlines.

The great concentrations of heavy metals and other potentially toxic substance in sludge are a major hazard when dumped into the ocean because control over their disposition is lost once they have been dumped. The result is a distinct threat to ocean ecology, including the endangering of food fish near the shore.

In inland cities, sludge is most often incinerated or used in landfills.

Digested sludge is settled in beds and dried until it is ready to be collected and spread on fields.

Compost Science *photo*

But land for fill sites is quickly running out, and so is the natural gas used for the incinerators which still remain the most common means of disposing of sludge. Air pollution control legislation has already caused many sludge incinerators to be shut down for failure to meet federal standards.

Obviously, sludge production will continue to increase in volume each year, while traditional disposal methods show less and less capability to handle that production. The obvious answer is to compost our sludge, and to use it as a soil conditioner/fertilizer.

Our sewage treatment plants produce three major kinds of sludge—raw, digested, and activated. Raw sludge is produced in the

In this plant, after the sludge is screened out into settling beds, the remaining effluent is showered over a two-acre 10-foot-deep trickling filter bed of crushed stone. The filtered, purified liquid is returned to a nearby water supply, in this case a river.

Compost Science *photo*

primary treatment of sewage by means of gravity settling. Digested sludge has been subjected to anaerobic fermentation in a digester. Activated sludge has been produced in the aerobic secondary treatment process. Digested sludge may be air-dried, centrifuged, and/or heat-dried. Activated sludge may be heat- or air-dried.

Sludge Chemistry

Benefits to the land which result from spreading dried digested sludge are very similar to those which result from spreading garden compost. When soil is enriched with sludge, it aggregates better, holds water better, and handles air and gases like carbon dioxide better. Sludge is, in other words, a good soil conditioner.

The chief difference between sludge and garden compost is that sludge generally has a greater fertilizing value than ordinary compost. Total nitrogen concentrations in sludge range from 0.7 to 5.1 percent (dry weight); phosphorus, 1.1 to 6.1 percent; and potassium, 0.2 to 1.1 percent. On an N-P-K basis, then, sludge is usually superior to compost.

A History of Waste

The recent history of sludge seems to be one of missed opportunities. As long ago as 1884, a Dr. Henry J. Barnes reported to the Massachusetts Medical Society that "All the human and animal manure which the world loses, restored to the land instead of being thrown into the water, would suffice to nourish the world. These heaps of garbage at the corners of the stone blocks, these tumbrils of mire jolting the streets at night, these horrid scavengers' carts, these fetid streams of subterranean slime which the pavement hides, what is all this? It is the flourishing meadow, the green grass, the thyme and sage; it is game, it is cattle, hay, corn, bread upon the table, blood in the veins."

Dr. Barnes, despite his romantic appreciation of sludge, was fighting a losing battle in the Victorian age. In America, in the nineteenth century, the misuse of sludge was the product of two very important phenomena: the concentration of human populations into urban areas, and the development and increasing popularity of running water and sewage systems. Whereas, before the Civil War, urban cesspools were the recipients of human wastes, we gradually gained the affluence to enable us to "flush away" our wastes. The water closet, the flush toilet, became a Victorian nicety, and people of supposed good breeding never gave a thought to the final destination of their own wastes.

The situation in the first hundred years of our nationhood was vastly different. Our population was much smaller, and largely rural. Human wastes were stored in cesspools and privy vaults, and were periodically removed and taken to farms for application on the land. It was a sensible system which worked, and it became unworkable only when certain eastern cities became large enough to develop urban slums. The cesspools and privy vaults in these slum areas were not cleaned out regularly, leading to demands that running water and sewage systems be installed in all cities. These systems, while doubtless making a giant contribution to public health, dictated the misuse of human waste products which has persisted until the present day.

Modern Use of Sludge

Today, sludge is being returned to the land with increasing frequency, in response to pollution problems and new laws designed to solve those problems.

There are a number of forms in which sludge is applied. For purposes of simplification, however, we will consider only two—liquid

Lagoon-dried digested sludge is spread on farmland.

Compost Science *photo*

and dry. In liquid, sludge is used either in its natural state or with water added to it. Liquid sludge or slurry can be pumped into tank trucks which then spray it onto farm fields, parks, pastures, or waste land. There, it can either be left on the surface or plowed in after having dried. Sludge slurry can be used with various irrigation systems, or it can be pumped by gravity or pressure into furrows and covered, or incorporated directly into the top 8 inches of soil with a sub-sod injection. There are also several other methods for applying and incorporating liquid sludge.

Sludge can also be applied in dry, digested form. Here, the final product is granular, resembling finished compost. This method has the advantage of allowing for better timing of application, because dry sludge can be stored. Because of its lighter weight, dry sludge is less expensive to transport.

Composting Sludge

Composting has several important advantages over conventional anaerobic digestion and drying as a method for disposing of sludges and as a method of producing nutrient-rich soil conditioners. According to Clarence Golueke, "Composting broadens the variety of uses to which sludge can be applied, by converting it into an easily workable and storable product suitable for large-scale farming and for the home garden."

The composting process stabilizes excess quantities of nitrogen, converting soluble forms to temporarily insoluble and slowly soluble ones. In this way the danger of nitrogen leaching from land and contaminating waters is greatly decreased. By adding high-carbon materials to nitrogen-high sludge, compost also gives a more balanced addition to the soil, permitting a higher degree of nitrogen assimilation by soil microorganisms.

When sludge is composted with other ingredients, the heavy metal concentration in it becomes diluted. Heavy metal concentration and pathogens are the two greatest dangers surrounding the use of sludge as a fertilizer and soil conditioner. Dr. Rufus Chaney of the U.S. Department of Agriculture, Beltsville, Maryland, says "Grass and plants grown with composted sludge contain about one-half the cadmium of plants grown with uncomposted sludge." One reason for this may be that composting raises the pH level and in more alkaline conditions metals tend to be bound in unusable forms.

Sludge Composting in the United States

The composting of sludge has been making good headway in the United States. Eliot Epstein, of the Biological Waste Management and Soil Nitrogen Laboratory, Agricultural Environmental Quality Institute, Beltsville Agricultural Research Center, has summarized current progress as follows.*

There are two primary methods of sludge composting in the United States, the windrow system and the Beltsville Aerated Pile Method.

THE AERATED PILE METHOD

The Beltsville process, developed by engineers at the U.S. Department of Agriculture research center at Beltsville, Maryland, consists in essence of mixing sewage sludge with a bulking material such as wood chips and then composting in a stationary pile for 21 days while air is drawn through the mass. Wood chips, shredded paper, paper pellets, leaves, peanut hulls, and automobile fluff have all been used as bulking materials. The paper and paper pellets were obtained from a resource recovery plant at Cockeysville, Maryland, following air classification. The automobile fluff consisted of shredded foam rubber and fabric material recovered after metal removal. Following mixing of the bulking material with sludge, the researchers construct an aerated pile as shown in figure 1.

A loop of perforated plastic pipe 10 centimeters in diameter is laid on the surface and covered with 30 centimeters of wood chips or unscreened compost. This comprises the base of the pile. The sludge-wood chip mixture is then placed in a pile on the prepared base, after which the pile is blanketed with a 30-centimeter layer of screened compost for insulation and odor control. Fifty tons of wet sludge produce a pile of triangular cross section, which is approximately 16 meters long, 7 meters wide, and 2.5 meters high. The loop of perforated pipe is then connected by solid pipe to a ⅓-h.p. blower controlled by a timer. Aerobic composting conditions are maintained by drawing air through the pile. The effluent air stream is conducted into a small pile of screened, cured compost, where odorous gases are effectively absorbed. The blower is operated intermittently to provide oxygen levels between

*Reprinted with permission from *Compost Science*, September/October, 1977.

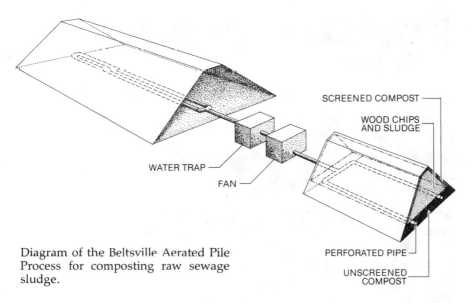

SCREENED COMPOST

WOOD CHIPS
AND SLUDGE

WATER TRAP

FAN

Diagram of the Beltsville Aerated Pile
Process for composting raw sewage
sludge.

PERFORATED PIPE

UNSCREENED
COMPOST

5 and 15 percent during the composting period. The sludge-wood chip mixture is composted in the pile for 21 days, during which time the sludge is stabilized by the rapid decomposition of volatile organic solids, and odors are abated.

A modification of the aerated pile is the aerated extended pile, in which each day's sludge delivery is mixed with wood chips and placed in a pile which utilizes the shoulder (lengthwise dimension) of the previous day's pile, forming a continuous or extended pile. The extended pile causes a major reduction in the compost area, the amount of blanket material required, and the wood chip requirement for the pile base.

Cities as diverse as Durham, New Hampshire; Bangor, Maine; Camden, New Jersey; and Windsor, Ontario, have begun using the aerated-pile method of sludge composting developed at Beltsville.

PROJECTS EMPLOYING WINDROW COMPOSTING

One of the oldest composting processes in the United States is windrow composting. The longest and best-known operation of this type is the one conducted by the Los Angeles, California, County Sanitation District in conjunction with the Kellogg Supply Company. Dewatered, digested sewage sludge is mixed with dry sludge and placed in a windrow. The sludge is composted in the windrow under aerobic

Finished sludge compost is dry and crumbly in texture.

Compost Science *photo*

conditions for variable time periods ranging from 21 days in summer to 40 days in winter. The windrows initially are 4 feet deep and 10 feet wide. The material is turned by Cobey Roto-Shredder machines twice daily for the first five days, then once daily to insure adequate amounts of oxygen. When the compost is ready, the Kellogg Company hauls it to their facilities for screening and bagging. The product is sold under the trade name of "Nitrohumus."

Composting of sewage sludge is a viable and economic alternative to sludge disposal. It is important, though, that industrial contamination be kept at a minimum so that the final product is a valuable resource.

Sludge-Refuse Compost

From the point of view of sheer economy, the composting of sewage sludge (which is high in nitrogen) with municipal refuse (which is high in carbon) would seem a perfect solution to many urban headaches. Even a city which bagged the finished compost and distributed it free to citizens would come out ahead.

The first pilot-scale experiments with sludge-refuse compost were conducted in the 1950s by the University of California at Berkeley, and other studies were carried out in the Los Angeles area.

According to Dr. Golueke, "It has been estimated that the output of compostable refuse from an average city would accommodate about one-third of its output of digested sludge. Therefore, if the sludge were relieved of about two-thirds of its water, all of the sludge could be composted without difficulty, provided it could be thoroughly mixed with the absorbent."

Composting of refuse and sludge has so far been given much more serious attention abroad than in the United States. Professor Gedaliah Shelef of the Technion-Israel Institute of Technology in Haifa has noted that the changes in living standards and compost technology make composting of combined refuse and sludge feasible. Aeration and mixing, he says, are made easier at higher sludge moisture contents because of the presence of coarse material like plastic and tin cans which are normally sorted out of refuse before composting.

Many of the barriers to further development of sludge compost plants in this country today are problems of institutions and public opinion, not of technology.

Health and Safety

There are two reasons you should be informed about the health and safety of using sludge. The first is that as a gardener, homesteader, or farmer, you may want to use some of this valuable soil builder and fertilizer on your garden, in your fields, or in your compost pile. You can buy digested or composted sludge products at a hardware or garden supply store or, if you are lucky and live in a town the right size, you may even get digested sludge free at your municipal treatment plant. If you need larger amounts of sludge, for a farm or homestead, you may be able to contract with a sewage treatment plant for dry or liquid sludge if you have, or can rent, a truck or tank truck to carry it. Occasionally, you may find a plant that will deliver and/or apply the sludge. In any case, it's important to check all public health ordinances affecting your area and, if possible, to discuss your plans with your neighbors before making arrangements for sludge, whether you or someone else does the job. It would also be wise to learn all you can about applying the material and using it correctly.

If the age of technology and "miracle" developments has taught us anything, it is to be cautious consumers. Even if something is free, it's no bargain if it endangers our health or the health of our land. So the first reason for learning about sludge safety is to protect our own health and the health of the soil.

The second reason we should be informed is that a public battle is shaping up over sludge use, a battle which carries over into all of composting practice. As composters we will have to have informed answers for those who try to scare us back to chemical fertilizers by using public health arguments, and this will be true whether or not we, ourselves, use sludge.

Using Sludge in the Garden

The topic of using sewage sludge in the garden is currently causing much controversy and conversation. Based on the research up to now, and conversations with many of the researchers, the editors of *Organic Gardening* feel we can safely recommend application of most digested sewage sludges in the garden.

Most potential sludge users are concerned about pathogens being transmitted in the sludge. This concern stems from the many episodes of persons developing health problems from eating food fertilized with human manure. There is considerable difference between raw human wastes and sewage sludge. Sludge is the end product of the waste treatment process. This process is designed to greatly reduce the pathogen content of the incoming sewage. In almost all cases the sludge you receive will have already been activated (aerobic bacterial treatment) and subjected to a period of biological breakdown. The waste would then be settled, and later placed on sand drying beds for a period of time. All this treatment renders most viruses inactive. Further, the act of storing sludge, or composting it, kills off most surviving pathogens. At this time we have not been able to find any research that would support the claim of pathogen persistence in sludge that has undergone composting and storage. Any sludge that has been composted, or activated, dried and stored for a period of time may be considered safe from pathogen contamination. If you have access to raw sludge, you should compost and store it for at least a year before using it.

PATHOGENS IN SLUDGE

Pathogens survive for periods of varying duration in soil and their survival time is determined by their genetic makeup, the moisture content and temperature of the soil, soil pH, sunlight, organic matter present, and other soil organisms present in soil to compete with them.

SURVIVAL TIMES OF VARIOUS PATHOGENS IN THE SOIL AND ON PLANTS

Organism	Medium	Survival Time
Ascaris ova	soil	Up to 7 years
	vegetables	25 to 53 days
Salmonella typhosa	soil	29 to 74 days
	vegetables	31 days
Cholera vibro	spinach, lettuce	22 to 23 days
	nonacid vegetables	2 days
Endamoeba histolytica	vegetables	3 days
	soil	8 days
Coliforms	grass	14 days
	tomatoes	35 days
Hookworm larvae	soil	6 weeks
Leptospira	soil	15 to 43 days
Polio virus	polluted water	20 days
Shigella	tomatoes	2 to 7 days
Tubercle bacilli	soil	6 months
Typhoid bacilli	soil	7 to 40 days

In general, wet, cold, shaded, humus-rich soil with low microorganism populations most favors pathogen survival. Because of the many factors affecting survival time, no hard and fast rules can be laid down to determine a time when a given sludge is safe for all uses. However, Dr. Golueke believes that a year of storage will get rid of all the pathogens likely to be found in sludges so long as conditions in storage do not favor pathogen recurrence. Composting at home, though, can reduce the time needed for pathogen destruction.

Viruses may survive 28 to 170 days, again depending upon conditions of storage or soil. Much more study needs to be made of virus survival. Some biologists believe the omnipresence of viruses, the difficulty of filtering and cultivating them, and their ability to undergo mutations pose special problems in sludge. Pathogen counts from sludge can easily include nonvirulent viruses which qualify the reliability of the procedures.

There seems to be general agreement that composting destroys pathogens. All living organisms have temperature points beyond which they cannot survive. Dr. Golueke compiled a table of the thermal death points of various pathogens and parasites and proved theoretically that the temperatures reached in aerobic composting exceed all these thermal death points. "No harmful microorganisms," he says, "could survive the composting process *provided* all organisms were exposed to the bactericidal conditions prevailing inside the pile at some time during the course of the process." His findings have been proven experimentally by others.

For example, recent investigations at Johnson City, Tennessee, in conjunction with an EPA project showed that (1) pathogenic bacteria that may be associated with sewage sludge and municipal refuse were destroyed by the composting process after being inserted into windrows; and (2) *M. tuberculosis* was normally destroyed by the fourteenth day of composting if the temperature had averaged 149°F. (65°C.). In all cases, the organisms were destroyed by the 21st day. In further research with sludge-treated soils conducted by the National Environmental Research Center in Cincinnati, Ohio, various sludges were applied at the rate of 1 gallon per square foot. The results of the study showed a maximum survival time of 16 weeks for salmonella species and 21 weeks for *Pseudomonas aeruginosa.*

HEAVY METAL POLLUTION

Some sewage sludges, mainly those receiving industrial effluent, may have high levels of heavy metals that render them unsafe for garden use. Some sludges may have metal contents so high that they will actually retard plant growth. As a potential user of sludge, you must be concerned with these heavy metals. The ideal solution is to have the polluting industries stop dumping chemicals into the sewage system. Some towns have greatly reduced the heavy metal content of their sludge by isolating the company putting such wastes into the system and making them install antipollution equipment at the plant. Once the metals are mixed with the sludge, it is almost impossible to remove them. The problem must be controlled at the source.

The four metals you should be most concerned with are zinc, copper, nickel and cadmium. The first three are important because they are phytotoxic (poisonous to plants) at relatively low levels, and cadmium is of concern because plants tend to accumulate it in their leaves, and it has adverse effects on humans, with the body building up a toxic amount over a period of time. For that reason, sludge with relatively high levels of cadmium should never be used on food crops, and sludge containing high levels of zinc, copper or nickel should be carefully monitored to avoid a toxic buildup both in soil and plants.

When speaking of high or low levels of heavy metals in sewage sludges, the amounts discussed are incredibly small, owing to their high toxicity. For instance, a sludge considered to have a high cadmium content may have 75 parts of cadmium for every million parts of sludge. The test to determine heavy metal content of a sludge is strictly a laboratory matter.

When discussing limits for these metals, we can give only general figures, because the actual uptake of a metal by a plant will depend on many factors—the pH of the soil, type of plant grown, cation exchange capacity of the soil, to name a few. There are many things we do not know about the way heavy metals behave in the soil. For example, we do know that composting sewage sludge reduces the amount of cadmium a plant will absorb, but no one as yet knows why.

Thus, for a general guideline, on a dry weight basis, the limits in the chart below have been determined safe. As yet, no federal agency has settled on limitations for heavy metal content of sludges. The U.S. Department of Agriculture has done most of the research into the topic, but the agency does not want to be responsible for establishing and possibly enforcing the eventual final guidelines. The figures given are the result of U.S. Department of Agriculture work, and establish total yearly accumulations on a kilogram-per-hectare basis.

Cadmium	5 to 20
Zinc	250 to 1,000
Copper	125 to 500
Nickel	50 to 200

In most cases, if the sludge you will be using has been analyzed, the results will be in a parts per million basis. In that form, the upper limit for cadmium would be 25 ppm for sludges to be used for food crops, and 50 ppm for any to be used on ornamentals or tree crops. At those limits the sludge could be applied on a regular basis for many years without harmful buildup in the soil. If you cannot get a copy of an analysis of the sludge—unless you are absolutely sure there are no industries dumping into the system—you should not use it. But you *should* pressure town officials to have the sludge analyzed—and dumping laws enforced.

Another way of telling whether a sludge is safe is the zinc-cadmium ratio. If there is one part of cadmium for every 100 parts of zinc, you may use the sludge. At this ratio, the zinc would kill off the plants if there was enough cadmium in the sludge to harm you or your animals. If this happens, the soil would have to be limed to a high pH, and soil and plant samples analyzed, but human health would not be endangered. For that reason, we recommend always finding out the cadmium and zinc content of the sludge you will be using on a parts-per-million basis or milligrams-per-kilogram ratio, then calculate the cadmium-zinc ratio.

The last area of concern is the presence of industrial chemicals. Such items as PCB's and PBB's are noted problem-causers in sludge, due to their being taken up by plants and passed along in the food chain. Ask the director of the sanitation plant where you will be getting your sludge if these chemicals are present. If the sludge contains more than ten parts per million of PCB or PBB, we do not recommend you use it. Luckily, this should not be much of a problem for most people.

Concerning the actual usage of sludge, we recommend that it be used as any other manure. It is best applied in the fall and allowed to winter over, or applied in the early spring with four to six weeks of time in the soil before planting. For safety, you should keep the soil at a pH of about 6.5 to further inhibit metals uptake. Don't apply fresh sludge to root crops that you'll be harvesting that year and eating raw, or crops such as leafy green vegetables that you'll be picking shortly after application.

If you are interested in using sewage sludge, by all means urge your local municipality to stop industrial users from dumping pollutants which could result in potentially dangerous sludges. Clean sludge is the same as clean water; it is good for plants; while polluted sludge is the same as polluted water; it is not good for plants.

17

Composting Industrial Wastes

Industrial wastes—and especially the organic wastes from the food, clothing, lumber, and paper industries—represent a resource of tremendous potential value to America's garden and farm lands. Unfortunately, like both garbage and sludge, industrial wastes have traditionally been mismanaged or wasted. When garbage and sludge are mismanaged, the consumer pays the price in higher taxes. When industrial wastes are mismanaged, the consumer usually pays through higher prices for the products he buys, or through higher taxes when government cleans up the lands and waters polluted by industry.

Despite the abuse heaped upon private industry for its pollution activities, the private sector has occasionally shown both courage and creativity in its approach to wastes, often leading government efforts in this area. Especially when markets can be found for industrial wastes, industry will cooperate fully in meeting public demand for wastes. Prime examples for many years have been buckwheat hulls, cocoa bean shells, peanut shells, and sugar cane wastes, all of which are bagged and marketed to gardeners as mulches.

A few manufacturers and industries have been especially farsighted in investigating and practicing methods of composting their organic wastes. In 1953, Lederle Laboratories, a pharmaceutical company in Pearl River, New York, began investigating composting as a means of disposing of pharmaceutical sludge. The sludge was found to have a year-round C/N ratio of about 15:1. It contained manure from stabled animals, wastes from the fermentation of antibiotics, animal livers and other organs from which extracts had been made, and sanitary sewage from 4,000 employees. A mixture of 65 percent sludge, 25 percent barn manure containing straw bedding and sawdust, and 10 percent wood sawdust was made, and for every 100 pounds of the mixture one-half

367

pound of ground phosphate rock was added. The sludge was dewatered on vacuum filters using lime as a coagulant, until it contained between 50 and 60 percent water. Sawdust not only acted as an absorbent, but also helped to bring down the pH of the sludge from 8.0 or 7.5 to 7.5 or 6.5.

The procedure that was developed in small-scale experiments was to seed each mixture with a 10 percent addition of the batch which was begun the previous day. After this addition, the mixture was shredded and stored for 24 hours. Each day this process was repeated until a point of partial stability had been reached in six days. The total windrowing time was 150 days.

In 1955 a ten-acre plot was designated for windrow operations with a five-month turnover of materials. A shredder which could treat 30 cubic yards of compost per hour was put into operation. This was used with a 1-cubic-yard capacity front-end loader. Windrows were laid out 25 feet wide, 300 feet long, and an unusual 15 feet in height.

After composting for five months, the material was moved to small cone-shaped piles for further drying, and then reshredded in a warehouse. The finished compost was used on the grounds of the company or sold to a local dealer for distribution as a soil or lawn conditioner. The laboratory found composting to be the most practical method for treating, disposing of, and using its wastes.

A municipal composting plant in Blaubeuren, Germany, was set up and is now in operation due to the influence of the mill manager and part-owner of a large cement plant. The manager-owner, Dr. E. Spohn, believes in returning the land, which has been stripped for calcareous rock ore, to agricultural use.

A research laboratory at the cement plant and an experimental farm supervised by Dr. Spohn perform tests on the use of compost. At the refuse facility, municipal refuse is rasped and then composted in windrows for three to six months with one or two turnings.

This is an encouraging example of an industry that has taken full responsibility for repairing damage it has done to land.

Types of Industrial Waste

In general, the term "industrial wastes" refers to all wastes produced on industrial premises or arising from industrial processes. These include all excess materials discarded by manufacturers as non-reclaimable or uneconomical to reclaim. They may be solid, semisolid, liquid, or gaseous. There is an almost inexhaustible number of different types of industrial wastes and, since new manufacturing processes are constantly being introduced, new wastes are continuously appearing. Wastes, however, sometimes become the raw materials of new processes. More and more industries are directing research toward finding new by-product uses.

One way of categorizing industrial wastes is to divide them into organic and inorganic groupings. By and large, inorganic wastes are not suitable for composting. In most cases they contain little or no nitrogen, and the carbon they contain is not in a form usable by microorganisms in their metabolism. There are, however, exceptions to this rule, as we will see later.

It is the organic wastes of industry that cause the problem. Water-soluble organic waste may be unsuitable for landfill, because of the danger of the leaching of nitrogen and other chemicals to ground and surface waters. Organic wastes are also potential sources of infection. They can cause odors and attract pests as they decay.

On the other hand, it is organic wastes that contribute most to the soil if they are composted properly. Composting is not always the most economical way of dealing with organic wastes, but it is, except in the case of toxic wastes, the most ecologically responsible way.

Organic wastes can be further categorized into those wastes high in nitrogen and those with a low-nitrogen content. High-nitrogen wastes will decompose rapidly, but to be properly composted they must be mixed with high-carbon material at a ratio of 25 to 30 parts of carbon to one of nitrogen. Since, as we have seen in studying garden compost materials, there are abundant sources of carbon, both in nature and from industry—from dried leaves or sawdust to municipal refuse—it should be easy to find complementary ingredients for waste of high nitrogen. With low-nitrogen wastes, it may be necessary to "seed" the mixture with high-nitrogen wastes such as animal manures.

WASTES OF THE FOOD INDUSTRY

In looking for high-nitrogen wastes, the first place to go is the food industry—packing houses, slaughterhouses, stockyards, fish processing companies, canneries, distilleries, dairies, and breweries.

We've already discussed (in Chapter 13) the problems of disposing of feedlot manure and the need to take certain steps, such as drying or mixing with absorbent material, when composting manure.

Slaughterhouse Wastes

It has been estimated that for small slaughterhouses that do not process any by-products themselves, the compostable waste will be as much as 50 to 80 pounds on a dry basis per ton of meat processed. Large plants, which, as we know, claim to use every part of the pig but the squeal, have much less waste—an average of 25 to 40 pounds per ton. In large modern plants most of the wastes are in the form of a liquid sewage.

According to Harold B. Gotaas in his book *Composting*, wastes in rural slaughterhouses consist of blood, unsalable meat, intestines, offal, paunch manure (the vegetable waste found in the digestive tract of the slaughtered animal), hoofs, and other materials. He gives the following table for the contents of this material:

	Percent
Moisture content	75–80
Organic matter (dry basis)	80–95
Nitrogen (dry basis)	8–11
Phosphorus as P_2O_5 (dry basis)	3.0–3.5
Potassium as K_2O (dry basis)	2.0–2.5
Carbon (dry basis)	14–17
Calcium as CaO (dry basis)	3.0–3.5

In Switzerland, Beccari cell systems, which were described in the last chapter, are used for composting slaughterhouse wastes. These cells consist of concrete silos or pits with wall aeration and water drainage. Decomposition takes place over six months until the end product resembles stable manure in nutritional value. Beccari cell composting, which is partly anaerobic, works best for paunch manure, intestines, small pieces of meat and trimmings, while bones, hoofs, large chunks of meat, and whole carcasses are not suitable unless they are first ground.

Tankage, (the correct name for the refuse of slaughterhouses and butcher shops, exclusive of blood, which has been processed to free it of fats) has a nitrogen content of between 5.0 and 12.5 percent. The phosphoric acid content is usually around 2 percent, but it may be higher if bones are included. Gardeners can sometimes obtain tankage for addition to home compost piles. Local slaughterhouses are the best places to look for it. Blood meal or dried blood, bone meal, and hoof and horn meal which are especially rich in nitrogen, may also be obtained commercially for use in home compost.

Steamed bone meal is made from green bones (those recently received from the slaughterhouse) which have been steamed or processed to remove fats. It has less nitrogen than raw bone meal. Bone black is charred bone. It is used by the sugar refining industry as a filter and is sometimes ground for sale with sugar residues in it. With the sugar residues its nitrogen content can be 2 percent. It also contains trace elements.

Wastes from the Fishing Industry

The clean-up of waste liquors and scrap produced in fish reduction processes began as a measure to control pollution, but has since become a very profitable industry in itself. Reclaimed fish solubles once thrown away now account for 20 to 25 percent of the total production value of fish products. The tobacco industry is a heavy user of fertilizers produced from fish residues, and fish emulsion fertilizer made from fish solubles is widely used by gardeners. Stockwater from the wet processing to remove oil from fish is now vacuum evaporated and the solids are used in pet foods and animal feeds. Although industry's gain is composting's loss in this case, it does represent an efficient means of using waste.

Fish scrap is over 7 percent nitrogen on a dry basis, and contains almost the same amount of phosphorus. Dried ground fish is free from fat, but fish scrap contains much oil and therefore breaks down more slowly when composted. In tropical regions where citrus or banana wastes are available near fish canneries, composting of combined fish and fruit residues has been successfully carried on. It is usually done in pits because of the odor problem. Cannery fish scrap can also be used in agricultural composting. Some farmers sprinkle fish scrap with quicklime before adding it to compost to reduce problems from odor and oil. Shellfish waste is sometimes also available to farmers near processing plants.

Cannery Wastes

Dr. Golueke points out in *Biological Reclamation of Solid Wastes* that cannery waste presents problems in composting because of its high moisture content. For example, peach and apricot wastes have a moisture content of about 85 percent. He suggests incorporating these wastes with an absorbent material of porous structure which will give a balanced C/N ratio to the compost. He says:

> Sawdust, straw, and rice hulls can be reused repeatedly with cannery wastes because they are resistant to decomposition and can be sifted out of finished compost. Because much of the high carbon material is removed with this method, a higher than normal C/N ratio is permissible.

A National Canners Association study suggests 1,000:1 as a permissible ratio when composting peach or apricot residues with sawdust. Nitrogen may be added in the form of manure, urea, or green vegetable matter.

Other cannery or food processing wastes which lend themselves to composting are citrus wastes, especially skins which are rich in phosphorus and nitrogen; apple pomace; asparagus trimmings; castor pomace from the making of castor oil; beet wastes from canneries or the sugar industry; coffee chaff; spinach wastes; olive residues from oil pressing; pea pods; tea leaves; spice marc; buckwheat hulls; filter cake from sugar refineries; cane waste; whey; cocoa shells; tung oil pomace; rice hulls; residues of yeast and malt companies; starch waste; and gelatin waste. These materials were discussed in Chapter 6.

Winery Waste

The leftovers from wineries, consisting of the pressed parts of grapes, also contain yeasts and bacteria which accelerate composting. Their nitrogen content is around 1 percent. As is the case for composting cannery waste, special care must be taken to remove excess water from grape pomace before it is composted. Grape waste usually leaves the winery in sludge form.

In Switzerland, grape sludge is dehydrated by means of a vibrating sieve condenser similar to the kind used in sedimentation plants. To counteract the acidity of the pomace, lime is used. When the sludge is dry enough to be handled with a spade, it is mixed with an equal quantity of shredded municipal refuse and composted in large piles. Grape sludge adds much to the nutritional quality of the refuse compost and speeds its decomposition.

The following table, taken from an article by Dr. Rudolf Braun

entitled, "Utilization of Organic Industrial Wastes by Composting,"
(*Compost Science*, Autumn, 1962) shares the contents of the Swiss grape
sludge:

COMPOSITION OF THE SPADEABLE (DRY) AND
UNFERMENTED SEDIMENTATION SLUDGE

Material	Percent
Water content	84.0
Total organic matter	70.5
Inert organic matter	17.5
Effective organic matter	53.0
Soluble humus substance	17.9
Total nitrogen	1.62
Phosphorus as P_2O_5	0.59
Potash as K_2O	0.36
Calcium as CaO	3.9
Magnesium as MgO	0.33
pH value before lime treatment	5.9
pH value before composting	7.0

A combination of pressed grapes, feathers, and hair has been
composted in more than one operation in Switzerland.

Brewery and Distillery Wastes

After hops have been extracted by a process using water, the
brewery leftover is called spent hops. In their wet state, spent hops are
75 percent water, 0.6 percent nitrogen, and 0.2 percent phosphorus. In
the more reliable dry weight measure, nitrogen amounts to 2.5 to 3.5
percent and the phosphorus about 1 percent. Spent hops are rich
enough in nitrogen, and decompose rapidly enough that they make a
good compost ingredient. Dried spent hops also have value as a mulch.

Some breweries will sell or donate spent hops for use in compost
piles.

Another brewery waste is the material left over from the mashing
process. This material, called brewers' grain, is composed of grain parts.
It decays readily and contains almost 1 percent nitrogen, but it must be

mixed with absorbent material to compost well. Similar grain material can be found at whiskey distilleries.

Peanut Hulls, Rice Hulls, and Soy Wastes

Peanut shells and soybean wastes are unusually high in nitrogen as compared with other vegetable by-products. Peanut shells, in fact, contain 8.6 percent nitrogen by analysis on a dry basis. Manufacturers of peanut and soy products, however, like those of fish products, now use much of what used to be waste as part of their edible products.

Rice hulls are lower in nitrogen, but they are an excellent source of potassium and they decompose rapidly in compost if a strong nitrogen source is used with them.

WASTES OF THE CLOTHING AND FABRIC INDUSTRIES

Leather Industry Wastes

The wastes from tanneries and the shoe, accessory, and leather clothing industries are particularly rich in nitrogen. Leather dust varies from 5.5 to 12 percent nitrogen, and also contains a considerable amount of phosphorus. Raw hides are as high as 13 percent nitrogen.

In France, leather waste is treated either with acid or alkaline solutions to reduce it to a form that can be used in fertilizer, or it is composted.

Tanning makes the nitrogen compounds in leather refractory and causes leather scraps to take a long time to break down when composted. Chemists at the College of Agriculture in Poona, India, found that acid treatment with 2.5 percent sulfuric acid prior to composting speeded the decomposition of both vegetable- and chrome-tanned leathers in compost. With chrome-tanned leather, hydrochloric acid is also used successfully.

Tanbark is a residue resulting from the process of tanning leather by vegetable methods. In earlier times it was made from the bark of hemlock, oak, and chestnut trees. Today, when vegetable products are used in tanning, they are usually made from wattle, mangrove, myrobalans, and valonia, plants imported from South America, Africa, India, and Asia Minor. Tannins are extracted from these plants under steam pressure. The waste material is ground, screened, dumped, composted, and sold commercially for garden use and mulching. Tanbark is moderately high in nitrogen, containing up to 1.7 percent. It is also rich in trace minerals.

Some Other Animal Wastes

Feathers from the poultry industry are high in nitrogen—up to 15 percent—and will decompose rapidly if kept quite moist. They can be used as an absorbent with moist, but high-carbon wastes. Hair and fur are more difficult to compost because they are resistant to decay. Fine clipping or grinding and adequate moisture hasten the process.

The gelatin and glue industries which use hoof and horn material also produce high-nitrogen compostable wastes.

Animal Fiber Textile Wastes

Wool waste or "shoddy" has been used by English farmers living in the vicinity of woolen textile mills since the early days of the industrial revolution. Generally the moisture content of wool wastes is between 13 and 20 percent and the nitrogen content 2 to 4 percent.

A Swiss named Ernst Baumann who owned an orange plantation in Spain developed a method whereby 10 tons of woolen refuse per year were mixed with stable manure and municipal garbage and composted.

Hat manufacturers and others who make or use felt have waste composed of hair and wool which may contain up to 14 percent nitrogen. Like hair, felt requires much moisture and an abundance of bacteria to decompose quickly. Manure provides a good combining substance for composting felt waste.

Silkworm cocoons contain about 10 percent nitrogen and over 1 percent potassium. By-products from silk mills are useful in composting.

Textile Wastes from Vegetable Fibers

When we move from the wastes of animal to those of vegetable products, the high-nitrogen character of the wastes generally disappears. To achieve a proper balance for composting most vegetable wastes, we must add material of high-nitrogen content. Though more difficult to obtain, nitrogen sources are available in manure, tankage, garbage, sewage sludge, and several other wastes. There are major exceptions to the general rule that animal sources are richer in nitrogen. Cottonseed meal, peanut shells, and soy wastes, are three high-nitrogen vegetable wastes.

Cotton Wastes

Cotton textile mills produce a large amount of cotton dust, especially in their blowrooms. In India, this dust has been found to average 20 to 50 tons per year per 25,000 spindles. The waste consists of unrecoverable cotton fibers and broken cottonseed coats.

The chemical analysis is as follows, according to A. D. Bhide of the Central Public Health Engineering Research Institute, in Nagpur, India:

CHEMICAL ANALYSIS OF RAW COTTON DUST

Item	Percent by Weight
Moisture	8.0
Organic matter	70.0
Carbon	41.0
Nitrogen	1.40
Phosphorus as P_2O_5	0.60
Potash as K_2O	1.20
C/N ratio	29.28/1
pH	6.2

The table shows that the waste has an N-P-K value higher than average municipal refuse.

In India, cotton waste has been composted in large windrows under 5 feet high with a moisture range of 50 to 60 percent. The process takes 20 days with turning on alternate days. The material is sufficiently clean so that it creates no nuisance in composting.

Cottonseed burrs are a source of potash. When combined with other waste products of cotton mills, they can be piled in the open and will decay to compost humus without further additions.

Cottonseed meal is made from cotton seed which has been freed from lint and hulls and has the oil extracted from it. Cottonseed cake is a rich protein food widely used in animal feeds. The meal has an acid reaction which makes it valuable for treating alkaline soil and for use in growing acid-loving crops. Cotton seed is rich in nitrogen, containing around 7 percent.

Cottonseed hulls and hull ashes are widely used in composting and may be purchased commercially by farmers and gardeners. They are good potassium sources, containing 15 to 23 percent.

The Texas State Department of Health developed a system of composting cotton gin trash which accomplishes the return to the soil of all parts of the cotton plant except the blossom and the seed. The process is comparatively low in cost. In addition its use has almost eliminated the incineration of cotton wastes which was once a serious air polluter.

Jute and flax residues may also be composted, though preliminary water soaking may be necessary to help break down resistant fibers. Manure, sewage sludge, or garbage can be used in composting these fibers, or in composting cotton wastes.

WASTES OF THE LUMBER AND PAPER INDUSTRIES

Experts have determined that there is more waste of lignin or wood fiber than of any other by-product of industry. Most of this comes from the paper and pulp mills, but the woodworking and wood-using industries such as saw- and planing-mills also contribute wood fiber waste.

Wastes of the cellulose, paper, and carton industries are often in chemically treated slurry form, which contributes to difficulty in using them to compost. Some of these wastes, along with small pieces of wood, sawdust, shavings, and ground bark, can be used in the manufacture of new products such as pressed fiber sheets and boards, and insulating materials.

Forestry also produces lignin waste from small branches, twigs, bark, chips, and sawdust. Forestry services in various countries have successfully composted this waste.

In the chapter on sewage sludge, we saw that wood chips are used in the U.S. Department of Agriculture composting projects in Beltsville, Maryland, as a high-carbon absorbent which, after being composted with sludge, can be recycled for repeated use.

The main problems with wood wastes are that their C/N ratio is extremely high and that they are resistant to bacterial action. In order to compost them, it is necessary to add an organic material with a high nitrogen content. Any material with a nitrogen level over 2 percent may be used if it is mixed in equal parts with the sawdust or wood chips. A high protein material like fish meal can be used in a ratio of one part meal to ten parts sawdust. It is also necessary to provide a ready energy source for bacteria to use before they have broken down the lignin or cellulose enough to allow it to provide their carbon. This energy source will aid in the initial breakdown of the material. Many organic materials can supply quick energy in the form of soluble sugars. Among these materials are cannery wastes, spent hops, ground pea vines or pods, garbage, or sugar beet or cane wastes.

Several wood-related industries in this country and abroad have abandoned or dismissed composting as a means of waste disposal because untreated wood scraps composted alone, even under the best conditions, may take as much as three years to produce a relatively stable humus.

In Switzerland, the time for composting wood waste has been reduced to five to six months in experiments conducted by the Swiss Federal Forestry Experimental Station and the International Research Group on Refuse Disposal. The experiments used urea or sewage sludge as a nitrogen source. Branches and leaves were chopped in small pieces, and household garbage provided an energy source and a source of bacteria. Piles were turned and re-formed at intervals.

At the University of Washington, sawdust, wood chips, and bark were experimentally composted with stable manure, sewage sludge, spent brewers' mash, and fishery refuse. A mixture of two parts wood waste to one part organic wastes proved to be most efficient.

In composting industrial wood wastes such as sawdust or wood shavings, cane sugar may be added to provide fuel for microorganisms before the carbon in the decay resistant lignin has become available to them. Sugar has been used in laboratory experiments, but a waste material such as bone black which has been used as a filter in sugar refining, or cane or beet residue would be more practical in large-scale practice.

A group of researchers at the University of Wisconsin successfully composted sawdust in four to five weeks by treating it with gaseous ammonia and then neutralizing it with phosphoric acid. The treated sawdust was then inoculated with a particular type of fungus.

You will recall that in a compost pile it is the fungi and actinomycetes that take over in the final and cooler stages of decomposition, and that these microorganisms concentrate their particular attention upon resistant cellulose and lignin materials. Though inoculums are generally ineffective, there is some evidence that inoculations of *Coprinus ephemerus*, a fungus that specializes in cellulose decomposition, may be effective in reducing treated sawdust. Wood materials are not natural sources of bacteria like other compost ingredients, so they may be the exception to the general rule about inoculums.

The Wisconsin experiment was conducted first in aerated barrels, then in windrows. Sawdust compost made in either manner has an exceptional ability to absorb and assimilate other nutrients.

The particle size of wood waste material is important to composting.

Coarse chips take a long time to decompose, but sawdust, if too fine, tends to pack and exclude air. A mixture of shavings, chipped wood, and sawdust is most satisfactory.

WASTE OF THE CELLULOSE INDUSTRY

During the past decade, the cellulose industry has experienced tremendous expansion. This expansion has influenced not only the paper industry, but also textile, food, pharmaceutical, and fermentation industries. The recovery of cellulose by chemical means has, however, created a major problem in dealing with spent wastes, particularly sulfite liquor, which is the principal waste product of cellulose extraction.

In cellulose extraction, debarked woods—usually spruce, pine, beech wood, or occasionally straw—are boiled under pressure in a calcium bisulfite solution which contains free sulfuric acid. The process dissolves the lignin out of the raw material and exposes the cellulose fiber.

When the sulfite liquor produced by cellulose extraction gets into a stream or river, it causes serious pollution problems. Schemes for using the waste, which in addition to sulfites also contains lignin, have thus far all been prohibitively expensive.

In Uzwil, Switzerland, tests have been conducted using sulfite liquor as a supplement in the composting of kitchen refuse. Refuse is hammermill-ground in a municipal plant and then composted in large piles. Sewage sludge is also added if conditions require it. The sulfite liquor which is mixed with the refuse has a C/N ratio of over 300:1 and a pH of 3.0.

Piles in the project have a moisture content of 43 percent. It has been found that the addition of spent sulfite liquor had little influence on the speed at which municipal refuse could be composted or on the physical composition of the piles, though the mass of the material was increased. The garbage, however, effectively neutralized the low pH of the liquor. The pH of the garbage was 8.6, and that of the total mixture 8.4. The finished compost had beneficial influence on the plants treated with it, an influence as good if not better than that of unmodified garbage compost.

These experiments illustrate the possibilities for cooperation between municipal composting or refuse disposal plants and the producers of industrial waste.

The following table of compostable organic wastes and their sources appeared in an article by Rudolf Braun in *Compost Science.** Dr. Braun was Secretary of the International Research Group on Refuse Disposal, in Zurich, Switzerland.

INDUSTRIAL WASTE OF FOREMOST ORGANIC COMPOSITION SUITABLE FOR COMPOSTING

Industries	Kind of Waste
1. Food and packing industry	
Sugar factories	pulp, sludge, slurries
Starch factories	pulp, fibrous material
Canning industry	pulp, refuse of fruits & vegetables
Chocolate factories	cocoa, nutshells, fats
Malt & yeast plants	spent slurries, filtrate residue
Breweries	spent mash, filtrate residue, hop waste
Wineries & distilleries	press residue, fruit pits, filtrate residue
Slaughterhouse, meat-packing industry	confiscated carcasses, meat refuse, bones, horns, hoofs, waste from intestines, etc.
2. Industries with vegetable & animal residues as raw material	
Pectin factories	fruit pulp, sugar, filtrate residue
Factories cleaning & preparing intestines	scraps of intestines, fat
Factories cleaning & preparing hair, bristles, feathers	hair, bristles, feathers similar to that of slaughterhouses
Factories using up cadavers, knackeryards	
Wood alcohol distilleries	lignin, spent slurries, filtrate residue
3. Wood-cellulose and paper mills, wood pulp mills, saw mills, planing mills	
Cellulose mills	chips, shavings, sawdust, bark fibers, spent liquor

*Reprinted with permission from *Compost Science*, August, 1962.

Paper and carton factories	cellulose fibers sludge
4. Textile plants	
Fulleries, clothweaving factories	wool, hair, fiber
Textile processing plants	waste from impregnation, waxes, paraffin
Artificial fiber & chemical yarn mills	viscose residue, sludge
5. Leather & glue factories	
Tanneries, leather-processing plants	hair, pieces of skin & leather, sludge, phobaphene
Glue & gelatin factories	same
6. Pharmaceutical industry	
Antibiotics, alkaloid plants	fermentation tank sludge, filtrate residue, spent liquors, mother slurries
7. Petroleum industry	crude oil, crude sludge, filtrate residues

Inorganic Wastes

PETROLEUM INDUSTRY WASTES

Wastes from oil and natural gas production are usually disposed of through incineration. The industry also has many by-products for the use of primary wastes.

Russian experts have found, however, that in certain rock formations rich in oil, and in the waste products of the petroleum industry, there are substances which stimulate the growth of plants. Alkaline wastes, oil slate, and bituminous rock increase the ability of soil to assimilate phosphorus and nitrogen ions and raise the intensity of microorganism activity and biochemical processes. According to Rudolf Braun of Zurich, these influences are particularly ascribed to the naphthalene acids and mineral oils which also spur the development of *Azotobacter* and increase the antibiotic action of certain molds. In Switzerland, experiments are being conducted to find means of using these petroleum residues in composting.

CELLOPHANE AND GLASS FRIT

Research at Rutgers University has shown that waste cellophane flakes are useful as a mulch and add bulk to compost, producing a product comparable to commercially prepared peat. Cellophane is made from wood pulp, but is low in nutrients.

Agricultural experiment stations in Florida and California have found that a glass compound called frit supplies trace and minor elements to soil—sodium, potassium, iron, and calcium. Neither cellophane nor frit contains enough nitrogen or available carbon to be used as active ingredients of compost, however.

STEEL BY-PRODUCTS

A waste material of steel manufacture, ferrensul, shows promise as a source of several trace minerals—calcium, sulfur, magnesium, iron, and manganese.

Basic slag is also a steel-making by-product, It comes out of the milling operation, and contains phosphorus and calcium. When composted with manure, basic slag releases phosphoric acid usable by plants. Slag is alkaline in reaction. It must be ground fine before use and should be composted with acid ingredients if it is to be used on alkaline or neutral soil.

KILN DUST FROM CEMENT FACTORIES

Cement kiln dusts have about the same ability to promote yields of alfalfa and to raise the pH levels of acid soils as pulverized limestone. This was the conclusion of a study made by D. M. Carroll, C. J. Erickson, and C. W. Whittaker. Their findings indicate that cement dust can be used in place of limestone when acid wastes are composted. Like lime or powdered limestone, however, cement dust used in large quantities will drive nitrogen from compost piles as ammonia.

Another compost-related use of cement kiln dust, which was investigated at Pennsylvania State University, is in the vacuum filter processing of sewage sludge. Kiln dust was shown in experiments conducted at the University to be more effective than lime for removing water from sludge when it was used in quantities slightly larger than is normal for lime use. Additional phosphorus and magnesium in the kiln dust would also supply these nutrients to digested sludge or sludge compost.

State agricultural colleges and commercial laboratories are often willing to test industrial wastes to determine if they are suitable for composting.

Appendix

Manufacturers of Composting Equipment

Shredders

Allis-Chalmers
Outdoors Leisure Products Div.
P.O. Box 512, 1126 South 70th
Milwaukee, WI 53201

Amerind-MacKissic
Box 111
Parker Ford, PA 19457

Ariens
111 Calumet & 655 West Ryan St.
Brillion, WI 54110

Atlas Tool & Mfg. Co.
5151 Natural Bridge Ave.
St. Louis, MO 63115

Bolens Div. FMC Corp.
Urban/Suburban Power
  Equipment Div.
215 S. Park St.
Port Washington, WI 53074

Columbia
P.O. Box 2741, 5389 W. 130th St.
Cleveland, OH 44111

Gilson Brothers Mfg. Co.
Box 152
Plymouth, WI 53073

Hahn, Inc., Agricultural Products
  Div.
1625 N. Garvin St.
Evansville, IN 47711

International Harvester
401 N. Michigan Ave.
Chicago, IL 60611

Jacobsen Mfg. Co.
1721 Packard Ave.
Racine, WI 53403

F. D. Kees Mfg. Co.
Box 775, 700 Park Ave.
Beatrice, NB 68310

Lindig Mfg. Corp.
 Box 111, 1877 W. County Rd. C
St. Paul, MN 55102

McDonough Power Equipment
  Co.
Macon Rd.
McDonough, GA 30253

Magna American Corp.
Box 90, Highway 18
Raymond, MS 39154

MTD Products, Inc.
P.O. Box 2741, 5389 West 130th St.
Cleveland, OH 44111

Osborne Mfg. Co.
P.O. Box 29
Osborne, KS 67473

Red Cross Mfg. Corp.
Box 111, 124 S. Oak St.
Bluffton, IN 46714

Roof Mfg. Co.
1011 W. Howard St.
Pontiac, IL 61764

Roper Sales Corp.
1905 W. Court St.
Kankakee, IL 60901

Roto-Hoe & Sprayer Co.
100 Auburn Rd., Route 87
Newbury, OH 44065

Royer Foundry & Machine Co.
158 Pringle St.
Kingston, PA 18704

Sears, Roebuck, & Co.
925 S. Homan Ave.
Chicago, IL 60624

Toro Co.
8111 Lyndale Ave. South
Bloomington, MN 55420

W-W Grinder Corp.
2957 N. Market St.
Wichita, KS 67219

Winona Attrition Mill
1009 W. Fifth St.
Winona, MN 55987

Composters

Derby Composter Co.
Box 21
Rumson, NJ 07760

Gardening Naturally (Earthmaker)
Industrial Park
Stockbridge, MA 01262

Global Services, Inc.
(Compostumbler)
Department P
P.O. Box 185-A College Park
Lewisburg, PA 17837

Rotocrop (USA) Inc.
604 Aero Park
Doylestown, PA 18901

Bibliography

Abraham, George, and Abraham, Katy. *Organic Gardening Under Glass.* Emmaus, Pa.: Rodale Press, 1975.

Allaby, Michael, and Allen, Floyd. *Robots Behind the Plow: Modern Farming and the Need for an Organic Alternative.* Emmaus, Pa.: Rodale Press, 1974.

Annual Review of Microbiology, The. Mortimer P. Starr, editor. Palo Alto, Calif.: Annual Reviews, Inc., Vol. 30 (1976).

Berkowitz, J. B.; March, F.; and Horne, T. *Individual Solid Waste Classification Systems: Final Report.* Washington, D.C.: Environmental Protection Agency, 1975.

Best Ideas for Organic Vegetable Growing. Editors of *Organic Gardening and Farming.* Emmaus, Pa.: Rodale Press, 1969.

Breidenbach, Andrew W., and Federal Solid Waste Management Research Staff. *Composting of Municipal Solid Wastes in the United States.* Washington, D.C.: Environmental Protection Agency, 1971.

"Carter Pledges Strong Backing for Environment." *EPA Journal* 3 (June 1977): 2–3.

Compost Science (quarterly). Emmaus, Pa.: Rodale Press, 1960–1977.

Conrat, Maisie, and Conrat, Richard. *The American Farm: A Photographic History.* San Francisco: California Historical Society; Boston: Houghton Mifflin Co., 1971.

Dindal, Daniel L. *Ecology of Compost: A Public Involvement Project.* Syracuse: New York State Council of Environmental Advisers, State University of New York, College of Environmental Science and Forestry, 1972.

385

Encyclopedia of Organic Gardening, The. Staff of *Organic Gardening and Farming.* Emmaus, Pa.: Rodale Press, 1959.

Foster, Catharine Osgood. *Organic Flower Gardening.* Emmaus, Pa.: Rodale Press, 1975.

Foster, Catharine Osgood, compiler, and the *Organic Gardening and Farming* staff. *Terrific Tomatoes: All About How To Grow and Enjoy Them.* Emmaus, Pa.: Rodale Press, 1975.

"Fuel Gas from Solid Waste." *EPA Journal* 3 (March 1977): 11.

Getting the Bugs Out of Organic Gardening. Organic Gardening and Farming editors. Emmaus, Pa.: Rodale Press, 1973.

Goldstein, Jerome. *Sensible Sludge: A New Look at a Wasted Natural Resource.* Emmaus, Pa.: Rodale Press, 1977.

Golueke, Clarence G. *Biological Reclamation of Solid Wastes.* Emmaus, Pa.: Rodale Press, 1977.

Golueke, Clarence G. *Composting: A Study of the Process and Its Principles.* Emmaus, Pa.: Rodale Press, 1972.

Gotaas, Harold B. *Composting: Sanitary Disposal and Reclamation of Organic Wastes.* Geneva: World Health Organization, 1956.

Hang, Y. D., and Woodams, E. E. "Baked-Bean Waste: A Potential Substrate for Producing Fungal Analyses." *Applied and Environmental Microbiology* 33 (1977): 1293–94.

Hart, Samuel A. *Solid Waste Management/Composting: European Activity and American Potential.* Cincinnati: U.S. Department of Health, Education, and Welfare, Public Health Service, Consumer Protection and Environmental Health Service, Environmental Control Administration, Solid Wastes Program, 1968.

Hegazi, N. A., and Leitgeb, S. "*Azotobacter* Bacteriophages in Czechoslovakian Soils." *Plant and Soil: International Journal of Plant Nutrition, Plant Chemistry, and Soil Microbiology* 45 (October 1976): 379–95.

Ilyaletdinov, A. N.; Enker, P. B.; and Yakubovskii, S. E. "Participation of Heterotrophic Microorganisms in Removal of Heavy Metal Ions from Effluent." *Microbiology* 45 (1976): 1092–98.

Jackson, P. M. "An Economic Study of Domestic Waste Management." *Solid Wastes* 65: 276–82.

Johns, Glenn F., compiler, and editors of *Organic Gardening and Farming*. *The Organic Way to Mulching: Using Natural Ground Coverings for Soil Improvement*. Emmaus, Pa.: Rodale Press, 1976.

Lindberg, S. E., and Turner, R. R. "Mercury Emissions from Chlorine Production Solid Waste Deposits." *Nature* 268 (July 14, 1977): 133.

Logsdon, Gene. *The Gardener's Guide to Better Soil*. Emmaus, Pa.: Rodale Press, 1975.

Logsdon, Gene. *Homesteading: How to Find New Independence on the Land*. Emmaus, Pa.: Rodale Press, 1975.

Meyers, P. G. "Selection of Advanced Solid Waste Disposal Techniques." *Public Works* 106: 70–71.

Millar, C. E. *Soil Fertility*. New York: John Wiley and Sons, Inc.; London: Chapman Hall, Ltd., 1955.

Minnich, Jerry. *The Earthworm Book*. Emmaus, Pa.: Rodale Press, 1977.

National Center for Resource Recovery. *Resource Recovery from Municipal Solid Waste*. Lexington, Mass.: Lexington Books; Toronto and London: D. C. Heath and Co., 1974.

Ogden, Samuel. *Step-by-Step to Organic Vegetable Growing*. Emmaus, Pa.: Rodale Press, 1975.

Olkowski, Helga, and Olkowski, William. *The City People's Book of Raising Food*. Emmaus, Pa.: Rodale Press, 1975.

Organic Fertilizers: Which Ones and How to Use Them. Staff of *Organic Gardening and Farming*. Emmaus, Pa.: Rodale Press, 1973.

Organic Gardening and Farming Magazine (monthly). Emmaus, Pa.: Rodale Press, 1962–1977.

Organic Matter and Soil Fertility. Amsterdam: North Holland Publishing Co.; New York: John Wiley and Sons, Inc., 1968.

Pavoni, J. L. *Handbook of Solid Waste Disposal*. New York: Van Nostrand Rinehold Co., 1975.

Pfeiffer, Ehrenfried. *Bio-Dynamic Farming and Gardening*. New York: Anthroposophic Press, 1943.

Poincelot, Raymond P. *The Biochemistry and Methodology of Composting*. New Haven: The Connecticut Agricultural Experiment Station.

Poincelot, Raymond P. *Gardening Indoors with House Plants*. Emmaus, Pa.: Rodale Press, 1974.

Porteous, A. "Domestic Refuse: Its Composition, Properties, Recovery Potential, and Disposal Methods: Present and Future." *Chemical Pollution* (1975): 23–47.

Rainbook: Resources for Appropriate Technology. Editors of *Rain*. New York: Schocken Books, 1977.

"Recovering Wastes." *EPA Journal* 3 (1977): 8–9.

Rodale, J. I. *Pay Dirt*. Emmaus, Pa.: Rodale Press, 1959.

Rodale, J. I., and staff of *Organic Gardening and Farming*. *The Complete Book of Composting*. Emmaus, Pa.: Rodale Press, 1971.

Seldman, Neil N. *Garbage in America: Approaches to Recycling*. Washington, D.C.: Institute for Local Self-Reliance, 1975.

Skitt, John. *Disposal of Refuse and Other Waste*. New York: Halsted Press, John Wiley and Sons, Inc., 1972.

"Soil and Pollution: Interview with Eckardt C. Beck, Deputy Assistant Administrator for Water Planning and Standards." *EPA Journal* 3 (1977): 6–7.

Stoner, Carol Hupping, editor. *Goodbye to the Flush Toilet: Water-Saving Alternatives to Cesspools, Septic Tanks, and Sewers*. Emmaus, Pa.: Rodale Press, 1977.

Stout, Ruth, and Clemence, Richard. *The Ruth Stout No-Work Garden Book: Secrets of the Famous Year-Round Mulch Method*. Emmaus, Pa.: Rodale Press, 1971.

Suberkropp, K., and Klug, M. J. "Fungi and Bacteria Associated with Leaves during Processing in a Woodland Stream." *Ecology* 57 (1976): 707–19.

Swift, M. J. "The Ecology of Wood Decomposition." *Science Progress* 64 (Summer 1977): 175–99.

Sykes, Friend. *Food, Farming, and the Future*. London: Faber and Faber; Emmaus, Pa.: Rodale Press, 1951.

Vivian, John. *The Manual of Practical Homesteading*. Emmaus, Pa.: Rodale Press, 1975.

Waksman, Selman A. *Humus: Origin, Chemical Composition, and Importance in Nature.* Baltimore: The Williams and Wilkins Co., 1938.

Waksman, Selman A. *Principles of Soil Microbiology.* Baltimore: The Williams and Wilkins Co., 1927.

Index